GUIDES FOR THE JOURNEY

John Macmurray
Bernard Lonergan
James Fowler

David G. Creamer

University Press of America, Inc.
Lanham • New York • London

Copyright © 1996 by
University Press of America,® Inc.
4720 Boston Way
Lanham, Maryland 20706

3 Henrietta Street
London, WC2E 8LU England

Library of Congress Cataloging-in-Publication Data

Creamer, David G.
Guides for the journey : John Macmurray, Bernard Lonergan, James
Fowler / David G. Creamer.
p.   cm.
Includes bibliographical references and index.
1. Macmurray, John, 1891-. 2. Self (Philosophy) 3. Lonergan,
Bernard J. F. 4. History--Philosophy. 5. Philosophy. 6. Theology,
Doctrinal. 7. Fowler, James W. 8. Christian education--Philosophy.
9. Faith development. I. Title.
B1647.M134C74   **1996**   191--dc20   95-45294 CIP

ISBN 0-7618-0181-2 (cloth: alk: ppr.)
ISBN 0-0-7618-0182-0 (pbk: alk: ppr.)

*To the Creamer family
from whom I continue to learn about
the journey of life and faith*

*To my brothers in the Society of Jesus
fellow pilgrims with Ignatius*

Table of Contents

Tables

Preface

I have written this book as an introduction to the lives and thought of John Macmurray, Bernard Lonergan, and James Fowler. I think their congruent thought is helpful in interpreting our lives and the world in which we live them at this juncture in human and earth history. Their work ought to be made more generally accessible.

Specifically, I have in mind my students in Education and Religion at the University of Manitoba and others I have met in workshops, talks, and small adult faith communities. Accordingly, I am *not* presuming the reader has a familiarity with philosophy or the meaning of technical terms used. So as not to interrupt the flow of the text I have provided a glossary of names and key terms.

I use quotations from Macmurray, Lonergan, and Fowler in my presentation because I want to give the reader a flavor for the texture and depth of their work. I have included endnotes as guides for further reading as well as a bibliography and index. A list of abbreviations used in the book is also provided.

My thanks to J. Bowler, R. Boys, J. Costello, F. Crowe, G. Drobot, J. Emslie, J. English, E. Frigo, G. Leach, P. Malone, M. Matic, D. Swirsky, & J. Veltri for reading various drafts of this book and offering constructive suggestions. Special thanks to my colleague D. Lenoski for grammatical corrections, to M. Matic and G. Broesky for carefully checking quotations, and to M. Caligiuri for his computer wizardry.

David G. Creamer, S.J.
October, 1995

Acknowledgments

Permission to quote from John Macmurrray's *The Self as Agent* and *Persons in Relation* has been granted by Humanities Press International, Inc., Atlantic Highlands, NJ. Permission to quote from Bernard Lonergan's *Method in Theology* has been granted by the Lonergan Trustees.

The poem Bernard Lonergan, S.J. is reprinted with the permission of John F. Kinsella, S.J. and America Press, Inc., 106 West 56th Street, New York, NY 10019; originally published in *America*'s September 11, 1993 issue. The author thanks Ruth McLean for permission to quote sections of her poem "Awoken."

John Macmurrray's photograph (12) is courtesy of the John Macmurray Collection, Regis College, University of Toronto. The photograph of Bernard Lonergan (50) is used with the permission of the Lonergan Archives, 15 St. Mary Street, Toronto. James W. Fowler kindly supplied his photograph (112).

List of Abbreviations

Becoming: Fowler, James W. *Becoming Adult, Becoming Christian: Adult Development and Christian Faith*. San Francisco: Harper & Row, 1984.

Collection: Lonergan, Bernard. *Collection*. Volume 4 of the *Collected Works of Bernard Lonergan*. Edited by Frederick E. Crowe and Robert M. Doran. Toronto: University of Toronto Press, 1988. *Collection* was first published in 1967.

Desires: Gregson, Vernon, ed. *The Desires of the Human Heart: An Introduction to the Theology of Bernard Lonergan*. Mahwah, NJ: Paulist Press, 1988.

Enterprise: Crowe, Frederick E. *The Lonergan Enterprise*. Cambridge, MA: Cowley Publications, 1980.

Freedom: Macmurray, John. *Freedom in the Modern World*. Atlantic Highlands, NJ: Humanities Press International, 1992. *Freedom in the Modern World* was first published in 1932.

Insight: Lonergan, Bernard. *Insight: A Study of Human Understanding*. Volume 3 of the *Collected Works of Bernard Lonergan*. Edited by Frederick E. Crowe and Robert M. Doran. Toronto: University of Toronto Press, 1992. *Insight* was first published in 1957.

Interpreting: Macmurray, John. *Interpreting the Universe*. London: Faber & Faber, 1933.

Lonergan: Crowe, Frederick E. *Lonergan*. Outstanding Christian Thinkers Series. Series Editor Brain Davies, OP. Collegeville, MN: The Liturgical Press, 1992.

Method: Lonergan, Bernard. *Method in Theology*. Toronto: University of Toronto Press for Lonergan Research Institute, 1990. *Method in Theology* was first published in 1972.

Old & New: Crowe, Frederick E. *Old Things and New: A Strategy for Education*. Atlanta: Scholar's Press, 1985.

Passages: Droege, Thomas A. *Faith Passages and Patterns*. Philadelphia: Fortress Press, 1983.

Pastoral: Fowler, James W. *Faith Development and Pastoral Care*. Philadelphia: Fortress Press, 1987.

Pensées: Pascal, Blaise. *Pensées*. London: Penguin Books, 1966. *Pensées* was first published soon after Pascal's death in 1662.

Persons: Macmurray, John. *Persons in Relation*. Atlantic Highlands, NJ: Humanities Press International, 1991. *Persons in Relation* was first published in 1961 by Faber & Faber, London.

Promise: Palmer, Parker. *The Promise of Paradox: A Celebration of Contradictions in the Christian Life*. Notre Dame, IN: Ave Maria Press, 1980.

Search: Macmurray, John. *Search for Reality in Religion*. Swarthmore Lecture Pamphlet. London: Friends Home Service Committee, 1969. The Swarthmore Lecture was first published in 1965, the year of its presentation, by George Allen and Unwin Limited.

Second Collection: Lonergan, Bernard. *A Second Collection*. Edited by William F.J. Ryan and Bernard J. Tyrrell. Philadelphia: The Westminster Press, 1974.

Self: Macmurray, John. *The Self as Agent*. Atlantic Highlands, NJ: Humanities Press International, 1991. *The Self as Agent* was first published in 1957 by Faber & Faber, London.

Stages: Fowler, James W. *Stages of Faith: The Psychology of Human Development and the Quest for Meaning*. San Francisco: Harper & Row, 1981.

Third Collection: Lonergan, Bernard. *A Third Collection: Papers by Bernard J. F. Lonergan, S.J.* Edited by Frederick E. Crowe, S.J. New York: Paulist Press, 1985.

Topics: Lonergan, Bernard. *Topics in Education*. Volume 10 of the *Collected Works of Bernard Lonergan*. Edited by Frederick E. Crowe and Robert M. Doran, revising and augmenting the unpublished text prepared by James Quinn and John Quinn. Toronto: University of Toronto Press, 1993. These lectures were delivered at Xavier University, Cincinnati, in August, 1959.

Transforming: Liddy, Richard M. *Transforming Light: Intellectual Conversion in the Early Lonergan*. Collegeville, MN: The Liturgical Press, 1993.

Understanding: Lonergan, Bernard. *Understanding and Being.* Volume 5 of the *Collected Works of Bernard Lonergan.* Edited by Elizabeth A. Morelli and Mark D. Morelli; revised and augmented by Frederick E. Crowe with the collaboration of Elizabeth A. Morelli, Mark D. Morelli, Robert M. Doran, and Thomas V. Daly. Toronto: University of Toronto Press, 1990. *Understanding and Being*, the Halifax Lectures on *Insight*, was first published in 1980.

Chapter 1

Introduction

If the modern world has begun our emancipation from magic, superstition, and arbitrary belief, it has also brought us to the foot of a bridge over a great abyss. Behind us lies the comfortable world of secure belief. Some who have caught a glimpse of the abyss will want to return to the world of security; they will give themselves, uncritically, once again to the faith of their childhood. . . . Others, more critical in their judgments, will refuse to go back. Some of these will attack the precipice *without* a bridge, believing naively in their own invincibility, and some will but stare into the pit of empty endlessness and wait out their lives.

But most, I suspect, will close their eyes and busy themselves with the endless tasks of daily life . . . but without much real sense of what life is all about. And — what is worst of all — without much real passion for the lives they live.

This . . . is for those who refuse to abandon the quest and are willing to test out some bridges, shaky though they may be, to see where they will lead.[1]

Overview

The past quarter century has been one of unprecedented change in the world in which we live and the understanding we have of our place in it. In 1969, human beings walked on the moon for the first time and looked back to see a world without any borders; the earth as a beautiful but tiny and fragile blue and white ball suspended in the black void of space. Today, jet travel puts any spot on that globe just a day away and with e-mail and the Internet those same places are just seconds away! This shrinking of our world makes us aware of a whole range of complex issues and problems that heretofore were not part of our consciousness. Traditional groupings and relationships between people are in flux, cancer and AIDS loom as major killers, and the gap between rich and poor nations continues to grow. Moral questions are becoming increasingly complex. We do not even have agreement on when human life begins or ends. Ecological issues ranging from the disposal of toxic waste to the depletion of the stratospheric ozone layer and the disappearance of countless plant and animal species are paramount. For the first time, the entire planet faces an ecological crisis largely brought about by over consumption and exploitation on the part of the Western world:

> If today is a typical day on planet earth, humans will add fifteen million tons of carbon to the atmosphere, destroy 115 square miles of tropical rainforest, create seventy-two square miles of desert, eliminate between forty to one hundred species, erode seventy-one million tons of topsoil, add twenty-seven hundred tons of CFCs to the stratosphere, and increase their population by 263,000. Yesterday, today, and tomorrow.[2]

Added to all of this is the questioning and confusion within our religious traditions. It is commonplace to point out that Western civilization is now "post-Christian" and suffers from a "crisis of meaning." How are we to understand the past few decades; have we lost our way? The Hebrew scriptures caution that "where there is no prophecy, the people cast off restraint" (Proverbs 29:18) and the prophets in our midst today warn that "the major actions to stabilize the vital signs of earth and stop the hemorrhaging of life must be made within the next decade or two."[3]

During the Rubik's Cube craze several years ago one of my friends discovered that each little square got its color from a sticker that could be peeled off. And so, when twisting and turning could not quite achieve uniform color on each of the six sides of the cube, he completed the puzzle by peeling and sticking little squares of color as required! There is this tendency in all of us, it seems, to look for simple solutions as our response to complex situations and problems.

This tendency promotes reductionism — religious fundamentalism at one extreme and secularism at the other. Within my own faith tradition, the Roman Catholic church, we seem to be polarizing into two camps. Reminiscent of Popes Pius IX and Pius X who censured the "world" and things "modern," some withdraw into a Catholic fundamentalism seeking to "restore" the church to its earlier triumphal power and glory. Others adapt to the modern, secular world to the point where they begin to wonder, 'Do we even need religion?' There appears to be a clash between conserving religious tradition and opening ourselves to things contemporary and scientific. And then there are those few still faint voices — this book introduces three of them — who call us to journey far beyond both *classicism* and *modernism* towards a world community rich in diversity but living harmoniously with one another and the planet.

Twenty-five years ago I was introduced to the thought of Bernard Lonergan in an undergraduate philosophy course and several years later, during graduate school, to the philosophy of John Macmurray and the developmental approach to faith put forward by James Fowler. Over time I have come to appreciate the potency and broad applicability of their respective critical investigations. I believe that these three scholars are helpful in discerning the path along which human beings are called to travel as we approach the new millennium.

The Roman philosopher and statesman Boethius (c. 480–c. 524) observed that 'each age is a dream that is dying *and* one that is coming to birth.' Looking back over the history of human thought we see that, as one way of making sense of the world proved inadequate to the task at hand and began to collapse, another was already beginning to appear. So, as the European medieval religious synthesis (Scholasticism) proved unable to accommodate the findings of Copernicus, Newton, and Darwin, modern philosophical and scientific approaches emerged. Today, by and large due to the growth of modern science and our awareness of human subjectivity and historical consciousness, contemporary Western culture no longer rests on the certainty of absolute truth. But we still have a *desire* for certitude, at the same time recognizing the limitations of science and technology when it comes to providing answers for our spiritual hunger. We live, as it were, in an age when the old dream, while dying, is not yet dead and the new dream, having been conceived, is not yet born. So what is the way forward?

It is my conviction that the works of John Macmurray, Bernard

Lonergan, and James Fowler represent something of the new ways of 'knowing' and 'being' that are coming to birth in our day. Each one recognizes that there need not be a clash between living in continuity with tradition *and* openness to authentic creativity. Real knowledge is not a choice between *what was* and *what is* but is a paradoxical relationship between both old and new. An exploration of the new *both/and* convergence in their thought, in opposition to earlier *either/or* approaches to human knowing, will be a major focus of this book.

Personal Stories

> The life of each of us is a story in progress — a story taking form and living out a narrative structure (*Becoming* 135).[4]

My mentor from graduate school, Dr. Edmund V. Sullivan, wrote at the end of the Acknowledgments section of one of his books: "I depart from the usual 'I do not hold all of those listed above responsible for my ideas.' I hold them all responsible. My ideas are formed by the company I keep."[5] Dr. Sullivan's words sum up my sense of how I have come to hold and teach the views I do. A major influence on my thinking, Dr. Sullivan's courses at the Ontario Institute for Studies in Education (OISE) in Toronto introduced me to the work of John Macmurray and James Fowler. Moreover, Dr. Sullivan re-acquainted me with the thought of Bernard Lonergan which I had earlier dismissed as obscure and irrelevant to real life. What you will be getting in these pages, therefore, is an introduction to the company I have kept with Macmurray, Lonergan and Fowler over the past quarter century. I write about their lives and their thought, not from a neutral or disinterested stance, but, with the conviction that they have something worthwhile to say to us as we journey through life in the last years of the twentieth century.

What I offer in these pages is also influenced by the company I kept before arriving at this point in my life; my youth in Saint John, New Brunswick; undergraduate days at St. Mary's University in Halifax, Nova Scotia; teaching as a young Jesuit at Gonzaga High School, St. John's, Newfoundland; studying theology in the ecumenical context of the Toronto School of Theology (TST); and more recently as a high school administrator in Winnipeg and now professor in Education and Religion at St. Paul's College, the University of

Manitoba.

Accordingly, I want to begin by sharing four of *my* stories; four of "the strange and fateful 'moments'"[6] which say something about who I am, what I have brought to my reading and study of these three figures, and the difference they have made in my life. I do this at the outset because I believe that my personal history; my religious, cultural, and educational milieu have shaped my voice. In these pages, my selection of topics, my weighing of evidence and evaluation of people and events, my vision and values will constantly be heard. Ultimately, I believe, there is no such thing as a neutral approach to meaning questions — the central themes of this work reflect, and in part arise from, the central themes and movements of my life. I am formed by the company I keep!

My first story begins with twelve years of Catholic education in Saint John. As a boy growing up, I went to Catholic schools not because Catholicism was a strong influence on our family but because, in New Brunswick where one had to choose between a Catholic and 'Protestant' school, we certainly knew we were not Protestant! My religious education was provided by the *Baltimore Catechism*,[7] the prime vehicle used for the moral and religious instruction of North American Catholics before the Second Vatican Council (1962–65). This formal, rather dry and authoritarian, albeit clear and concise, book set forth the basic beliefs of Catholics. We were required to memorize and give intellectual assent to "The Faith" thus expressed. In those days before Jean Piaget revolutionized the way we understand childhood, it was believed that a child of seven or eight could be taught the same things as an adult. A teacher might have to use simpler language but abstract concepts could be taught; after all, children were just "miniature adults." Accordingly, in Miss Luney's Grade 2 class at St. Peter's School (1953–54), I memorized the truths of the Catholic faith about the Trinity.

Related to this point about rote learning is the fact that as I graduated from St. Malachy's High School (1964) in Saint John, I won an award for Religion. The award had nothing to do with how I lived my faith but was for successfully answering questions on an examination paper. An ability to memorize, not religious practise, seemed to be the measuring stick of my Catholicism. It struck me as odd, even then.

In the fall of 1976, as part of my divinity studies, I enrolled in the 'Trinity' course at Regis College in the Toronto School of Theology. I recall that the professor, Frederick Crowe, S.J., a published expert on the subject, opened his first lecture by saying that he 'really didn't know much about the Trinity — the Trinity is a mystery.' It popped into my head that he should have met Miss Luney because she knew *everything* about the Trinity! Looking back, I think I left Grade 2 believing God was a triangle or shamrock; God was Irish in any case! What was missing from much of my religious education in Catholic schools was a sense of life as a faith *journey* and a sense of the ineffable mystery of God's self communication and desire for a personal relationship with me.

A second story, related to these earlier incidents from school days, comes from my early teaching experience (1971–74) as a young Jesuit at Gonzaga High School, St. John's, Newfoundland. I taught Chemistry, General Science, World History, Geography, and Religion at various grade levels. As part of the school's Grade 11 religion program, we designed a program (Awareness Day) around the Last Judgment passage in Matthew's gospel dealing with the separation of sheep from goats on the basis of their treatment of the "least ones" (Matthew 25:31–46). Once during the year, each class would be divided into small groups to spend a morning visiting selected local government and church related service agencies. After a "poverty lunch" in various settings, the students returned to the school to spend the afternoon in a large group sharing of the experiences of the day. Each Awareness Day ended with Mass (focusing on the theme of social justice as integral to faith) and a simple communal supper.

Over the next decade I returned to St. John's on various occasions and often met with students from my teaching days at Gonzaga. Invariably, they would speak with great affection about their Awareness Day experience. Hardly ever was there any reference to their Religion *classes*; on occasion I met students who couldn't even remember that I had taught them Chemistry! This experience says something profound to me about the limits of knowledge that is not used or lived — it is one thing to *know* the truth; it is quite another to *live* it.

My third story concerns my interest in, or more accurately lack of interest in, Philosophy. As a science undergraduate at St. Mary's University (1964–68) I was required to take two philosophy courses during the four year degree program. I hated the experience. While I can still recall the boring lectures in the introductory course (Philosophy 201, 1965–66), I needed to check my transcript to make sure I had, in fact, taken a second philosophy course. I had (Philosophy

302 in 1966–67). My transcript reveals that I passed only after a supplemental examination in September, 1967, which probably accounts for my lack of memory of the experience!

In August, 1969, I joined the Jesuit Order and soon found that philosophical studies were a required part of the regimen. Fortunately, my two courses at St. Mary's did not go for naught and I was required to take just one semester at the University of Guelph, Ontario (Winter, 1971). One of those courses was on the philosophic thought of a Canadian Jesuit, Bernard Lonergan. I passed the course but it made little sense to me and seemed totally irrelevant. I had read somewhere that philosophy offered 'unintelligible answers to insoluble problems' and adopted that characterization as my own. My negative evaluation of philosophy, and of Lonergan in particular, was only confirmed when I heard the great man himself give a lecture at Ignatius College, Guelph (1970), on the 'Meaning of Meaning' — it was totally beyond me! As I moved from Guelph I hoped I had moved away from philosophy forever!

My fourth story explains my reacquaintance with the thought of Bernard Lonergan through that of Macmurray and Fowler. It begins with a workshop I attended at Ewart College, Toronto (February, 1978), while I was doing graduate studies at OISE. It was my introduction to James Fowler and his theory of "faith development." I was immediately drawn to Fowler's work because I saw his field of study as of practical value. Because of my own eclectic studies in science, humanities, and education, I was also attracted by its interdisciplinary character, blurring the artificial boundaries we have erected between disciplines. In the case of Fowler's research interests, the boundary was between psychology and religion and much of my own work in recent years has been at this interface.

At OISE, Dr. Sullivan introduced me to the philosophy of John Macmurray which initially held no fascination.[8] I applied Macmurray's belief that "it is always legitimate to ask, of any theory which claims to be true, what practical difference it would make if we believed it" (*Self* 23)[9] to philosophy and concluded that it made no practical difference to me! Over time, however, I came to see that Macmurray's work sought to replace the modern idea of philosophers as thinkers isolated from the world, their philosophy a "bubble floating in an atmosphere of unreality" (*Self* 78), with a personalist philosophy emphasizing relationship and action. Macmurray took seriously the questions (and answers) of earlier philosophers (notably the rationalism of René Descartes and the idealism of Immanuel Kant) but he also took *my* experience seriously: "When philosophy is alive it grows straight out of human life" (*Freedom* 44).[10] Macmurray's was a philosophy with *practical* implications. I was hooked![11]

Armed with this background, I returned to Bernard Lonergan and found a methodology adequate to the task of continuing Macmurray's effort to elucidate the nature of personal existence. As I began teaching graduate students in the Faculty of Education at the University of Manitoba, their initial reaction to the idea of studying philosophy was negative (as was mine before them) but they were soon won over by Macmurray, Lonergan, and Fowler, none of whom they had previously encountered. I have since introduced elements of the thought of all three thinkers into my undergraduate teaching with positive results. This encouraging response to my classes is in part responsible for this work.

Conclusion

Each of these personal stories say something to me about a shift that is taking place in my lifetime, both within Western culture and the Christian tradition to which I belong — a shift from the pre-modern, classical, worldview to the modern, historically conscious, worldview. The acceptance and integration of this shift has not come easily in my own life and, if my interaction with people tells me anything, it is that this is not an easy paradigm shift for most of us. But it is a transition we must make to get on with the journey of life. It has been, for me, a movement from *uncritical* reliance on authorities and dogma, to an appreciation of what Lonergan calls the "new learning" (*Topics* 16–17)[12] and the importance of living with, and learning from, one other in community. John Macmurray, Bernard Lonergan, and James Fowler have been three of my mentors in this process; their lives and work are testimony to the importance, necessity, and value of the shift. They come from different times and places and are the product of different religious and educational backgrounds, yet they communicate a complementary vision of the human project. In each case, their vision extends beyond the shift out of classicism and into modernity to a way of living in harmony with one another and the planet that in times past was the dream of a few visionaries and even now is grasped by only a few.

Because I believe that the central themes and resonances of the work of Macmurray, Lonergan, and Fowler reflect, and in part arise from, the central themes and movements of their lives and times, my consideration of each will begin with a biographical sketch followed by an exposition of their basic thought. A concluding chapter will attempt to draw the basic themes of the book together into a parcel convenient for carrying on life's journey.

Notes

1. Russell Pregeant, *Mystery Without Magic* (Oak Park, IL: Meyer Stone Books, 1988), 17.
2. David W. Orr, *Ecological Literacy: Education and the Transition to a Post-modern World* (Albany, NY: State University of New York Press, 1992), 3.
3. David W. Orr, *Ecological Literacy: Education and the Transition to a Post-modern World* (Albany, NY: State University of New York Press, 1992), 20.
4. The reference in brackets (*Becoming* 135) is to James W. Fowler, *Becoming Adult, Becoming Christian: Adult Development and Christian Faith* (San Francisco: Harper & Row, Publishers, 1984), 135. Quotations from this work will henceforth be indicated as here (*Becoming* 135).
5. Edmund V. Sullivan, *Critical Psychology and Pedagogy: Interpretation of the Personal World* (Toronto: OISE Press, 1990), xvii. Currently, Dr. Sullivan is Coordinator of a program in Community and Global Transformation Studies (an interdisciplinary approach to global ecological and social issues and global education) in the Department of Curriculum at the Ontario Institute for Studies in Education, Toronto, Canada.
6. Paul Tillich as quoted by Robert Coles in *Walker Perry: An American Search* (Boston: Little, Brown & Company, 1978), x.
7. See chapter 7, notes 18 and 19.
8. I never met John Macmurray. In graduate school, at Dr. Sullivan's invitation, I attended a meeting of the John Macmurray Society (founded 1971 in Toronto) which soon broke up as the keynote speaker was taken away by ambulance after suffering a suspected heart attack.
9. The reference in brackets (*Self* 23) is to John Macmurray, *The Self as Agent* (Atlantic Highlands, NJ: Humanities Press International, 1991), 23. Quotations from this work will henceforth be indicated as here (*Self* 23).
10. The reference in brackets (*Freedom* 44) is to John Macmurray, *Freedom in the Modern World* (Atlantic Highlands, NJ: Humanities Press International, 1992), 44. Quotations from this work will henceforth be indicated as here (*Freedom* 44).

11. I agree with E. F. Schumacher who quotes St. Augustine as writing "Man has no reason to philosophize except with a view to happiness" (E. F. Schumacher, *A Guide for the Perplexed* (London: Sphere Books Ltd, 1978), 5.

12. The reference in brackets (*Topics* 16–17) is to Bernard Lonergan, *Topics in Education*, vol. 10 in the *Collected Works of Bernard Lonergan*, ed. Frederick E. Crowe and Robert M. Doran (Toronto: University of Toronto Press, 1993), 16–17. Quotations from this work will henceforth be indicated as here (*Topics* 16–17). By "new learning" Lonergan does not just mean an *addition* to accumulated knowledge in a subject area but a *transformation* of our very understanding of the nature of the discipline in question. The physics of Albert Einstein, for instance, is not just an addition of material to Newtonian physics but a transformation of the very nature of what we mean by "physics."

John Macmurray (c. 1958)

Chapter 2

John Macmurray (1891–1976)

I want to say something just in passing about the world we are living in, which is the really important period of history. We can regard this period of our history, I should say, as far greater than the Elizabethan period, but more like the period of the Ancient Greeks — the greatest period of history that the world has known. Lots of things are happening that have never happened before. It makes me wish I had not been born so early — I wish I had been born about now (John Macmurray, June 12, 1949).[1]

Early Years

John Macmurray was born in 1891 in Maxwellton, Kirkcudbright, in the extreme southwest of Scotland. While he was still a boy, his family moved to Aberdeen where he was educated at the Grammar School and Robert Gordon's College. Science was an interest from his teens and as a university student he took courses in science whenever he could. Later in life he allowed that a "solid grounding in science and scientific method has been of the greatest possible use to me not only as a philosopher . . . but at least as much in the religious field" (*Search* 11).[2] Summarizing his thoughts as a young man, Macmurray asked: "Could we not hope that through testing and modification we should arrive at a religion which science need not be ashamed to serve?" (*Search* 14).

Macmurray's religious upbringing was the traditional Calvinism of the Scottish church; he described his family as "deeply religious" and desirous of traveling to foreign mission lands. Filled with Christian fervor, he joined the Student Christian Movement (SCM) in 1909 when he enrolled as a student at Glasgow University. He organized bible study groups among students and addressed open air evangelical meetings. When his father died without achieving his goal of working in foreign missions, Macmurray volunteered for a mission career but was turned down.[3] It was while studying in Glasgow that he matured into the conviction that *reality is religious*, in that "religion is about human beings in relation,"[4] a view he was to live and defend throughout his life.

In October 1913, equipped with an honors degree in Classics from Glasgow, Macmurray went on to Balliol College, Oxford University, to study Philosophy. The outbreak of World War I interrupted his degree program.

World War I

Because he was struggling with the pacifist option (he was attracted to Quaker philosophy), Macmurray chose to serve with the Royal Army Medical Corps as a nursing orderly on the Western Front. Later, having discovered that a medic was as much a part of the fighting machine as any soldier, he accepted a commission as a lieutenant with the Queen's Own Cameron Highlanders. Wounded in the defense of Arras during the final German attack in 1918, he was awarded a Military Cross and sent home. As the war ended he returned to Oxford to finish his interrupted studies, taking his final Master of Arts examinations in the summer of 1919.

Reflecting on the war years, Macmurray tells us that he and many of his contemporaries "went into war in a blaze of idealism, to save little Belgium and to put an end to war" only to discover "stage by stage . . . that war was simply stupidity, destruction, waste and futility." "We became," he says, "critical, skeptical and sometimes cynical" (*Search* 18–19).

A key event in the life of John Macmurray occurred during home leave in the autumn of 1916.[5] He had been invited to preach in a church and took advantage of the occasion to speak (in full uniform) on the need for reconciliation among warring parties following the cessation of hostilities. His words were met with a hostile and cold reaction from the congregation. It is to this unhappy event that Macmurray traces his refusal to be associated with denominational Christianity: "I spoke and wrote thereafter in defense of religion and of Christianity; but I thought of the churches as the various national religions of Europe" (*Search* 21). "I stand as a Christian," he said, "but outside all the Churches."[6] Macmurray explains this bold statement:

> When I say that I am a Christian I mean, therefore, that I stand in the contemporary world for and with the movement that Jesus originated. When I say that the effect of this is to set me outside all the Churches, I mean to imply that at the present time, and in their contemporary condition, the Churches do not stand in and with that movement.[7]

The war years had a significant impact on the development of Macmurray's thought. War was an alienating, destructive experience, quite opposite to that of personal relationship ("friendship") which is the underlying motif of his writings. Further, his negative experience in the wartime pulpit caused him to live on the fringes of organized religion throughout his professional life even as he championed Christian ideals.[8]

Professor of Philosophy

Following demobilization, Macmurray considered working with the newly formed League of Nations[9] but, believing that his emerging philosophical ideas were relevant to daily life, he decided on a career as a professor of philosophy. In a letter written ten years later to Rev. Richard Roberts (an early mentor), Macmurray wrote: "I think I am entering a field which is absolutely virgin soil for the philosopher, and calling for a reconstruction of modern philosophy from top to bottom. . . . I'm only trying to pioneer and blaze a philosophical trail in this new continent of being"[10] He was aware as he set out that he was taking "the road less travelled"[11] and that his work would probably be rejected or at least ignored by his contemporaries. Harboring no illusion about doing more than pointing the way towards an adequate modern philosophy, he accepted a one year appointment as a lecturer in Philosophy at Manchester University (1919–20). Then, between

March, 1921 and November, 1922, Macmurray taught Philosophy at the University of Witwatersrand, Johannesburg, South Africa.

From 1922–28 he was Fellow and Classical Tutor at Balliol College, Oxford where his first essay was issued by the Aristotelian Society in 1925.[12] In subsequent publications during this period, his enduring interest in the relationship between science and religion is already evident.[13]

In 1928 Professor Macmurray accepted a position in Philosophy at London University College where he lectured and wrote until 1944. During his London tenure he became a BBC radio celebrity and began publishing in earnest.

Typical of a number of British intellectuals in the 1930s, Macmurray undertook a serious study of the writings of Karl Marx. Over the next several years, in a series of articles and books highlighting the Marxist emphasis on action and social relations, he argued that a synthesis of the key elements in Marxism and Christianity was not only possible but desirable.[14] In later works from the period, a fading of sympathy towards Marxism is apparent in his critique of the Marxist understand-ing of religion ("opiate of the people") as incorrect. Dialectical materialism was an inadequate tool for interpreting the world which Macmurray had come to know as essentially *personal.* As a result of these interests and writings, throughout the 1930s and 1940s Macmurray maintained connections with British labor unions and even acted as the spokesperson for a group called The Christian Left. The preeminent position his philosophy gives to action over knowledge can be traced to these years.

Radio Personality and Author

During the summer of 1930, in an attempt to take philosophy to the people, Macmurray delivered a series of twelve BBC Radio talks relating to the philosophical questions of the times. Titled "Reality and Freedom," they were surprisingly well received:

> Few would have expected that at the height of a beguiling summer and at the unlikely hour of eight of the evening twelve broadcast talks on Philosophy would have produced a miniature renaissance among thousands of English listeners. In that sense, at least, the talks made broadcast history. The pamphlet which introduced them . . . became a 'best-seller.'[15]

In large part due to the considerable correspondence these and a subsequent series of four talks on "The Modern Dilemma" (January, 1932) generated, they were published as Macmurray's first book, *Freedom in the Modern World*, which appeared in the Spring of 1932.[16] In 1935 he published a second collection of lectures, *Reason and Emotion*, which went through several editions.[17]

Macmurray has said that the whole of his adult life was concerned to explicate the character of Christianity. *Clue to History*,[18] for instance, one of Macmurray's early and most difficult works, unfolds how Christianity, ensnared in a Greco-Roman understanding of consciousness (theoretical, aesthetic, technical, pragmatic), had conceived of Jesus as a kind of Greek philosopher. Macmurray offers the corrective that Jesus, in continuity with Hebrew consciousness and the Hebrew prophetic tradition (religious, communal, practical), was not a philosophical *thinker* according to the Greek ideal but a person who *acted.*

Macmurray studied Descartes, Kant and Hegel, concluding that idealist religion is *unreal*, and he found kindred spirits in Soren Kierkegaard and Martin Buber. In his introduction to *Reason and Emotion*, John E. Costello, S.J. tells this anecdote about Macmurray and Buber: "In his one and only meeting with Martin Buber, after three hours of conversation Buber is reported to have said, 'I see no point on which we differ. It is simply that you are the metaphysician and I am the poet.'"[19] Of Buber, Macmurray wrote, "I met him once and was wholly at one with him."[20]

Communal experiments in education were another focus of his attention, particularly at Wennington, a Quaker school in Yorkshire (founded 1940). In its "effort to make the school itself a society of friends," Macmurray wrote, "the development of the personal lives of their pupils" was the primary focus at Wennington. [21] Seeking, as did the faculty at Wennington, to bridge the gap between "intellectual achievement" (thinking) and "admirable character" (doing) proved to be a major theme of Macmurray's life.

Lecturer

From 1944–57 Macmurray was Professor of Moral Philosophy and later Academic Dean at Edinburgh University. As in London, students overflowed his lectures. World War II veterans were especially attracted to his thought.

During his tenure in London and Edinburgh, Professor Macmurray traveled extensively to present lectures; notably, at Yale University in the United States[22] and Queen's University in Kingston, Ontario, Canada.[23] At the apex of his career, Macmurray was invited to deliver the prestigious Gifford Lectures for 1953–54 which he titled "The Form of the Personal." These were subsequently published as *The Self as Agent* (1957)[24] and *Persons in Relation* (1961).[25] They represent Macmurray's mature philosophical thought and will be the major focus of the next chapter of this book.[26]

Retirement

John Macmurray retired from Edinburgh University in 1957 after almost four decades of teaching and writing. Although he had been familiar with the Society of Friends since the period between the wars, it was only after retirement that he formally applied for and was accepted into full membership. "I became increasingly unsatisfied in my isolation," he reported (*Search* 28). In 1965, speaking "not as a philosopher but as a person to persons, as a Christian to Christians and . . . as a Quaker to Quakers" (*Search* 3), Macmurray delivered his Swarthmore Lecture, "Search for Reality in Religion," a moving personal confession of faith. A major focus in this lecture was the perennial question as to the relationship between faith and reason. In the next chapter we will consider in some detail Macmurray's under-standing of the philosopher as "necessarily involved in a commitment which has itself a religious quality" and the argument set forth in his Swarthmore Lecture that "faith and reason have more in common than we are inclined to allow" (*Search* 2 & 3).

Macmurray moved to Buckinghamshire, England, in the late 1960s. He died in Edinburgh on June 20, 1976 and was buried in the Quaker village of Jordans. A year later, a friend and student of his thought wrote:

> We keenly miss the presence of this *real* person. Our toothy video-tape world has all too few of his kind whose only ulterior motive in communicating is to do the truth, textured with seasoned experience, expert research, and the wisdom born of wide-ranging, unhurried and unflinching reflection.[27]

John Macmurray is remembered as a deep but clear and original twentieth century philosopher of ethics and religion. With the reissuing of five of his most important works between 1991 and 1993 there is a renewed interest in his thought which we try to unpack in the next chapter.

Notes

1. This quotation is from a transcript of an address delivered by John Macmurray during a Sunday evening assembly at Wennington School, June 12, 1949. It is part of the John Macmurray Collection, Regis College, University of Toronto, Canada.

2. The reference in brackets (*Search* 11) is to John Macmurray, *Search for Reality in Religion*, Swarthmore Lecture Pamphlet (London: Friends Home Service Committee, 1969), 11. Quotations from this work will henceforth be indicated as here (*Search* 11). The Swarthmore Lectures are sponsored by Swarthmore College, a Society of Friends foundation in Swarthmore, Pennsylvania. The title of the Lecture, "Search for Reality in Religion," is "virtually descriptive of Macmurray's philosophical career" (A. R. C. Duncan, "No Man is an Island . . .," *Listening: Journal of Religion and Culture* 10, no. 2 [Spring, 1975]: Note 4, 53). See also, Thomas E. Wren, "John Macmurray's Search for Reality," *Listening: Journal of Religion and Culture* 10, no 2 (Spring, 1975): 1 which views Macmurray's Swarthmore Lecture as "virtually descriptive of his entire life." Macmurray describes himself as "having always been a staunch supporter of science" (John Macmurray, "Science and Objectivity," *Listening: Journal of Religion and Culture*, [Spring, 1975]: 8). He credits his scientific training for his ability to reject the dogmatic claims of theology which do not stand up to critical analysis.

3. Albert H. Nephew, "The Personal Universe," *Listening: Journal of Religion and Culture* 10, no. 2 (Spring, 1975): 99. In this respect, as in others, it strikes me that Macmurray's life parallels that of Eric Liddell, the 1924 Olympic sprinter from Scotland, the subject of the 1981 Academy Award winning film, *Chariots of Fire*.

4. This quotation is taken from a 1967 BBC radio talk of John Macmurray, "What Religion is About." It is found in Kenneth Barnes, Kathleen Lonsdale, and John Macmurray, *Quakers Talk to Sixth Formers: A Series of Broadcasts* (London: Friends Home Service Committee, 1970), 51. Clearly, Macmurray does not intend the term *religion* to be understood as synonymous with theology or any system of beliefs (*Search* 14–15).

5. On an earlier leave in 1916 he married Betty who survived him. The Macmurray's had no children.

6. John Macmurray, "Here I Stand," a somewhat autobiographical talk found in the John Macmurray Collection, Regis College, University of Toronto, Canada. It is not dated. Macmurray's critique of religion at this time in his life recalls Lonergan's comment: "I for one would object to the identification of religion with self-centered religion. . . . the function of religion is not to make man self-centered but to complete his self-transcendence" (*Second Collection* 158–59). Human authenticity lies in this self-transcendence (*Second Collection* 155).

7. John Macmurray, "Here I Stand," John Macmurray Collection, Regis College, University of Toronto, Canada.

8. As we shall see more clearly in our exploration of his philosophical thought in the next chapter, "Macmurray held firmly to a personal faith in Christ and in the power of the Christian gospel as the single most potent force available to transform human hearts and human society in the direction of the justice and love that our human nature desired and required" (John E. Costello, S.J., Introduction to *Reason and Emotion* by John Macmurray [Atlantic Highlands, NJ: Humanities Press International, Inc., 1991], x).

9. He had great hope that the League of Nations could prevent future war. See A. R. C. Duncan, "No Man is an Island . . .," *Listening: Journal of Religion and Culture* 10, no. 2 (Spring, 1975): 43.

10. John E. Costello, S.J., Introduction to *Reason and Emotion* by John Macmurray (Atlantic Highlands, NJ: Humanities Press International, 1992), xi and xiii. In this attitude, Macmurray was like Bernard Lonergan who set out to reconstruct a methodology for Roman Catholic philosophy and theology. Both Macmurray and Lonergan can be thought of as "personalist" philosophers (*See* **Personalism/ist** in Glossary).

11. This is the title of a Robert Frost poem which was echoed in the classic best-seller *The Road Less Traveled* by M. Scott Peck (New York: Simon & Schuster, 1978).

12. John Macmurray, "Is Art a Form of Apprehension or a Form of Expression?," *Proceedings of the Aristotelian Society* (Supplement 5, 1925): 173–89. Macmurray remained active in the Aristotelian Society until the late 1930s.

13. For example, in "Objectivity in Religion" (in *Adventure: The Faith of Science and the Science of Faith*, ed. B. H. Streeter [London: Macmillan, 1927]), Macmurray sets forth questions about the nature of religion which were to prove central in later publications.

14. In part, this same sympathy motivates Liberation Theology, a largely Roman Catholic phenomenon originating in Latin America. Liberation Theology combines Biblical and Marxist themes in its critique of oppressive social, economic, and political structures.

15. C. A. Siepmann, Foreword to *Freedom in the Modern World* by John Macmurray (Atlantic Highlands, NJ: Humanities Press International, 1992), xxxvi.

16. A second edition of *Freedom in the Modern World* was published in 1935 and various editions appeared down to 1968. In 1992, Humanities Press International reissued the book "in the belief that the problems Macmurray examines and his close reasoning towards a solution, are just as relevant today" (back cover of 1992 edition). In addition to the 1930 and 1932 lecture series, the book included the pamphlet distributed by the BBC as preparatory reading to the 1930 lectures, "Today and Tomorrow: A Philosophy of Freedom," and an original concluding essay, "The Final Summary: Self-Realization," in which Macmurray tackles his critics. Macmurray's last BBC radio series, during Lent 1964, evidenced that the main mission of Jesus was to free human beings from fear.

17. Other publications by Macmurray in the 1930s and 1940s include: *Interpreting the Universe* (1933), *Philosophy of Communism* (1933), *Creative Society* (1935), *Structure of Religious Experience* (1936), *The Boundaries of Science* (1939), *Challenge to the Churches* (1941), *Constructive Democracy* (1943), all first published by Faber & Faber Limited, London, England. *The Clue to History* (1938) was published by the Student Christian Movement Press in London.

18. John Macmurray, *The Clue to History* (London: Student Christian Movement Press, 1938).

19. John E. Costello, S.J., Introduction to *Reason and Emotion* by John Macmurray (Atlantic Highlands, NJ: Humanities Press International, 1992), xix.

20. Letter to Stanley Peck, July 21, 1972, in the John Macmurray Collection, Regis College, University of Toronto, Canada.

21. This is taken from the concluding paragraph of "They Made A School," a handwritten manuscript by Macmurray, dated December 4, 1968. It is found in the John Macmurray Collection, Regis College, University of Toronto, Canada. The same collection also contains an "Address to Wennington Students," dated June 12, 1949. See also Kenneth C. Barnes, *Energy Unbound: The Story of Wennington School* (York, England: Williams Sessions Ltd., 1980). Wennington School is now closed.

22. Macmurray's Terry Lecture at Yale was published as *The Structure of Religious Experience* (London: Faber & Faber Limited, 1936). The Terry Lecture for 1937, "Psychology and Religion," was delivered by Carl Jung. In 1950, Erich Fromm was the Terry lecturer on "Psychoanalysis and Religion."

23. In 1949, Macmurray came to Canada to present "Conditions of Freedom," a set of lectures sponsored by the Chancellor Dunning Trust at Queen's University in Kingston. They have been published as John Macmurray, *Conditions of Freedom* (Toronto: The Ryerson Press, 1949) and reprinted in 1977 by the John Macmurray Society, Toronto.

24. John Macmurray, *The Self as Agent* (Atlantic Highlands, NJ: Humanities Press International, 1991).

25. John Macmurray, *Persons in Relation* (Atlantic Highlands, NJ: Humanities Press International, 1991). In a letter to Kenneth Barnes (founder and first headmaster of Wennington School), November 27, 1973, Macmurray, with reference to the Spanish translation of the Gifford Lectures, remarked "my clientele is broadening" (John Macmurray Collection, Regis College, University of Toronto, Canada).

26. In the first set of lectures, using a complex metaphysical argument, he demonstrates the primacy of action over thinking. In the second set of lectures he shows how the mutuality of persons ("'I' exist as only one element in the complex 'You and I'") brings doing (and not thinking) to center stage in human affairs. At the end of the lectures, having carefully developed his own philosophical standpoint, Macmurray tackles the key questions Gifford Lecturers are charged with answering: "What contribution does this philosophical study make to the problem of the validity of religious belief? Are there, or are there not, rational grounds for a belief in God?" (*Persons* 206). He argues that his new "more inclusive" philosophical standpoint ("I do" as including "I think") does indeed provide "rational grounds" for understanding that the world is personal and that God is the "Agent" whose "action" *is* the world; that is, we live in "a personal universe in which God is the ultimate reality" (*Persons* 224).

27. Philip Mooney, "Freedom Through Friendship, John Macmurray: In Memoriam (1891–1976)," *Friends Journal* (January 1, 1977): 4.

Chapter 3

Macmurray's Characterization of the Personal Life

All meaningful knowledge is for the sake of action, and all meaningful action for the sake of friendship (John Macmurray in *Self* 15).

Task of Philosophy

We have seen that Macmurray's choice of career as a professor of Philosophy was influenced by his earnest belief that "real philosophy . . . is the understanding of real human experience, and springs hot out of life itself" (*Freedom* 67). He understood and practiced philosophy, not as an intellectual exercise but in an effort to understand the meaning of the experience of real people struggling in this very real world to live together in community. Further, his philosophical positions grew out of the very fabric of his life; a strict Presbyterian youth and later abandonment of *organized* Christianity, wartime experiences and struggles, years spent in the university milieu, flirtation with Marxist thought and unions, and countless other experiences that helped shape his person. "Instead of saying that a philosophy is a way of life," he wrote, "it would be better to say that any way of life implies a philosophy" (*Self* 24). Because he believed that traditional academic philosophy had reached an impasse (unable to account for two world wars or come to satisfactory answers to the key questions of life), he brought a fresh philosophical approach to bear on the questions of his age, contributing to a philosophical Copernican Revolution.

The nature of the personal life was, for John Macmurray, the central issue of the twentieth century: "That we are living through a period of revolutionary change is already a commonplace. . . . To me it seems certain that the scale of change must dwarf the transformation of medieval into modern Europe" (*Self* 26).

The Gifford Lectures on Natural Theology, 1953–54[1] represent Macmurray's mature exposition of this new philosophical conceptualization — "the form of the personal" (*doing* is a more fundamental human category than *thinking*). In the Introductory to the Spring 1953 lectures (*The Self as Agent*), Professor Macmurray says: "The simplest expression that I can find for the thesis I have tried to maintain is this: All meaningful knowledge is for the sake of action, and all meaningful action for the sake of friendship" (*Self* 14–15). This chapter is an effort to uncover the profound meaning embedded in this deceptively simple sentence.

Macmurray maintained that "it is always legitimate to ask, of any theory which claims to be true, what practical difference it would make if we believed it" (*Self* 23); a question to ask yourself about *his* philosophical ideas as they unfold in these pages.

Survey of Western Philosophical Tradition

Contemporary philosophical positions can only be appreciated in the context of the history of philosophy.[2] Accordingly, Macmurray's thought must be situated within the Western philosophical tradition. We will begin with his analysis of modern Western philosophy as already having passed through two distinct phases, respectively dominated by a mechanistic metaphor (we are complicated machines) and an organic metaphor (we are complex animals).

Mechanical Metaphor

The first phase in modern Western philosophy, roughly corresponds to the growth of the physical sciences; Galileo Galilei (1564–1642) and Sir Isaac Newton (1642–1727) being two of the better known figures of the period. In philosophical terms, Macmurray says, this phase covers the period from René Descartes (1596–1650) to David Hume (1711–1776).[3] It is to this philosophical tradition, with roots in fourth century B.C. Greece (Plato and Aristotle), that we owe our tendency to identify rationality as *the* peculiarly human attribute.

During this first period, according to Macmurray's analysis, the central concern of philosophy was to understand and explain matter (i.e., its *form*). The essence of human nature was *thinking* (the human being was a thinking thing, a "mind in a machine") and knowledge of the external world resided in the human mind. According to this view, what we knew as a result of contemplative thought was *objective* and real; what we knew only from sense experience was *subjective* and, hence, unreliable, illusory or imaginary. The universe was viewed as a collection of inert chunks of matter (stars and planets) and tiny particles (atoms) operating "mechanically;"[4] philosophy was theoretical and analytic (deductive) with "substance" (thing) as its key concept. A concrete example may help to clarify the point.

Our eyes tell us that the sun circles the earth, rising in the east and setting in the west (just watch it!), yet we *know* that the earth moves around the sun. Accordingly, sense experience is unreliable. What we have come to see, however, is that both of these views, in their respective spheres are correct. To say that the sun rises and sets is to *describe* in ordinary language the movement of the sun as it *appears* to my eyes. To say that the earth moves around the sun in an elliptical orbit is to *explain*, in technical (i.e., mathematical) language, the *real* relationship between the earth and sun.

René Descartes (1596–1650)

Often called the father of modern philosophy, René Descartes approached his discipline with the understanding that to *think* was to *know*. This rational approach to philosophy discounted the senses as a reliable means for discovering truth. Employing a method of doubt (doubt is a form of thinking), Descartes' methodological skepticism led him to the one indubitable declaration "Cogito ergo sum" (I think, therefore I am). This "axiom" came to be viewed as the starting point for modern philosophy.[5]

All knowing was considered to be philosophy for the ancient Greek thinkers (*philosophos*, lover of wisdom), but with Descartes we see an effort to distinguish between philosophy and theology. Philosophy was the domain of human *reason* and theology, based on divine revelation, was the domain of *faith*.[6] Note that for Descartes, this distinction was not meant to discredit God or religion; he was in fact a believer, and his whole philosophical approach rested on God — because God is perfect, God could not deceive us and so the exercise of true reasoning will lead to truth. Descartes even offered a "proof" for God's existence (God is the Cause of the idea we have of God as Perfection).

David Hume (1711–1776)

In the work of the Scottish enlightenment philosopher David Hume, we see philosophy (already distinct from theology) further divided from science.[7] Hume attacked Descartes' rationalism and supported the view that knowledge can be derived through sense experience, i.e., empirically. Truth can be known in the physical world through the senses — *empirical* knowledge is knowledge of what is real. *Only* in the scientific realm, through the use of an inductive methodology, can we derive sure knowledge. The deductive relationship in rational philosophy between cause and effect, Hume argued, is not "necessary" but based on custom or habit.[8]

Note, however that although Descartes and Hume differ as to how the connection between the knowing subject and the object known is made (for Descartes, *mind* is the link, for Hume the link is *sense experience*) they hold in common the notion that, in the process of knowing, I (a subject) stand apart from the material world I seek to know (an object). It is this idea of the knower as radically distinct from what is to be known (subject/object split) which will be the focus of Macmurray's critique of the first phase of Western philosophy.[9]

Organic Metaphor

Over the seventeenth and eighteenth centuries it became apparent that while science and mathematics were appropriate for predicting and explaining events in the physical world, it was quite another thing to use material and mechanical categories as descriptive and predicative of the activity of living beings. Accordingly, a second phase of European philosophy can be discerned, roughly corresponding to the growth of the biological sciences; Robert Hooke (1635–1703) and Charles Darwin (1809–1882) being symbolic of the spirit of the age.

As representative of the second phase of philosophy, Macmurray chose the thought of the German idealist, Immanuel Kant (1724–1804), who sought to build a bridge between rationalism and empiricism, at the same time defending both from romanticism (emphasis on feeling over thinking). Before tackling Kant, we need to acquaint ourselves with this important antecedent.

Romanticism

The Romantic period in Western cultural history has its origins in the seventeenth century and extends into the nineteenth century. For the Romantics "reason" was that within us which produced science but it was "faith," our capacity for aesthetic experience, which really mattered and distinguished us from lower animals.[10] A 1930 publication expressed the essence of the Romantic critique of rational and empirical philosophy quite well:

> We are quite willing to be told that we are curiously carved pieces of the earth's crust, or strange dust-wreath vortexes, if we may add to the account *the something more which we know we are.* The whirling dust-wreaths of the street do not have longings. The bits of earth-crust which we throw about with our shovel do not yearn for what is not and then forthwith construct it. Desires and strivings, visions and ideals, emotions and sentiments, are as much a genuine part of us as are the iron and lime and phosphorus in our bodies. We have insights of what ought to be, appreciations of beauty, convictions of truth, experiences of love, and these things are not part of the earth's crust. They are not physical realities. They are not *results* of masses of matter in motion. They cannot be adequately explained mechanically.[11]

As the basis for our knowledge of the real, the Romantics, as it were, substituted the artist's point of view (ideas about the "true," the "good," the "beautiful") for the rationalist's mind and the scientist's empirical method. Neither rationalism nor empiricism leave any room for affectivity (feelings, emotion). The productive spontaneity of the imagination (an artistic activity which combines elements of experience in a way that is not given in experience) underlies all experience, the Romantics said, and particularly all cognitional activity (knowing). It is this synthetic and artistic movement which is the wellspring of knowledge for the Romantics.

Immanuel Kant (1724–1804)

According to John Macmurray, Kant's publications represent "the most adequate of modern philosophies" for two reasons — because Kant was correct in his critique of rational thinking which dominated the first phase of philosophy, and because modern philosophies since Kant are derivative of his thought (*Self* 39).[12] Before proceeding with Macmurray's critique of this second, "organic," phase of Western philosophy we must consider, briefly, Kant's idealist philosophy. At the outset, however, I should remind you that Kant is reported to have sent an early draft of his *Critique of Pure Reason*[13] to a colleague who returned it unfinished with the comment that he was afraid if he went on to the end he might become insane. You are warned!

Critical of the classical philosophical position (rationalism), Kant held that it was not possible to gain knowledge of the world by thought alone. However, he also knew, contrary to the views expounded by British empiricists, that sense experience by itself does not give true knowledge of the world either. For Kant, knowledge comes as a result of a *synthesis* between what we experience by means of our senses ("phenomena") and concepts ("categories") of pure thought which exist in our minds and are imposed on phenomena to make sense of the world. It is true, Kant says, that unless an object is apprehended by the senses we could not even become aware of it but at the same time it is equally true that there is more to knowing than just taking a good look at what is already out there — without interpretation, sense experience is blind! Further, we can *think* as we please but if we are trying to get at truth there is only one way to proceed and that, Kant contends, is to acknowledge that we think according to categories existing in the mind. One can say, for instance, that '1 + 1 = 3,' but to count correctly there are rules that prescribe the method and describe the process to be followed.

In his *Critique of Pure Reason*, Kant first proposed that "space" and "time" are given to everyone as "*a priori* pure intuitions;" i.e., they are absolute, independent of, and prior to, any sense impression. Second, serving as a kind of basic conceptual apparatus for making sense of the world, he proposed twelve "categories of thought" organized according to quantity (unity, plurality, totality), quality (reality, negation, limitation), relation (substance, causality, interaction), and modality (possibility, existence, necessity). We "construct" the world we know (i.e., knowledge is "synthetic") but we do so in accordance with laws of thought. Without categories of understanding we would not be able to form a concept of the object out there and hence not be able to *know* it. An example may prove helpful at this point.

David Hume had used a game of billiards to illustrate that there was no *necessary* connection between cause and effect. It is a habit of mind, he said that makes us assume that one ball striking another in a particular spot will move it in a predictable direction. Kant, concerned to preserve a role for reason in the knowing process, understands the billiard shot quite differently. For Kant, the intuitions of space and time allow the sense impression of one ball on the table being struck by another to be conveyed to the mind. Here the quantitative category "plurality" registers the two balls, the qualitative category of "reality" registers that one ball strikes the other in a certain way, the relational category of "causality" understands that the struck ball will go in a certain predictable direction, and the modal category of "necessity" understands that this will occur in the same way each time one ball strikes another in the same way.

Even if the example has not proven to be helpful, I trust it makes clear that according to Kant, knowing depends on an integration of sense data about what is "out there" with categories of understanding. But there is a catch! Kant's view is that the categories of understanding are in the *mind* of the knower rather than features of things as they are in themselves. Accordingly, what we know through this process is the world only as it *appears to us* (the practical world of phenomena) and not the world as it *is in itself* (the real world of noumena) which is beyond the limits of human knowledge. Yet, although Kant denies the Cartesian view that we can have knowledge of *things in themselves*, he does not repudiate reason as such but just points out its limitations.

Further, Kant says that, although reality cannot be perceived in experience, the existence of an absolute moral law or "categorical imperative" must be presumed: "Two things fill the mind with ever new and increasing admiration and awe," Kant wrote in *The Critique of Practical Reason*, "the starry heavens above and the moral law within."[14] Traditional metaphysical arguments for the existence of God, the soul, immortality, free will and similar issues, Kant pointed out, were also beyond the limits of reason which is legitimately employed only in knowing the phenomenal world.

So, for Kant, knowing is not the simple, straightforward, mechanical activity it was for Descartes (pure reason) and Hume (sense experience). His complex understanding of the knowing process involves *both* sense experience of an object out there *and* a knowing of that object by means of inner categories of the mind. In this way he sought to stake out a middle ground which held together the positive elements in rationalism and empiricism and at the same time defended both from the attacks of romanticism which argued that feeling was a more basic human category than was thinking.

This achievement accounts for Macmurray's assessment of Kant's thought as the "most adequate of modern philosophies." The philosophical problem Kant wrestled with, as Macmurray formulates it, was the "form" or conceptualization of the "organic" (it is more than just mechanical "thing") and his answer to the question was a synthesis of elements of both rationalism and empiricism. But, in his efforts to defend rationality against the influence of romantic sensitivity (heart before head), Kant is not able to make the connection between a thing as it *is* in itself and that same thing as it *appears* to me. He is forced to conclude that although there is indeed a real, noumenal, world "out there," as mere "thinking things" we can never know it but only the phenomenal world of appearances. Macmurray summarizes Kant's predicament as follows:

> Knowledge is, in some sense, the discovery of what exists independently of any activity of ours. If we construct our knowledge, if it depends at all upon a spontaneous, inventive activity of the mind, then there is no escape from the conclusion that we can never know the world as it is in itself, independently of our ways of apprehending it. . . . Reality as it is in itself is unknowable. This is the famous doctrine of the Thing-in-itself, of the noumenal world, and it is Kant's denial of knowledge (*Self* 46).

Kant is correct, Macmurray contends, to critique rationalists for their attachment to the mind of the subject and the empiricists for their fixation on the object as known through the senses. He is even correct in his explanation that the object we have grasped through the senses is at least partially known in terms of categories of the mind (i.e., subjectively) but, and this is Kant's difficulty, he is not able to show that the *real* object out there and the knowledge of that object which I have in my mind correspond. Kant's distinction between what is real 'out-there' and what is real 'only in the mind' is unacceptable for Macmurray because it makes the mind a place of unreality and illusion where each of us is, as it were, locked up like a prisoner in solitary confinement (*Self* 39–61).[15]

Note that Kant, like his predecessors, primarily understands the knowing subject to be separate from what is to be known. It is a critique of this separation of subject and object which lies at the heart of Macmurray's effort to rethink the starting point of philosophy as that of the self as an *agent* (involved with and for others in action) rather than that of the self as an isolated *thinker* absorbed in thought.

Insights derived from nineteenth century evolutionary biology, helped to move us away from perceiving human beings as simply "thinking things" to understanding them as "organisms" actively involved in their knowing. To have arrived at this point is a great achievement but, as Macmurray points out, we were too easily seduced by the ability of the new organic metaphor to explain human behavior. A powerful advance on the understanding of what it is to be a human being offered by the earlier mechanical model, the organic metaphor, Macmurray insists, is also limited because of its attempt (denying 'self' and 'human consciousness') to explain the human person exclusively in organic categories:

> The root of the error is the attempt to understand the field of the personal on a biological analogy, and so through organic categories. . . . We are not organisms, but persons. The nexus of relations which unites us in a human society is not organic but personal (*Persons* 45–46).[16]

We will now turn to a consideration of Macmurray's critique of our Western philosophical tradition and his understanding of the "personal."

Macmurray on the Western Philosophical Tradition

Macmurray's Gifford Lectures begin with a general statement that they focus on his two major criticisms of our Western philosophical tradition (applicable to both the mechanical and organic metaphors) — it is "theoretical" and "egocentric."[17] In turn, we will unpack each of these appraisals.

Modern Philosophy as "Theoretical"

Modern philosophy is *theoretical*. It assumes that a human being ('self') is primarily a *thinking* 'subject' for whom the world is the 'object' to be *known*. Against this "presupposition," Macmurray argues that a thinking subject is derivative of a doing subject (an 'agent'). By proposing[18] that we substitute "I do" for "I think" as our starting point, *The Self as Agent* seeks to "shift the center of gravity in our philosophical tradition" from the theoretical to the practical (*Self* 85).

Macmurray's foundational critique of our Western philosophical heritage centers on our habitual understanding of the knower as being distinct from the object to be known in the human knowing process. For Descartes, the knower stood apart from the object, thinking about it. For Hume, the knower stood apart from the object, collecting empirical data about it through the senses. For Kant, the knower took sense data from out there into his/her mind where the mind's categories processed the raw data in order to understand it. Although each of these positions came under attack by the Romantics, they also stood apart from the object to be known, merely substituting feeling as the basis for human knowing.

Rationality, Macmurray agrees is *one* human quality; it is "the capacity for objectivity, and . . . it is the possession of this capacity which distinguishes persons from whatever is sub-personal" (*Interpreting* 127–28).[19] And, even though he speaks of rationality as "the essential characteristic of personal consciousness," for Macmurray, rationality means much more than just thinking: "It is the essence of personal consciousness as such. Rationality is not a peculiar characteristic of the intellect. It is equally characteristic of the emotional life. . . . art and religion are just as rational as science or philosophy" (*Interpreting* 131). *Being* is more foundational than knowing; who we *are* is far more important that what we *know*. Here, of course, Macmurray is integrating the insights of the Romantics into his position (something Kant was loathe to do).

Knowing, then, for Macmurray, is more than mere intellectual activity; *knowing what to do* certainly involves more than just interpreting sense experience (empiricism). Feeling is integral to knowing and acting: "there is no *a priori* reason . . . why at the personal level, feeling should not be as much an element in cognition as sense. For it is a person who knows in acting, not his mind or his thought, and feeling, like sense, is a necessary element in any personal consciousness" (*Self* 126).

Accordingly, Macmurray proposes *action*, not thought, as the fundamental category for understanding what it is to be human. In ordinary speech when we absentmindedly make a mistake we say, 'I'm sorry, I wasn't thinking about what I was doing' — the implication being that if I *was* thinking about what I was doing I would have done it right! "Knowledge is that in my action which makes it an action," Macmurray says, "and not a blind activity" (*Self* 129). Our very use of language, then, lends support to Macmurray's argument that while thought does not include action, action by its very nature includes thinking. The "I do" contains the "I think," of necessity; we solve our day-to-day problems by "taking thought." Moreover, the "I do" includes the "I *know* that I do." In fact, as he points out, thinking is not something that just happens to me but something that I *do!*[20] In Macmurray's view, and here is where the practicality of his philosophical approach is apparent, our theoretical activities *ought* to have their origin in practical requirements and theoretical results, if they are meaningful at all, are solutions to *practical* problems. Macmurray refers to "purely theoretical" activities as "purely imaginary" (*Self* 21).[21] To sum up, action is an *inclusive* concept whereas thought is an *exclusive* concept.

Macmurray's philosophy, then, is not just a theory of knowledge but of action! Action is a full concrete activity of the Self employing *all* our capacities whereas thought is constituted by the exclusion of some of our powers and a withdrawal into an activity which is less concrete and less complete. It is important to remember, however, that a theory of knowledge is derived from and included within a theory of action. Avoiding the dualism of theoretical philosophies (subject as separate from object), Macmurray points out that the self that reflects and the self that acts is the same self; action and thought are *contrasted* (not split) modes of its activity.

Table 3.1

I DO	=	I KNOW	+	I MOVE
ACTION	=	KNOWLEDGE	+	ACTIVITY (*Self* 128)

Modern Philosophy as "Egocentric"

Macmurray's second criticism of our European philosophical tradition is that it is *egocentric*. Logically, he deduces, we ought to expect that the emergence in our century of a scientific human *psychology* would be paralleled by a transition from an organic to a *personal* philosophy. Resting on the assertion that *the Self is neither a substance nor an organism, but a person* (person is inclusive of both substance and organism), the "form of the personal" would be the "emergent problem" (*Self* 37). This is the transition Macmurray champions but it is not easy to achieve because his interpretation of the term "personal" involves a letting go of the egocentric point of view. Simply put, the self does not exist in isolation but as part of the unit 'You and I.'

In my teaching I use an example which may help to clarify what Macmurray means by his use of the term *personal*. As I understand it, if you were placed at birth on a deserted island where you were the only human being and somehow grew to maturity, you would know that you were a different kind of creature from the rats and chimpanzees; you might know too that this difference consisted in your rationality. But according to Macmurray's understanding, although you might know what it is to be *human* (rational) you could not know what it is to be a *person* until another human being arrived on the island and befriended you. The notion of person is only realized in relationship with at least one other human being.

Having established in the 1953 Gifford Lectures that the self exists not as a thinking subject but as 'agent' (actor, doer), Macmurray argued in the following year's lectures that the 'agent self' can exist only in dynamic relation with other human beings who are also agents. The thesis he defended is "that the Self is constituted by its relation to the Other; that it has its being in its relationship; and that this relationship is necessarily personal" (*Persons* 17).

> The idea of an isolated agent is self-contradictory. Any agent is necessarily in relation to the Other. Apart from this essential relation he does not exist. But, further, the Other in this constitutive relation must itself be personal. Persons, therefore, are constituted by their mutual relation to one another. 'I' exist only as one element in the complex 'You and I' (*Persons* 24).

To substantiate this view, *Persons in Relation* (Gifford Lectures, Spring, 1954) sets out Macmurray's criticism of *egocentrism*. For Macmurray, a foundational problem with the traditional point of view adopted by our philosophy is the idea that a human being is, in essence, a 'self' in the moment of *private reflection*, by definition cut off from the world he/she seeks to know. A formal dualism is thus created between the subject and any object of his/her concern; between thought and action, between reason and emotion, between theory and practice. Any philosophy which takes the 'I think' as its first principle, Macmurray contends, must remain formally a philosophy without a second person; a philosophy which cannot be conceived relationally; 'You *and* I.' Against this understanding of the 'self' as a solitary and isolated thinking thing,[22] Macmurray sets forth the view that the 'self' is a *person*, and that human existence is *constituted* by the relationship of persons.[23]

Thinking about another person or seeing another person in terms of the organic metaphor, for example, can never amount to *personal knowledge of* that other person. The possibility of persons *in relation* (involving action, emotion and practice) is therefore unattainable. But, when we start from the standpoint of action, Macmurray argues, there is an *essential* relation between thought and action (theory and practice) which is that thought is included in action.

Form of the Personal

Macmurray begins his argument with a consideration of the prototypical relationship in our lives, that between a mother and her baby.[24] He does this, in part, to counter the "widespread belief . . . that the human infant is an animal organism which becomes rational, and acquires a human personality, in the process of growing up" (*Persons* 44). If the organic metaphor can be proven inadequate as an explanation for human behavior at infancy, he reasons, then it follows that it must also be inadequate as an account of human maturity.

Macmurray's argument is that the new born baby's "total helplessness" indicates that infants are "made to be cared for." Animals are more or less endowed instinctually with what they need for survival in the environment into which they are born. We might similarly expect new born babies to be endowed with what they need for survival in the environment into which they are born. But, because the organic metaphor is not an exhaustive description of humanness, a baby's adaptation is to "a complete dependence upon an adult human being." Further, this need which the baby has for care, Macmurray points out, "is not simply biological but personal, a need to be in touch with the mother, and in conscious perceptual relation with her."[25]

Relationship is *constitutive* of human living for Macmurray: "We need one another to be ourselves. This complete and unlimited dependence of each of us upon the others is the central and crucial fact of personal existence" (*Persons* 211). The idea of an isolated agent is self-contradictory; any agent is necessarily in relationship. Apart from this essential relation an *agent* does not exist. Further, personal relationship is not only a possibility, in action, but necessary. We act with and for others.[26] Morality, Macmurray points out, "is essentially social" (*Persons* 116).

Persons are *constituted* by their mutual relation to one another. 'I' exist only as one element in the community 'You and I' which constitutes both the 'You' and the 'I.' You tell me who I am as a *person*. "I need you to be myself" (*Persons* 150). The emerging ecological worldview supports this principle of the *mutuality* of the personal; we are who we are only in and through our relationships with other human beings, all creatures, and the planet itself. The intrinsic value of community is honored and there is a growing recognition in the emerging world order that the best way to serve individuals is to improve community.

"Friendship," the word Macmurray prefers to love as descriptive of the true nature of personal relationships, is a central concept in his exposition of the "form of the personal." Friendship is "the real relationship of one person with another independently real person."[27] Friends can take off their masks and be wholly themselves in the presence of others. "To be a friend," as Macmurray puts it, "is to be yourself for another person."[28] One characteristic of friendship which he holds dear is the freedom inherent in the relationship: "All knowledge of persons is by revelation. My knowledge of you depends not merely on what I do, but upon what you do; and if you refuse to reveal yourself to me, I cannot know you, however much I may wish to do so" (*Persons* 169). Friendship is not forced. Macmurray's second set of lectures survey the field of the personal from the standpoint of action, the distinguishing quality which sets us apart as human beings. The aim of *Persons in Relation* is to discover how this ultimate fact can be generalized in reflection. For Macmurray, meaningful relation-

Table 3.2

HISTORY OF WESTERN PHILOSOPHY AS REVELATORY OF THREE LEVELS OF HUMAN CONSCIOUSNESS [29]

	PRE-MODERN Classical Greece Descartes to Hume	MODERN Kant Rousseau/Hegel	POST-MODERN[30] John Macmurray Bernard Lonergan
Self as . . .	SUBSTANCE	ORGANISM	PERSON
Reality as . . .	SCIENTIFIC	ETHICAL	SPIRITUAL[31]
Philosophical Problem	FORM OF THE MATERIAL	FORM OF THE ORGANIC	FORM OF THE PERSONAL
Philosophy	MATERIALISTIC	IDEALISTIC	EXISTENTIAL
Science	PHYSICAL/ MATHEMATICAL	BIOLOGICAL	HUMAN/ PSYCHOLOGICAL
Scientist	GALILEO	DARWIN	FREUD
World view	MECHANICAL	ORGANIC	PERSONAL
Primacy of the . . .	THEORETICAL (THINKING)		PRACTICAL

ship depends upon meaningful action; the two are symbiotically related. I can know another person *as a person* only by entering into a personal relationship with that other person. Without this I can know that person only by observation and inference; only as an object or thing. An activity of reflection is never completed until it is *expressed* and "a morally right action is an action which intends community" (*Persons* 119).[32]

The question which underlies any philosophical inquiry into action is not the organic question, 'How can we *know* what is right to do?' but the personal question, 'How can I *do* what is right?' Implicit in this, Macmurray proposes, is the idea that without another human being no *action* (Action = Knowledge +Activity) is possible: "The possibility of action depends upon the Other being also agent, and so upon a plurality of agents in one field of action" (*Self* 145). To *act* is to work cooperatively with others and it is impossible to live rationally and communally without such cooperation.

Science

Several of Macmurray's early essays dealt with his abiding interest in the relationship between science and religion. One, titled "Christianity — Pagan or Scientific?" is critical of traditional Christianity with its emphasis on the certainty and unchangeable nature of dogma and sympathetic towards what he calls "scientific Christianity:"

> . . . a Christianity which lives experimentally, holding all its doctrines as liable to modification or even rejection, accepting all its rules of organization and its laws of conduct, as simply so much result of human experience to be used as working hypotheses and experimented with incessantly for their own development and reshaping.[33]

"Beyond Knowledge"[34] goes even further, arguing that the attitude of science is, in fact, the attitude of genuine faith. Science was the topic of one of John Macmurray's last published essays, "Science and Objectivity."[35] Here, he presents two points about the nature of science: (a) the scientific method by its very nature is a "paradigm of self-transcendence"[36] and (b) the findings of science are not certain[37] but always tentative, probable, "radically hypothetical."[38]

One of the more important theoretical consequences of the shift in John Macmurray's philosophy from the theoretical (thinking) to the practical standpoint (action) is that we no longer see the sciences as independent bodies of truth but as human performances, as something that human beings do.

This is a relatively new understanding of science. In the nineteenth century, for example, the German atheistic philosopher, Ludwig Feuerbach, after referring to Copernicus as the "first revolutionary of modern times" proclaimed that the natural sciences had "dissolved the Christian world view in nitric acid."[39] Until well into our own century, science more or less lived by Feuerbach's condescending attitude, secure in its belief that *only* science could know reality with certainty. Today few scientists make this claim.

Classical physics (Isaac Newton) understood matter to be comprised of tiny material atoms which in turn contained still smaller particles (electrons revolving around a nucleus composed of protons and neutrons). In many respects the inner world of the atom, like the planetary system, was understood to operate mechanically according to precise mathematical laws. Since theoretical physicist Albert Einstein (1879–1955) authored his generalized theory of relativity (1915), science has abandoned the mechanical model of reality and is busy revising its theory. The world is no longer understood in terms of tiny material particles moving with mathematical precision but in terms of relationship between entities, no longer in terms of certainty but in terms of probability. This new attitude towards scientific inquiry provides crucial support for Macmurray's argument and is a point of congruence between his philosophy and that of Bernard Lonergan.

Religion and God

Search for Reality in Religion[40]

Characteristic of philosophy and theology in Macmurray's day was the widespread acceptance of an impassable gulf between *faith* and *reason* (traceable to Descartes). Outside of the narrow confines of religion, the supremacy of reason was taken for granted and it was more or less agreed (often even within religion) that knowledge of the divine, if there was such a thing, could only be attained in transcendent religious experiences. Because "religious" experiences were considered by rationalist definition to be "non-rational," there was no point at which faith and reason could meet. Faith was *un*-reasonable, then, and atheism the only logical conclusion a *reasonable* person could hold; religion was an "illusion," Sigmund Freud said,[41] echoing the sentiments of his age. Macmurray disagreed:

> The view that there is no path from common experience to a belief in God; that religion rests upon some special and extraordinary type of experience apart from which it could not arise — this seems to me hardly credible (*Self* 19).

Where atheistic existentialism finds human relationship an insoluble problem and all human projects doomed to frustration and ultimate meaninglessness, the theistic alternative, Macmurray avows, issues from the hope of an ultimate unity of persons in fellowship, which gives meaning to human effort. His philosophy's very conceptualization of the personal directs our attention to *real* religion. Religion, as Macmurray understands it, is a universal *human* experience "bound up with that in our experience which makes us persons and not mere organisms" (*Persons* 156).

Drawing on an understanding of a progressive unfolding of Western philosophy through material, organic, and personal phases, Macmurray advances the view that reality unfolds in three spheres, scientific, aesthetic (ethical), and religious (spiritual). In his view, the first two are subordinate to (but included within) the third, religion, which is essentially "interpersonal." In fact, for Macmurray, "religion is about the community of persons" (*Persons* 157). True religion, he says, is about working to achieve an all embracing world community.

The field of personal relationships is the field of religion, for Macmurray. In *Search for Reality in Religion*, he goes so far as to speak of community not only as the friendship which ought to exist among human beings but also as our proper relationship with God.[42] Moreover, friendship ought to characterize the relationship between humanity and the God given natural world (*Search* 34).[43] Friendship is not just the ideal relationship among human beings but it is also the paradigm for right relationship to the planet. Both are forms of the community of all existence: "The two forms of dependence — upon other people and upon nature — are interwoven and inseparable. They constitute the community of all existence."[44]

God

"Objectivity in Religion" (*Adventure* 177–215)[45] sets forth questions and principles which were to prove central to Macmurray's later thought. Having dismissed the traditional proofs for God's existence, Macmurray asks: "Is the supreme reality of the world properly described as God or as matter or as life, or in some other way?" (*Adventure* 182–83). Arguing, as we have seen, that reality is essentially religious (i.e., interpersonal) and understanding that "the whole of religion is rooted in the idea of God" (*Adventure* 181), Macmurray argues that to describe the supreme reality of the world as God is to say that "the ultimate reality of the universe is such that it can satisfy religious demands. God is therefore necessarily personal. . . . There can be no question of an impersonal God. The phrase is a contradiction in terms" (*Adventure* 183).

Our understanding of God as caring about creation implies that God is to be grasped as necessarily personal and the religious life as necessarily about personal relations, Macmurray maintains. Further, the shift in his philosophy from *I think* to *I do*, from the viewpoint of a disembodied thinker to that of a social, historical, embodied subject or agent, shifts the understanding of God from First Cause or Unmoved Mover to Person or Actor. The aim of Macmurray's Gifford Lectures was to set the stage for this new understanding of God: "In its full development, the idea of a universal personal Other is the idea of God" (*Persons* 164).

In his last lecture, Macmurray turns to the question set before each Gifford lecturer: "'What contribution does this philosophical study make to the problem of the validity of religious belief? Are there, or are there not, rational grounds for a belief in God?'" (*Persons* 206).

Macmurray begins to answer the question not with God but with human beings, specifically the Hebrew people, "the uniquely religious people of history" (*Search* 35). Note that he speaks of the Jewish people as *being* religious, not *having* a religion, as being in relationship with one another, with God, and with God's creation. God is creator of heaven and earth and all that exists including human beings made in the very *imago Dei* (image of God). God, in Macmurray's terminology, is the "original, unlimited and universal agent," an actor or doer. Human beings made in God's image are also free and creative agents. Of course, the relationship between ourselves as free and creative agents and God, the "original, unlimited and universal agent"

is personal (*Search* 44). God's first covenant with his people established this relational pattern: "I will be your God and you shall be my
people" (Jeremiah 7:23).[46]

Macmurray's philosophy, as we have seen, is in reaction to the
theoretical point of view. Accordingly, he begins his discussion of the
reality of God with a dismissal of earlier theoretical and egocentric
"proofs." It is clear to him that metaphysical proofs for God's existence make very little impact; they prove not the existence of God but
the existence of an *idea* or conception of God. At best, they arrive at
God as the Unmoved Mover, First Cause or Necessary, Intelligent and
Perfect Being[47] totally removed from our sphere of activity (dualism)
and lacking "any quality deserving of reverence or worship" (*Persons*
206–07).[48]

That we are not alone in the world is, for Macmurray, the "central
and crucial fact of personal existence." "We need one another to be
ourselves" (*Persons* 211).

> In ourselves we are nothing; and when we turn our eyes inward in
> search of ourselves we find a vacuum. . . . It is only in relation to
> others that we exist as persons; we are invested with significance by
> others who have need of us; and borrow our reality from those who
> care for us. We live and move and have our being not in ourselves
> but in one another; and what rights or powers or freedom we possess
> are ours by the grace and favor of our fellows (*Persons* 211).

Furthermore, what we know of another person we know because
they tell us. It is only a small step to transpose this notion to the
Judaeo-Christian understanding of God as one who has revealed God's
self as one who is with us; YaHWeH, Emmanuel.

To this point, we have traced Macmurray's argument that the
dynamic that makes the process of "mutual self-revelation" possible
is love (i.e., "friendship") through to his position that such love is the
"field of religion." He goes on, then, to point out that "from the
standpoint of the agent, which is the presupposition of our whole
argument, the question whether the world is personal is the question
whether God exists" (*Persons* 214). The question, Macmurray says,
is not 'Does God exist?' but 'Is what exists personal?' Resting on the
proposition that *doing* is more fundamental than *thinking* and that as
human beings we act in mutual relationship, his entire philosophy
aimed to demonstrate the "inadequacy of any impersonal conception
of the world" (*Persons* 218). Further, he established that the universe

itself must be personal (human beings are personal and part of the universe; therefore the universe is personal): "By shifting our standpoint from the 'I think' to the 'I do,' we have restored the reference of thought to action, and in the result have found that we are driven to conceive a personal universe in which God is the ultimate reality" (*Persons* 224).

Macmurray concludes his Gifford Lectures by recalling that philosophy in the Greek tradition left us with a theoretical and impersonal God lacking "any quality deserving of reverence or worship" (*Persons* 206–07) and modern philosophy, following in that tradition, "had been driven by its own logic in the direction of atheism" (*Persons* 224). He reminds us that shifting philosophy's starting point from the theoretical and egocentric to the personal led to the inevitable conclusion that there is "only one way in which we can think our relation to the world, and that is to think it as a personal relation, through the form of the personal." Of course for Macmurray, to see the world through this lens is to see it as the *act* of God. And, if God acts, God is Personal: "A personal conception alone is fully theistic and fully religious" (*Persons* 223). We are impelled, he says finally, "to conceive a personal universe in which God is the ultimate reality" (*Persons* 224).

Notes

1. The Gifford Lectures were later published as *The Self as Agent* and *Persons in Relation* and dedicated to his wife Betty. They were first published in London by Faber and Faber, in 1957 and 1961 respectively.

2. This is not the case for all disciplines; one can be a successful chemist, for instance, without knowing anything about the historical development of chemistry.

3. Bernard Lonergan also saw an initial phase of modern philosophy where "the primary focus of attention was cognitional activity." It was the period "from Descartes to Kant" who was a transitional thinker to the second phase where "there was a notable shift in emphasis" (*Third Collection* 242).

4. On the roof of the old observatory in Beijing, I marveled at various large mechanical representations of the solar system. How different this mechanical version of the universe is from James E. Lovelock's hypothesis that the planet is alive! See James E. Lovelock, *Gaia: A New Look at Life on Earth* (Oxford: Oxford University Press, 1979).

5. But how did Descartes get to be this thinking being? Macmurray would say that Descartes became a thinker as a result of his interactions with people and the world; i.e., relationally. Note that not all seventeenth century

thinkers were in total agreement with Descartes. Blaise Pascal (he and Descartes met) was drawn to science but he also knew that human beings were substantially more than calculating machines and that there is more to being human than rationality. He considered the heart (not mind) to be the core of human personality and in his *Pensées* wrote that "the heart has its reasons of which reason knows nothing" (*Pensées* 154).

6. In the thirteenth century, Thomas Aquinas had already made a clear distinction between philosophy (the work of human reason unaided by revelation) and theology (which takes revealed truth as its data) but he understood philosophy to be the handmaiden to theology, the 'queen of the sciences.' Descartes further distanced philosophy from theology but did not differentiate between philosophy and science.

7. The value of philosophy, for Hume, lies precisely in its ability to free us from the unhappy grasp of theology. In contrast with Descartes, Hume saw no philosophical arguments for God's existence because we cannot have empirical "experience" of God. Hume's most significant work, *A Treatise of Human Nature* (1739), was published when he was only twenty-eight. It was, however, a later and shorter work, *Inquiry Concerning Human Understanding* (1748), that was to attract the attention of Immanuel Kant (representative of the next phase of Western philosophy). Bernard Lonergan's *Insight* has been described as a modern day equivalent to Hume's *Inquiry Concerning Human Understanding*.

8. Bernard Lonergan uses David Hume to point out the contradiction between "a mistaken cognitional theory and the actual performance of the mistaken theorist." Lonergan wrote: "Hume thought the human mind to be a matter of impressions linked together by custom. But Hume's own mind was quite original. Therefore, Hume's own mind was not what Hume considered the human mind to be" (*Method* 21).

9. The mechanical world view is far from dead. During the 1991 Persian Gulf War the killing of human beings was referred to as "collateral damage." And, of course, we speak of the people working for a given company as "human resources."

10. Jean Jacques Rousseau (1712–1778) is representative of the romantic approach. His novel *Émile* (1762) champions education built on a child's natural interests and sympathies and *Confessions* (1782) describes Rousseau's romantic feelings of affinity with nature.

11. David M. Wulff, *Psychology of Religion: Classic and Contemporary Views* (New York: John Wiley & Sons, 1991), 153–54. Wulff is quoting Rufus Jones from William P. King, ed., *Behaviorism: A Battle Line* (Nashville, TN: Cokesbury Press, 1930), 21.

12. Some modern philosophers adopt Kantianism and some reject it outright. Others, while acknowledging Kant's contribution to the development of philosophy, critique and expand upon his thought in their efforts to take philosophy in new directions. Macmurray and Lonergan are in this category.

13. The problem for philosophy, as Kant saw it, was to distinguish science and morality from aesthetics. For this reason Kant wrote three critiques: the first about science (*The Critique of Pure Reason*), the second about morality (*The Critique of Practical Reason*) and the third about art (*The Critique of Judgment*). Throughout, he was concerned to defend rationality against attack from the Romantic and "faith" philosophers.

14. Macmurray argues that Kant's philosophy is flawed in that it appeals only to an *internal* rational principle or rule ("categorical imperative") for truth and right action. In Macmurray's view, it is possible for human beings to arrive at *real* truth and to make *real* decisions about what good actions to perform without recourse to law. As we shall see in chapter 5, Bernard Lonergan agrees with Macmurray.

15. Bernard Lonergan's critique of Kant (in *Insight*) is that, although he was well aware that knowing involved an understanding of experience, he did not move to the next level of consciousness where a judgment as to the validity of his understanding would bring him to truth, to reality. Lonergan and Kant are compared in Giovanni Sala, "The *A Priori* in Human Knowledge: Kant's *Critique of Pure Reason* and Lonergan's *Insight*," *The Thomist* 40, no. 2 (April 1976): 179–221.

16. The reference in brackets (*Persons* 45–46) is to John Macmurray, *Persons in Relation* (Atlantic Highlands, NJ: Humanities Press International, 1991), 45–46. Quotations from this work will henceforth be indicated as here (*Persons* 45–46).

17. *The Self as Agent* deals with Macmurray's first criticism and *Persons in Relation* with the second. The very titles of these works suggest something of the approach Macmurray will take in his critique of modern philosophy.

18. Note that what Macmurray sets forth is a *proposal*, the choice of which cannot be demonstrated but which will be verified in its unfolding power to explain.

19. The reference in brackets (*Interpreting* 127–28) is to John Macmurray, *Interpreting the Universe* (London: Faber & Faber, 1933), 127–28. Quotations from this work will henceforth be indicated as here (*Interpreting* 127–28). Macmurray first explores his more complete notion of rationality in chapter 6 of *Interpreting the Universe* and more succinctly in "The Nature of Reason," *Proceedings of the Aristotelian Society* 35 (1934–35): 137–48.

20. This is the conclusion of "Logic and Psychology," an unpublished paper in the John Macmurray Collection, Regis College, University of Toronto, Canada.

21. Macmurray also said that "the purely spiritual is the purely imaginary" (Postscript to *Green Pastures* by Mark Connelly [London: Delisle, 1963], 111) and elsewhere, "a purely spiritual world is a purely imaginary one" (Kenneth C. Barnes, *Energy Unbound: The Story of Wennington School* [York, England: William Sessions Limited, 1980], 29).

22. "When a person is 'thinged' only one aspect, or group of aspects, of his existence is recognized as real" (George R. Bach and Ronald M. Deutsch, "Of People, Images and Things," *Pairing* [New York: Avon Books, 1971], 76).

23. The agent-self, Macmurray states, is a logical abstraction and can only exist as a community of personal agents.

24. In support of the intersubjective nature of community, Bernard Lonergan writes that we were born of our "parents love" and "grew and developed in the gravitational field of their affection." He specifically mentions the primordial "bond of mother and child" (*Insight* 237). In the Western world today, we recognize that the "mother" might not be the biological mother but another loving primary care giver.

25. The quoted elements in this paragraph are all found in *Persons in Relation* between pages 47 and 49.

26. This is reminiscent of the work of Brazilian educator, Paulo Freire. Freire's thesis is that education is not a neutral process and ought to be cultural action for freedom. *Pedagogy of the Oppressed* (New York: Seabury Press, 1970), his most famous work, introduces the need for a pedagogy that liberates the oppressed and elaborates Freire's basic theme that, to be fully human, men and women must become subjects, agents.

27. Philip Mooney, "Freedom Through Friendship, John Macmurray: In Memoriam (1891–1976)," *Friends Journal* (January 1, 1977): 4. Because of Macmurray's Quaker background, "friendship" is a word charged with religious connotations of relationship, community, and love.

28. John Macmurray, "Ye Are My Friends," a 1943 address to the Student Christian Movement, issued as a pamphlet by the Friends Home Service Committee in 1943 and reprinted many times. It is quoted by Philip Mooney in "Freedom Through Friendship, John Macmurray: In Memoriam (1891–1976)," *Friends Journal* (January 1, 1977): 5. According to Macmurray, the emphasis in modern society on jobs and material goods (all we have left in Western society, it has been said, are *things* to buy) can in part be accounted for as a failure in friendship.

29. While using this chart, keep in mind that each successive historical period or "unity-pattern" of consciousness includes the viewpoint (s) of the previous period(s) or pattern(s) The biological perspective, for instance, is inclusive of the physical sciences and so we can have a discipline like biochemistry. Similarly, the human sciences make use of both the biological and physical sciences. And "organisms and persons, whatever more they may be, are certainly material objects" (*Interpreting* 102). For Macmurray, the central issue was not the historical periods themselves but the history of the development of human consciousness which they represent. It is also important to point out that each of the unity-patterns for seeing and thinking about reality represented by these three historical periods is still with us. *Interpreting the Universe* is an extended discussion of these ideas.

30. Macmurray uses the term "personal" to characterize the third period in the history of Western philosophy (inclusive of both the mechanical and organic). Because we tend to understand the term personal more narrowly than does Macmurray, I have chosen to use the term "postmodern" (*See* **Postmodern** in Glossary) to define the emerging era in philosophy. Although the term "postmodern" is variously defined, I take it to mean that which takes us beyond the failed assumptions of modernity. As I am using the term it refers to a sense that the "modern" is in need of reconception; a revisioning along holistic lines. Thomas Berry and others might use the term "ecozoic" (*See* **Ecozoic** in Glossary) to further emphasize that this intercommunion is not just among human beings but characterizes the entire earth community. In my view, Macmurray's understanding of "personal" and our use of the term "postmodern" are inclusive of "ecozoic."

31. Macmurray uses the term "religious" to describe the understanding of reality emerging in the third phase in western philosophy; religion as "about human beings in relation." In my experience, religion is often considered to be a negative word in contemporary western culture and so I have chosen the word "spiritual" as best capturing what Macmurray means by the term "religious" ("communal" would be another possibility but it lacks the transcendent dimension implicit in "spiritual").

32. This reminds me of M. Scott Peck's definition of love: "The will to extend one's self for the purpose of nurturing one's own or another's spiritual growth" (M. Scott Peck, *The Road Less Traveled* [New York: Simon and Schuster, 1978], 81). According to Macmurray's analysis, we possess two types of knowledge of people: our knowledge of people as *persons* and our knowledge of them as *objects*. The first depends upon and expresses a personal attitude to the other person, the second an impersonal attitude. When our attitude is personal, reflection will be philosophical; when it is impersonal, our reflection will be scientific. The first will yield a philosophy of the personal; the second a science of humankind (an anthropology).

33. John Macmurray, "Christianity — Pagan or Scientific?," *The Hibbert Journal* 24 (1926): 421–33.

34. John Macmurray, "Beyond Knowledge," *in Adventure: The Faith of Science and the Science of Faith*, ed. B. H. Streeter (New York: Macmillan, 1928).

35. John Macmurray, "Science and Objectivity," *Listening: Journal of Religion and Culture* 10, no. 2 (Spring, 1975): 7–23.

36. This phrase is quoted from Thomas E. Wren, "John Macmurray's Search for Reality: Introduction," *Listening: Journal of Religion and Culture* 10, no. 2 (Spring 1975): 3. In a similar vein, Abraham Maslow writes: "Some perceptive liberals and non-theists are going through an 'agonizing reappraisal' very similar to that which the orthodox often go through, namely a loss of faith in their foundational beliefs. Just as many intellectuals lose faith in religious orthodoxy, so do they also lose faith in positivistic, nineteenth-century science as a way of life. Thus they too often have the sense of loss,

the craving to believe, the yearning for a value-system, the valuelessness and the simultaneous longing for values which marks so many in this 'Age of Longing.' I believe that this need can be satisfied by a larger, more inclusive science, one which includes the data of transcendence" (Abraham H. Maslow, *Religions, Values, and Peak-Experiences* [New York: Penguin Books, 1970], 43–44).

37. Robert Coles challenges the notion of the objective, rational observer able to arrive at value-free knowledge. Critical thought is itself shaped and influenced; there can be no such thing as the autonomous rational Self. Knowing is never separated from the knower, nor does the knower stand apart from the complex web of society and culture in which he/she is embedded. The intellectual product is never totally distinct from the interpretive method that produced it. To appreciate this postmodern spirit is to appreciate the irony present in contemporary life (Bruce A. Ronda, *Intellect and Spirit: The Life and Work of Robert Coles* [New York: The Continuum Publishing Company, 1989], 32).

38. John Macmurray, "Science and Objectivity," *Listening: Journal of Religion and Culture* 10, no. 2 (Spring 1975): 7.

39. Ludwig Feuerbach as quoted in Hans Kung, *Freud and the Problem of God* (New Haven: Yale University Press, 1990), 3.

40. That Macmurray's religious commitment persisted is supported by the fact that his last essay, published by the Society of Friends in 1973, was titled "The Philosophy of Jesus."

41. Sigmund Freud hoped that humankind might one day so progress as to be able completely to do without the false consolation of religious belief. Religious doctrines, he wrote, "are illusions and insusceptible of proof. No one can be compelled to think them true, to believe in them. Some of them are so improbable, so incompatible with everything we have laboriously discovered about the reality of the world, that we may compare them . . . to delusions. . . . The riddles of the universe reveal themselves only slowly to our investigation; there are many questions to which science today can give no answer. But scientific work is the only road which can lead us to a knowledge of reality outside ourselves" (Sigmund Freud, *The Future of an Illusion*, ed. and trans. James Strachey [New York: W. W. Norton & Company, Inc., 1961], 31–32.

42. Gerald A. Largo, "Two Prophetic Voices: Macmurray and Buber," *America* 128 (March 31, 1973): 286. Macmurray was not alone in arguing that not *all* religion is illusory. Abraham Maslow concurs: "some others, still a small proportion, are finding in newly available hints from psychology another possibility of a positive, naturalistic faith, . . . a 'humanistic faith' as Erich Fromm called it, humanistic psychology as many others are now calling it. As John Macmurray said, 'Now is the point in history at which it becomes possible for man to adopt consciously as his own purpose the purpose which is already inherent in his own nature'" (Abraham Maslow, *Religions, Values, and Peak-Experiences* [New York: Penguin Books, 1970], 39).

43. "Man is . . . a part of nature; and we individual men and women are not merely members of the human community but elements of the natural world. We have in the end to face the question of our relation to the world. How is it to be conceived? How must we represent the world and the relation between ourselves and the world?" (*Persons* 212).

44. John Macmurray, *Religion, Art, and Science*, (Liverpool: Liverpool University Press, 1961), 58.

45. The reference in brackets (*Adventure* 177–215) is to John Macmurray, "Objectivity in Religion," in *Adventure: The Faith of Science and the Science of Faith*, ed. B. H. Streeter (New York: Macmillan, 1928), 177–215. The other references to *Adventure* in this paragraph are also to Macmurray's "Objectivity in Religion."

46. Macmurray's discussion of Christianity begins with a reminder that Jesus was a Jew, part of the most "uniquely religious people of history." Jesus lived not as a Greek philosopher in continuity with Plato and Aristotle but as one in continuity with the great Hebrew prophetic tradition of action. His teaching centered on the proclamation of the good news of the inbreaking on earth of the Reign of God coupled with the demand for a transformation in the way human beings relate to each other in keeping with the reality of God's reign. And yet, even in the New Testament we find evidence of the influence of Hellenistic thought on the first "followers of the way." Under the spell of Greek philosophy, the emphasis in the Christian community begins to shift from practice to theory, from action to thought, from following "the way" to professing certain orthodox beliefs. The theological definitions of the Councils of Nicaea, Constantinople, and Chalcedon are, in a real sense, a triumph of the theoretical point of view which comes to us from fifth century B. C. Athens. In the theologies of Augustine and Aquinas we *canonized* or at least *baptized* Plato and Aristotle!

47. This is shorthand for Aquinas' "five proofs" for God's existence.

48. Macmurray does, however, see value in the "argument from design" (*Persons* 207). A book by Brian Davies, *God and the New Physics* (New York: Simon and Schuster, 1983) would have pleased him.

Bernard Lonergan (c. 1970)

Chapter 4

Bernard Lonergan (1904–1984)

I am certain (and I am not one who becomes certain easily) that I can put together a Thomistic metaphysic of history that will throw Hegel and Marx, despite the enormity of their influence on this very account into the shade. I have a draft of this already written as I have of everything else.

. . . I think this is my work but I know more luminously than anything else that I have nothing I have not received, that I know nothing in philosophy that I have not received through the Society [of Jesus] (1935 Lonergan letter in *Transforming* 110–11, 113).[1]

Early Years

Bernard Joseph Francis Lonergan was born on December 17, 1904 in the town of Buckingham, Quebec. He was the first of three boys.[2] The Lonergans came from Ireland and by 1830 had settled on a farm near Buckingham where, with the exception of Bernard's grandfather, they integrated into the French speaking culture. Bernard's father was a civil engineer. His mother, Josephine Wood, descended from the United Empire Loyalists and was the daughter of a local wheelwright. As Bernard grew up in Buckingham his warm extended family also included his mother's parents and his mother's sister (*Lonergan* 3).[3]

In Lonergan's youth, Buckingham was a prosperous place, dominated by the sawmill at the waterfall on the Lièvre River, made famous in Archibald Lampman's (d. 1899) poem *Morning on the Lièvre*. The population of 3,000 was mostly Roman Catholic (about three-quarters of them French speaking). The Lonergan's were parishioners at the town's only Catholic church, St. Gregory Nazianzen, and Bernard attended St. Michael's, the local Catholic school for boys administered by the Brothers of Christian Instruction. His intellectual ability did not attract particular attention during elementary school although his brothers remembered that even as a boy he liked reading the stock market reports in the newspaper.

In the Fall of 1918, Bernard was sent as a boarder to Loyola College in Montreal, run by the English speaking Jesuits.[4] He completed the four year high school *Cours Classique* in two years, consistently winning the Governor General's Medal for placing first in his class. He was nicknamed "brains Lonergan."

Jesuit Formation

Bernard Lonergan entered the Jesuit Novitiate[5] at Guelph, Ontario, on July 29, 1922. He was in his eighteenth year. He later said that his decision to enter the Jesuit Order was taken on his ride out to a weekend discernment retreat: "I went out to the Sault [Montreal novitiate of the Jesuits of French Canada] to make a retreat, an election, and I decided on the street-car on the way out" (*Lonergan* 6). After two years of spiritual training in the Novitiate and his first vows as a Jesuit, Lonergan completed the traditional two year Juniorate course of classical studies. In the last of his four years at Guelph, he was asked to teach Latin and Greek to the Novices and mathematics to those entering the Juniorate program (*Lonergan* 7–12).

From 1926–29 he and other Canadian Jesuits studied Philosophy at Heythrop College,[6] Oxfordshire, England. The following year, with concentrations in classics, mathematics, and French, he completed his B.A. at the University of London (1930).

Formed spiritually over four years at Guelph and intellectually over four years at Heythrop, Lonergan was strengthened for his Regency at Loyola College, Montreal, where he taught a variety of subjects from 1930–33.[7] His teaching and other duties with the boarders allowed little time for creative thinking. He was able, however, to do "some reading" and write for the *Loyola College Review* which he edited during his three years at the school (*Lonergan* 18).

In the summer of 1933, Lonergan was assigned to theological studies at the Collège de l'Immaculée-Conception, Montreal (seminary of the French Canadian Jesuits). A few months later, and most significantly for Lonergan's future career, his Jesuit Provincial Superior transferred him to the Gregorian University in Rome to study philosophy and theology. He was ordained to the Roman Catholic priesthood on July 25, 1936 in the Jesuit Church of St. Ignatius, Rome, and received his Licentiate (Master's Degree) in Sacred Theology (S.T.L.) in 1937. Lonergan completed his Jesuit formation with Tertianship in Amiens, France (1937–38) before returning to the Gregorian where he pursued a Doctorate in Sacred Theology (S.T.D.) on the thought of Thomas Aquinas.

Lonergan considered his assignment to Rome a "magnificent vote of confidence" in his hopes for an academic career. Years later he would write to friends of his "breathless . . . enthusiasm for Rome" and love for "that 'timelessness' that characterizes life in the 'eternal' city" (*Lonergan* 20). Unfortunately, he was not quite so keen in his evaluation of professors at the Gregorian University who he described as assuming "that we lift static concepts off mental images much as if the mind were a sausage factory. Missing was insight, the notion of development and the personal dimensions of understanding."[8]

Bernard Lonergan left Rome just before the outbreak of war on the Italian peninsula and from 1940–46 taught theology at the College de l'Immaculée-Conception in Montreal. These years were the beginning of a teaching and writing career that was to span forty-three years.[9]

Genesis of *Insight*

From 1946–53 Lonergan taught at the Jesuit Seminary in Toronto and in 1949 began his magnum opus, *Insight: A Study of Human Understanding* (1957) which he wrote in English.[10] Lonergan explained the genesis of *Insight*. In 1945, he had given a course, Thought and Reality, at the newly founded Thomas More Institute for Adult Education in Montreal.[11] As a result of this experience he said "I knew that I had a book." Modestly, he often referred to the 750 pages of *Insight* as his "little book."[12]

In *Insight*, Lonergan sought to "transpose St. Thomas' position to meet the issues of our own day." He points to what these issues were and the task that needs to be done:

> Modernity lacks roots. Its values lack balance and depth. Much of
> its science is destructive of man. Catholics in the twentieth century
> are faced with a problem similar to that met by Aquinas in the
> thirteenth century. Then Greek and Arabic culture were pouring into
> Western Europe and, if it was not to destroy Christendom, it had to be
> known, assimilated, transformed. Today modern culture, in many
> ways more stupendous than any that ever existed, is surging around
> us. It too has to be known, assimilated, transformed.[13]

That he understood this task would prove to be the work of a lifetime
is clear from a remark in *Insight*: "To strike out on a new line and
become more than a week-end celebrity calls for years in which one's
living is more or less constantly absorbed in the effort to understand."[14] Frederick E. Crowe attests that the example *par excellence*
of such a person is Lonergan himself, "whose whole life has been one
of renouncement of the immediate small gain for the sake of the great
harvest of the future" (*Enterprise* 41).[15]

Insight was well received by religious and secular scholars.[16] It has
been published in Italian and translations are underway in six other
languages. It has achieved the status of a philosophical classic and is
one of those books that many people speak about but few have read
and even fewer have understood. Yet this is not too surprising because, although Lonergan's style is clear, "his dense, elliptical prose,
studded with references to Thomas Aquinas and modern physics,
makes its points in a methodical and mind-wearying manner. One
typical passage hammers home a conclusion with 'In the thirty-first
place . . .'"[17]

By the early 1960's *Insight* had attracted a great deal of attention
on university campuses across North America and study clubs grew up
to assimilate and expand its complex thought. *Time* magazine did two
stories on Lonergan (January 22, 1965 and April 27, 1970). The 1970
article, "The Towering Thought of Bernard Lonergan," opens with:
"Canadian Jesuit Bernard Joseph Francis Lonergan is considered by
many intellectuals to be the finest philosophic thinker of the 20th century."[18]

Generalized Empirical Method Applied to Theology

Gregorian University

In the fall of 1953, while *Insight* was in the editing and publication process, Lonergan returned to his alma mater, the Gregorian University in Rome, where he taught until 1965. Although the Professorship was prestigious, these years were not easy for Lonergan. His thinking had moved far beyond that taught and permitted in Catholic intellectual circles in Rome.[19]

> Lonergan himself clearly suffered, during his early career, because of the academic institutions and practices he inherited: "The situation I was in was hopelessly antiquated, but had not yet been demolished. . . . I taught theology for twenty-five years under impossible conditions." These conditions made it difficult not only to teach effectively but also to write creatively. Indeed, Lonergan himself found that most of the Latin theology he wrote early in his career was not "enduring" enough to bother translating into English.[20]

In the static and formal church environment of Rome in the decade before the Second Vatican Council, Lonergan was a ray of light for the scholarly and became an underground legend, a kind of cult figure, among Catholic seminarians who came to his classes in large numbers (650 in a lecture hall). The amusement of new students at "his sing-song voice and unmelodiously flat Latin pronunciation" was soon turned to despair at "his blithe unconcern for the frailties of lesser intellects:"

> Once, after failing to get a philosophical point across to his class, Lonergan brightened, said: "I think this will make it clear," [and] proceeded to cover the blackboard with differential equations. During a World War II discussion about the loss to mankind in bomb-gutted libraries, Lonergan argued that the important things were in people's minds, not in books. In answer, someone cited Shakespeare and got out a copy to cite lines at random. In each case, Lonergan identified the quotation, imperturbably reeled off the rest of the passage.[21]

Asked on one occasion where he got his ideas, Lonergan replied, "I read books"; asked how he found the books he answered "Luck."[22] On still another occasion, when queried as to why he didn't bring two conflicting passages in *Insight* into conformity, he replied: "Because I didn't have a word processor. When is a work finished? Not when it has reached perfection, but when you are sick and tired of correcting it."[23]

In Rome he published his major Latin theological treatises and solidified his interest in foundational questions rather than the day-to-day controversies in the church that seemed to capture the imaginations of other theologians. Lonergan was to devote his life to articulating a generalized method of inquiry and its implications for philosophy and theology, psychology, history, logic, mathematics, and economics. "In constructing a ship or a philosophy," he wrote in *Insight*, "one has to go the whole way; an effort that is in principle incomplete is equivalent to a failure" (*Insight* 7).[24] His own clear vision pointed to the need to overcome the terrible fragmentation of knowledge and life in modern times and the work of his lifetime was an effort to achieve an integrated view.[25]

During the Second Vatican Council (1962–65) he was among the theological experts (*periti*) who acted as teachers of the bishops.[26] Gerald Emmett Cardinal Carter of Toronto had this to say about Bernard Lonergan's contribution to the work of the council:

> I have always maintained that Bernard Lonergan was the hidden, valid source of much of the theology of the Second Vatican Council. I almost used the expression that he lurked in the Vatican Council giving advice to the *periti* who then paraded it in the council, generally through their Bishops. But one could never think of Bernie as lurking! That crazy laugh of his always gave me the impression that he was laughing at the world. And those who laugh at the world don't lurk. But what I would mean to say is that he never paraded his wisdom or for that matter his many contributions to other people.[27]

Method in Theology

Poor health brought Bernard Lonergan back to Canada (1965) to Regis College, the Jesuit Seminary, in Willowdale (a northern suburb of Toronto). It was discovered that he had lung cancer. He never returned to Rome, and after treatment (his right lung was removed) and lengthy recovery in Canada, Lonergan devoted himself mainly to research and writing.

At a plain wooden table in his spartan sixth floor room at Regis College, he drafted the theological sequel to *Insight* which was published in 1972 under the title *Method in Theology*. If *Insight* is Lonergan's answer to questions about the possibility and nature of human knowing, *Method* is his answer to a second problem having to do with the inadequacy of intellectual methods in the discipline he knew best, theology. So, despite his shy and somewhat insecure exterior, Lonergan dares to spell out the problem of theological method and offer the solution as well![28] The main ideas in both *Insight* and *Method* will be discussed in the next chapter.

Honors

In 1971–72, Lonergan was the Stillman Professor of Catholic Studies at Harvard University and a few years later (1975) he accepted the post of Visiting Distinguished Professor at Boston College where he conducted seminars, tutored students, and exchanged ideas with faculty.[29]

He received seventeen honourary doctorates (including one awarded at a special convocation for Lonergan and Karl Rahner (1904–1984)[30] at the University of Chicago in 1974) and numerous other awards. He was named a Companion of the Order of Canada in 1970.[31]

In April of 1970, the first major international congress on his work was held at St. Leo's College near Tampa, Florida. For four days, the 77 participants listened to 65 papers comprising more than 700,000 words (a "living *Festschrift*" to honor Lonergan's sixty-fifth birthday). Since 1970, numerous other conferences and workshops on his work have taken place in cities around the world, among them Halifax, Milwaukee, Ottawa, Toronto, Montreal, Boston, Rome, Philadelphia, Edmonton, Dallas, Dublin, and Mexico City.

A Lonergan Center was established in Toronto in the early 1970's (in 1985 it became the Lonergan Research Institute)[32] and Lonergan Centers exist in Montreal, Boston, Santa Clara (California), Sydney and Melbourne (Australia), Naples and Rome (Italy) Manila (Philippines) and Dublin (Ireland).

Since 1974, Lonergan Workshops have been held annually at Boston College.[33] They attract scholars from around the world and aim to expand and apply Lonergan's thought and methodology in new ways and in fields other than theology.

Method: Journal of Lonergan Studies has been published by

Loyola Marymount University of Los Angeles since 1983. It aims to promote scholarly, critical study of the ideas of Bernard Lonergan and to provide a forum for the dissemination of the results of such study. The *Lonergan Studies Newsletter*, initiated to celebrate Lonergan's seventy-fifth birthday, is a quarterly publication of the Lonergan Research Institute in Toronto. It lists publications related to Lonergan and also offers reviews, workshop and conference particulars, as well as news from the various Lonergan centers around the world.

The Lonergan Research Institute in Toronto, in cooperation with the University of Toronto Press, is in the process of editing the Collected Works of Bernard Lonergan in twenty-two volumes.[34]

Retirement Years

In March of 1983, Lonergan moved to the New England Jesuit Infirmary at Campion Center (Weston, Massachusetts) and then, at seventy-eight years of age, and in failing health, he willingly retired to the Canadian Jesuit Infirmary in Pickering, Ontario (his brother Greg joined him a few months later). "Scientist-humanist-philosopher-theologian" (*Enterprise* 2), Bernard Lonergan, died here of multiple ailments, on November 26, 1984 (just three weeks before his eightieth birthday).

At the time of his death Lonergan was largely unknown to the majority of Canadians, yet obituary tributes to his genius appeared in magazines and newspapers around the world from the Los Angeles Times, New York Times, Times of London, to the Hong Kong Sunday Examiner.

Bernard Lonergan has been acclaimed as one of the greatest thinkers of the twentieth century, a man "whose shadow has already fallen far into the next century."[35] *Insight* is routinely referred to as one of the most important works to be published in the world in this century. He is credited with having "closed a seven century gap in Catholic thought."[36] Many unabashedly call Lonergan one of the greatest thinkers of all time.

Although Lonergan spent eleven years of his life "reaching up to the mind of Aquinas" he once said that he did not think he had succeeded in climbing more than halfway up the mountain of Aquinas' achievements (*Insight* 769). In my view, we are not even halfway up the mountain of Lonergan's achievement and ten years after his death his thought still points us towards an intellectual, moral, and religious self-transcendence that we have yet to fully embrace.

Notes

1. This quotation is from a letter, dated January 22, 1935, which Bernard Lonergan wrote from Rome to his Jesuit Provincial Superior in Toronto. The reference in brackets (*Transforming* 110–11, 113) is to Richard M. Liddy, *Transforming Light: Intellectual Conversion in the Early Lonergan* (Collegeville, MN: The Liturgical Press, 1993), 110–11, 113. Quotations from this work will henceforth be indicated as here (*Transforming* 110–11, 113).

2. The second boy, Gregory, also became a Jesuit. Gregory typed much of the manuscript for *Insight*. Mark, the youngest, studied engineering and worked in industry.

3. The reference in brackets (*Lonergan* 3) is to Frederick E. Crowe, S.J., *Lonergan*, Outstanding Christian Thinkers Series, ed. Brian Davies, OP (Collegeville, MN: The Liturgical Press, 1992), 3. Quotations from this work will henceforth be indicated as here (*Lonergan* 3). *Time* (April 27, 1970, 11) recorded Lonergan as saying: "I've never been lonely. . . . A man is never lonely if he was loved by his mother."

4. In a public interview during the First International Lonergan Congress (1970), Lonergan described Loyola as follows: "The one [Jesuit boarding school] I went to in Montreal, in 1918, was organized pretty much along the same lines as Jesuit schools had been since the beginning of the Renaissance, with a few slight modifications. So that I can speak of classical culture as something I was brought up in and gradually learned to move *out of*" (*Second Collection* 209–10).

5. Jesuit terminology (Novitiate, Juniorate, Regency, and Tertianship) used in this chapter is explained in the Glossary.

6. Now part of the University of London, Heythrop was where English Jesuits took their Philosophy studies. Here Lonergan's first essays were published in the *Blandyke Papers*, the "Journal" of the College (*Lonergan* 12–17).

7. Lonergan was assigned by his Jesuit superiors to an extra year at Loyola, which he considered a serious and unjust rebuke at the time: "I had regarded myself as one condemned to sacrifice his real interests and, in general, to be suspected and to get into trouble for things I could not help and could not explain" (*Lonergan* 17).

8. *Newsweek*, April 20, 1970, 75. *Transforming Light*, by Richard Liddy, a student of Lonergan at the Gregorian in the early 1960s, charts Lonergan's early life including his "intellectual conversion" in the 1930s and the genesis of *Insight*.

9. Lonergan's work was *not* narrowly focused on Roman Catholic philosophy and theology. Essays and notes found among Lonergan's papers dating from the 1930s, ("File 713–History") make it clear that he was build-

ing a "philosophy of history" which, he wrote, "is as yet not recognized as the essential branch of philosophy that it is." Because his Roman studies were in theology, this philosophy of history project was put on a back burner (*The Lonergan Research Institute Bulletin*, no. 4, November 1989, 3). "File 713–History" further indicates "his interests to lie in the field of culture, philosophy of history, human sciences such as sociology, politico-economic questions, and the like" (*Lonergan* 24). A 1959 series of lectures on the philosophy of education (*Topics in Education*, vol. 10 in the *Collected Works of Bernard Lonergan*) which focused on the "new learning" testify to his relevancy in this field. A work on economics consumed the last years of Lonergan's life; it will be published as part of the *Collected Works of Bernard Lonergan*, University of Toronto Press.

10. Bernard Lonergan, *Insight: A Study of Human Understanding*, vol. 3 in the *Collected Works of Bernard Lonergan*, ed. Frederick E. Crowe and Robert M. Doran (Toronto: University of Toronto Press, 1992). *Newsweek* (April 20, 1970, 75) quotes Lonergan as saying: "Had 'Insight' been written in Latin . . . I might never have been allowed to publish it." The same article, "A Great Christian Mind," offered the following: "When he submitted his early treatise on the Trinity to Vatican censors for the church's traditional *nihil obstat* (a judgment that a book contains no doctrinal error), the unsigned manuscript finally was referred to the only scholar thought capable of judging it — Bernard Lonergan — who promptly stamped his approval."

11. The Thomas More Institute had been founded by his Jesuit friend, Eric O'Connor, an accomplished mathematician. Lonergan regularly offered courses and workshops there.

12. Lonergan was a quiet, shy, man who avoided personal publicity. Friends knew him as "an inveterate film goer . . . a man who loved music, Beethoven in particular, a hand of bridge, and who relaxed at night with a copy of *The New Yorker* magazine" (*The Toronto Star*, July 10, 1990, M4).

13. *Compass*, March, 1985, 19.

14. Quoted from The Lonergan Research Institute *Bulletin*, no. 4 (November 1989): 4.

15. The reference in brackets (*Enterprise* 41) is to Frederick E. Crowe, S.J., *The Lonergan Enterprise* (Cambridge, MA: Cowley Publications, 1980), 41. Quotations from this work will henceforth be indicated as here (*Enterprise* 41). The quotation continues: "We should be clear on the degree of sacrifice involved in such a decision. To withdraw from the hunt when there is quarry immediately before one and to postpone the pursuit while giving oneself to the forging of a new and vastly superior instrument; to be willing to spend one's entire life at the task, hoping that the long-term benefits will make it worthwhile, but knowing with certainty that one will not see the full harvest and realizing that at best one's efforts will be appreciated only by a small band of attentive readers and students; to live the long years perseveringly, hopefully, unwaveringly, in the labor of creating an adequate organon of incarnate spirit — that withdrawal, renouncement, willingness, decision,

and perseverance is not the act of a drifter or a self-seeker. It is an act of notable self-transcendence, one that we who share Fr. Lonergan's estimate of the momentousness of our times and of the magnitude of the task before us, should be able to appreciate."

16. *Insight* has been described as an "awe-inspiring" documentation of Lonergan's contribution to that job of knowing, assimilating, and transforming modern culture. One Lonerganian offered the following testimony as to the importance of *Insight*: "There are times I become quite discouraged with the state of the world, the church, and especially with the state of theology. I feel as though we've lost our bearings and aren't about to get them back. At such moments, there is only one remedy: I must return to my room and pick up Lonergan's *Insight*. I open it at random and read. Any section will do, just a few pages. Then I can sleep" (Bernard F. Swain, "Lonergan's framework for the future," *Commonweal* 112, no. 2 [January, 1985]: 46). In 1970, *Newsweek* called it "a philosophic classic comparable in scope to Hume's *Inquiry Concerning Human Understanding*" (*Newsweek*, April 20, 1970, 75). *Time* called it an "authentically towering masterpiece" which alone would have secured Lonergan a place in the history of thought (*Time*, January 22, 1965, 46). *Insight* has left its impact on philosophy and theology, education, mathematics, economics (a work nearing completion at the time of his death), sociology, (Lonergan wrote an article in 1935 arguing for a "Summa Sociologica.") and history ("File–713" in the Lonergan Archives).

17. *Time*, January 22, 1965, 46. The quote from *Insight* is on page 747.

18. *Time*, April 27, 1970, 10. Lonergan's obituary appeared in *Time* on December 10, 1984.

19. Lonergan was a strong defender of the need for intellectual freedom in the Catholic church: "one might as well declare openly that all new ideas are taboo, as require that they be examined, evaluated, and approved by some hierarchy of officials and bureaucrats; for members of this hierarcny possess authority and power in inverse ratio to their familiarity with the concrete situations in which the new ideas emerge; they never know whether or not the new idea will work; much less can they divine how it might be corrected or developed; and since the one thing they dread is making a mistake, they devote their energies to paper work and postpone decisions" (*Insight* 259–60).

20. Bernard F. Swain, "Lonergan's framework for the future," *Commonweal* 112, no. 2 (January, 1985): 47.

21. *Time*, January 22, 1965, 47.

22. *The Lonergan Research Institute Bulletin*, no. 5, November, 1990, 3.

23. *The Lonergan Research Institute Bulletin*, no. 6, November, 1991, 3.

24. The reference in brackets (*Insight* 7) is to Bernard Lonergan, *Insight: A Study of Human Understanding*, vol. 3 in the *Collected Works of Bernard Lonergan*, ed. Frederick E. Crowe and Robert M. Doran (Toronto: University of Toronto Press, 1992), 7. Quotations from this work will henceforth be indicated as here (*Insight* 7).

25. Lonergan seems to have worked all of his life as if he were preparing for another major shift in consciousness such as that involved in the transition from a classical to modern worldview. "His vision of the distant future was clear, his sense of the need [for a complete restructuring of knowledge] compelling, and his life's labor designed to meet that need at its most fundamental level" (*The Lonergan Research Institute Bulletin*, no. 5, November, 1990, 1).

26. Lonergan saw himself as "a Roman Catholic with quite conservative views on religious and church doctrines" (*Method* 332).

27. "Address by His Eminence Gerald Emmett Cardinal Carter," July 30, 1991, in *Companions of Jesus: Pilgrims with Ignatius* (Toronto: Canadian Institute of Jesuit Studies, 1991), 30.

28. A systematic Lonergan theology, he half-jokingly insisted, would be left for second-rate minds (*Time*, January 22, 1965, 47). Lonergan was reluctant to popularize or publish applications of his methodology to specific problems. A recent example of such an application is the collection of ten scholarly essays in *Lonergan and Feminism*, ed. Cynthia S. W. Crysdale (Toronto: University of Toronto Press, 1994). With regard to the general topic of applying Lonergan's thought, "The Genus 'Lonergan and' . . . and Feminism" by Frederick E. Crowe, in *Lonergan and Feminism*, is of particular interest.

29. During this period at Boston College, Lonergan got to know Hans-Georg Gadamer (they both lived in the Jesuit residence). In a conversation reported in *Method: Journal for Lonergan Studies*, Gadamer explains his relationship with Lonergan as follows: "He could talk; he was a fascinating talker. But he really couldn't discuss. But on a friendship-basis, we got along with one another very well" (M. Baur, "A Conversation with Hans-Georg Gadamer," *Method: Journal of Lonergan Studies* 8, no. 1 (March 1990): 2.

30. Lonergan and Rahner were born in the same year and both died in 1984. They were both Jesuit theologians.

31. Other awards and honors include: the Spellman Award from the Catholic Theological Society of America in 1949; the Aquinas Medal from the American Catholic Philosophical Association in 1970; the John Courtney Murray Award from the Catholic Theological Society of America in 1973; and the Aquinas Award from Aquinas College in 1974. Lonergan served as a theological expert during the Second Vatican Council, 1962–65, was a member of the International Theological Commission, 1969–74, and appointed as a consultor of the Vatican's Secretariat for Non-Believers in 1973. In 1975 he was named a Corresponding Fellow of the British Academy.

32. Lonergan Research Institute, 10 St. Mary Street, Suite 500, Toronto, ON, M4Y 1P9. The idea of an Institute was proposed (1984) by Robert M. Doran, S.J. Its first major project is the publication of the *Collected Works of Bernard Lonergan* (*Collection* xvii).

33. That same year (1974) Loyola College and Sir George Williams University merged to form Concordia University. Aware that gigantic universities can suffer, rather than profit, from their size, Lonergan College was established on the Loyola Campus in 1979. Operating at the undergraduate level, it teaches courses in the thought of Bernard Lonergan and offers its students an interdisciplinary seminar, unique in North America for its success. The seminar is based on Lonergan's method which not only includes but demands cross-disciplinary learning. To do otherwise is to contribute to the "pool of misunderstanding" that in Lonergan's thought lies at the source of so many of humankind's woes. Each year in the Lonergan College Seminar, a classic work is chosen for study (Bernard Lonergan, Northrop Frye, Carl Jung, Niccolo Machiavelli, Theresa of Avila, Charles Darwin). Every second Monday afternoon the College Fellows (15 professors from diverse departments and disciplines) meet with the year's seminar leader to discuss a segment of the classic, while the college undergraduates listen in. On the alternating Mondays, students meet in small groups with an assigned Fellow to extend the discussion of the previous week.

34. Five volumes (*Insight* 3, *Collection* 4, *Understanding and Being* 5, *Philosophical and Theological Papers* 6 and *Topics in Education* 10) have been released. The night before Bernard Lonergan died, Robert M. Doran (Associate Director of the Institute and co-editor of the Collected Works) told him that an agreement had been reached with the University of Toronto to publish his work (*America* July 27, 1991, 46).

35. One of his doctoral students in Rome said: "Not since Robert Bellarmine have so many been influenced by one Roman thinker." Another offered: "He's still 30 years ahead of his time" (*Time,* January 22, 1965, 47).

36. *Dictionary of Jesuit Biography: Ministry to English Canada 1842–1987* (Toronto: Canadian Institute of Jesuit Sources, 1991), 191.

Chapter 5

Lonergan's Understanding of Understanding

Thoroughly understand what it is to understand, and not only will you understand the broad lines of all there is to be understood but also you will possess a fixed base, an invariant pattern, opening upon all further developments of understanding (Bernard Lonergan in *Insight* 22).

Introduction

As Bernard Lonergan studied and taught in Rome and Canada, he came to a deepening awareness that the Roman Catholic scholastic theological tradition, a paradigmatic representative of the classical worldview, was "obsolete," "finished," "done for" and that a reconstructed theology was required. Further, he recognized that it was impossible to rebuild theology correctly until it was first established on a viable philosophical foundation. And so, by the time Lonergan had finished his doctoral studies at the Gregorian University in Rome, he was committed to nothing less than the total reconstruction of both Roman Catholic philosophy and theology. *Insight: A Study of Human Understanding* and *Method in Theology*, the major fruits of that effort to enhance the old with the "new learning," will be the main sources of our account of Lonergan's ideas in this chapter.

Basic to the thought of Bernard Lonergan is his effort to understand the nature of the human act of understanding; *insight* being the
key to unlocking the basic pattern whereby the fundamental nature of
reality is revealed to human beings. His analysis is of intentionality,
human acts informed by meaning — experiencing, imagining, remembering, desiring, wondering, inquiring, understanding, conceiving,
reflecting, evaluating, judging, deliberating, deciding, acting, loving.
More simply, the work of Lonergan's lifetime was to clarify and
unfold a methodological answer to the question 'What does it mean to
know?' Lonergan assumes that we *do* have an experience of knowing
because to claim that we do not know is at least to *know* that we do not
know, proving that knowledge is possible:

> Am I a knower? The answer yes is coherent, for if I am a knower,
> I can know that fact. But the answer no is incoherent, for if I am not
> a knower, how could the question be raised and answered by me? No
> less, the hedging answer 'I do not know' is incoherent. For if I know
> that I do not know, then I am a knower; and if I do not know that I do
> not know, then I should not answer.
> Am I a knower? If I am not, then I know nothing. My only
> course is silence (*Insight* 353).

Our initial focus in this chapter will be Lonergan's answers to four
questions: 'What am I doing when I am knowing?' (his cognitional
theory), 'Why is doing that knowing?' (his epistemology), 'What do
I know when I have done that?' (his metaphysics), and 'How am I to
decide what to make of myself?' (his existential ethics).[1]

Human Knowing

What am I doing when I am knowing? (cognitional theory)

Bernard Lonergan's investigation into the dynamics of human cognition (our "conscious intentionality") led him to propose that all conscious and intentional operations of knowing occur by means of a
dynamic interlocking pattern of experiencing, understanding, judging,
and deciding.[2]

Using a spacial metaphor, Lonergan speaks of four *levels* through
which the dynamic of conscious intentionality unfolds: the *empirical*
level of conscious attention to data, characterized by the operations of

our senses (seeing, hearing, touching, smelling, tasting) but including as well the interior senses (perceiving, imagining, anticipating, feeling, remembering); the *intellectual* level of consciousness, characterized by inquiry, insight (the act of understanding) and conceptualizing;[3] the *rational* level of consciousness, characterized by all operations of reflecting, grasping the evidence, and judging which are involved in verifying our understanding and judging the truth of what is; and the *responsible* level of consciousness characterized by deliberating, evaluating, and deciding about what good action ought to be done. This process brings us to a knowledge of reality. The real world for Lonergan is not simply the object of our understanding of experience (this is just thinking) but the object of judgments and decisions made in light of our understanding of this experience.

Before moving on, we will pause to consolidate our appropriation of the unfolding of what Lonergan refers to as the "generalized empirical method." I hope these two concrete illustrations of cognitional theory will suggest others to the reader.

First, consider how television star Peter Falk, as Lieutenant Columbo,[4] solves a murder case. What is unusual about a *Columbo* mystery is that at the outset we see the murder being planned and executed; we know who did it, as well as when, where, and how. Over the time remaining, we see Lieutenant Columbo's painstaking efforts to collect and assess evidence. His detective work moves from cigar puffing and head scratching at the complexity of the clues through a logical series of questions for intelligence — What happened? Why is this here? How does this fit? Where did that come from? Who could have done that? Columbo records *data* in his little black book, struggling to fathom how seemingly random pieces of evidence fit together. He goes off on tangents but endless questions raise suspicions and solve small puzzles until the penny drops and a flash of *insight* clarifies his *understanding* of the data. As he continues to scratch his head, search for matches in his shabby coat, and drive around in his old car, he surfaces questions for reflection (Is that really so? Am I certain?) and forms and tests hypotheses. Methodically he builds a case until he arrives at a possible, then probable, and finally certain *judgment* as to the true identity of the guilty party. In the final scene, he makes the arrest. Since we viewers know the identity of the guilty party from the very beginning of the show, why do we bother to watch *Columbo*? In my view, it is because of our fascination with the dynamics of human knowing, with the relentlessness of the process of understanding the evidence and arriving at the precise judgment that fits all of the facts beyond any doubt. *Columbo*, Lonergan would say, gives us an insight into insight.

The second example that I want to use is that of the film *Lorenzo's Oil*.[5] It begins in 1984 with the Odone family's growing consciousness of their five year old son Lorenzo's rare illness as its debilitating effects manifest themselves (*experience*). We follow them in their efforts to *understand* adrenoleukodystophy (ALD), initially in conversation with doctors and then in medical research libraries sifting through abstruse papers. The Odone's arrive at the stark realization that there are conflicting explanations for the cause and treatment of Lorenzo's rare disease. No consensus exists in the medical profession for how they ought to proceed. Lorenzo grows weaker and his family continues to try to understand the disease. At a turning point in the film, Lorenzo's father states that *understanding* is not enough. Although the Odone's have become experts and even organized an international conference on ALD, Lorenzo continues to weaken. The awareness dawns that they need to reflect on what they have understood and make a *judgment* about which explanation for Lorenzo's illness is correct and then *act* on it. They enter into a process of deliberation and assessment leading to the judgment that a particular by-product of common oils is the best course of treatment as it at least inhibits the progress of ALD. In the final minutes of the film the Odone's take the steps necessary to carry out their *decision*; Lorenzo begins to improve. Their discovery is communicated to other sufferers and what has become known as 'Lorenzo's oil' is still the best available treatment for adrenoleukodystophy.

From what we have seen to this point, I think it is clear that each step in the generalized empirical method builds on the preceding one: without the data of experience there is no possibility of inquiry and understanding; without a proper grasp of intelligibility (relationships and meanings), correct judgment is impossible; without having made a judgment as to what is so, no proper decision can be taken. According to Lonergan, as we achieve the goal of a particular level we go on, spontaneously, to the next. We don't go on, or at least can't *satisfactorily* go on, until the goal of a given level has been reached. So, every question for reflection presupposes that we have arrived at an answer to a question for intelligence; every question requiring deliberation and decision presupposes that we have answered yes or no to the reflective question, 'Is our understanding of the data correct?'[6]

These three levels are solidary. Without the first there would be no base for the second and no precise meaning for the third. Without the second the first could not get beyond elementary statements, and there could be no punch to the third. Without the third the second would be regarded as incredible, and the first would be neglected (*Insight* 7).

We are impelled to move from one level of consciousness to the next by wonder, by our intellectual curiosity, by means of that inborn human need to find answers to questions, all of which Lonergan calls our "detached, disinterested, unrestricted desire to know" (*Insight* 659).

A few years ago, I had occasion to meet a young university student from the former Soviet Union who was in Canada studying for the Orthodox priesthood. He explained to me that with the parting of the Iron Curtain his closed, controlled world had exploded. After only a few months in Canada he discovered so much that had happened in the world and even within Orthodox Christianity of which he was unaware. He told me that he "needed to know" and when I asked, "know what?" he replied "things; anything, everything, I just want to know." I immediately thought of Lonergan's detached, disinterested, unrestricted desire to know!

Each level of consciousness, according to Lonergan's account, is open to reality from a different standpoint. "The first level is open to reality as it can be experienced. The second level is open to reality as it is intelligible. The third level is open to reality as it is true. The fourth level is open to reality as it is *good*" (*Desires* 25).[7] In Lonergan's vision we human beings have within ourselves deep longings and desires for what is beautiful in our experience, for what makes sense, for what is true, and for what is good.

These four interlocking levels of human consciousness are "a rock on which one can build" (*Method* 19);[8] they constitute human consciousness and the *pattern* of the operations involved is *normative*. By this Lonergan means that in order to disprove what he is saying you would necessarily have to appeal to a *judgment* you have made that your *understanding* of a particular set of *data* is correct; in other words, you would *necessarily* have to use the process to disprove the process and so Lonergan concludes that "the possibility of a revision presupposes this analysis" (*Understanding* 143):[9]

If it is true that this is a structure that excludes the possibility of a revision, in the sense that any future revision in any concrete sense of 'revision' would presuppose knowing to be precisely a structure of this type, we have arrived at a fundamental invariant pattern. Any future advance in self-knowledge may fill out this pattern with further details, may enrich it with all sorts of conclusions; but to be a revision it has to preserve this pattern (*Understanding* 144).

The dynamic of the generalized empirical method grounds what Lonergan calls the "transcendental precepts" which guide the gradual expansion of human consciousness: *Be attentive, Be intelligent, Be reasonable, Be responsible*. There is, he suggests, an imperative quality to the dynamics of human consciousness. But, to suggest that human consciousness naturally unfolds attentively, intelligently, reasonably, and responsibly does not mean that we can't pass over or just pay cursory attention to one or another of the levels. We often do. We can, for instance, be unwilling to gather all of the data and seek to understand with the probability of an incomplete or erroneous insight. We can refuse to reflect reasonably and thereby make false judgments. We can choose not to act, to act apathetically, or even choose to do what is wrong. We can "impede or derail the deepest desires" of our human minds and hearts (*Desires* 22). For Lonergan, neglect of these transcendental precepts leads to alienation (*Method* 55).

Note that the spontaneous drive operating at each level of consciousness is in the form of a *precept* or imperative and not *necessity*; although we are called to be attentive to data, to probe intelligently, to reflect reasonably, and to decide responsibly, we need not respond to the call; we can choose to be inattentive, unintelligent, unreasonable, and irresponsible. Human freedom lies in that capacity for choice.

Why is doing that knowing? (epistemological theory)[10]

Medical researchers can dissect the human ear and see its intricate workings but they cannot *see* the inner act of hearing. Similarly, because the world of human consciousness (like hearing) is not something *out there*, it cannot be investigated empirically. Yet, even though human consciousness is not verifiable from *outside*, because the levels which constitute the process of human knowing are conscious (we are aware in our experiencing, aware in our understanding, aware in our judging, aware in our deciding), the human knower can answer this question about the validity of the knowing process from *inside*. Because the activity of knowing takes place within the consciousness of human beings who claim to have knowledge, knowers must decide whether their knowing is merely *subjective* (i.e., unreliable) or answer that they can know the truth about things as they exist apart from their own perceptions, i.e., *objectively* (reliably).

Lonergan's position on this question is rooted in an awareness that human consciousness is characterized by both outer and inner components. To focus, for example, on the dynamic operating on the empirical level, we are conscious of *what* we are attending to and we are conscious that *we* are attending to it. We are present *both* to the object of our inquiry *and* to ourselves. There is never just an isolated experience of something out there (rationalism, empiricism), but there is also a person, a *subject*, aware of doing the experiencing. The role of the human subject in the knowing dynamic is, as we shall see, key to Lonergan's argument for the possibility of *objectivity* in human knowing.

Before we proceed, allow me to offer one other example of this knowing process at work. When I completed my basic science degree I worked with two senior high school chemistry classes. The teacher assigned to teach chemistry had never taken a university science course and accordingly had no real *understanding* of the scientific method or of basic chemical procedures, reactions, and interconnections. But he had more or less memorized the textbook and did a credible teaching job except when it came to answering a student's question arising from confusion about definitions or explanations in the text. The only answers the teacher knew were those in the book; in fact, he had extraordinary recall. However, he was tied to the text and could not use different language to *explain* concepts or give alternative examples. He did not really understand the concepts himself and what was worse, he knew it; he *knew* that he didn't understand chemistry. It was at this point that I came onto the scene armed with my new Bachelor of Science degree in chemistry; i.e., armed with an *understanding* of the scientific method and the procedures of chemistry as well an acquired ability to offer alternative explanations and weigh the appropriateness of a student's rewording of a definition. The teacher I replaced would agree wholeheartedly with Lonergan that "until I have understood something, I haven't understood it, and I know I haven't understood it, and no amount of self-deception is going to really satisfy me" (*Desires* 19).

This story, I trust, helps to make the point that Lonergan's inquiry into the dynamic of human inquiry involves "self-appropriation;" we attend to the data of our consciousness (inside) even as we focus on data 'out there' which happens to be of interest. Key to a proper understanding and appreciation of Lonergan's achievement is this notion — all real knowledge requires that we *make our own* the structure of experiencing, understanding, judging, and deciding:[11]

> The dynamic cognitional structure to be reached is . . . the personally appropriated structure of one's own experiencing, one's own intelligent inquiry and insights, one's own critical reflection and judging and deciding. The crucial issue is an experimental issue, and the experiment will be performed not publicly but privately. It will consist in one's own rational self-consciousness clearly and distinctly taking possession of itself as rational self-consciousness. Up to that decisive achievement, all leads. From it all follows. No one else, no matter what his knowledge or his eloquence, no matter what his logical rigor or his persuasiveness, can do it for you (*Insight* 12–13).

Thus, in *Insight* we are counseled not to learn from the book but from reflection on our own human consciousness at work. For Lonergan, philosophy is what occurs in us; the *history* of philosophy is found in books. The philosophic evidence for Lonergan's position, then, lies within each one of us. The dynamic structure of knowing he has carefully uncovered is not *his* theory nor that of a philosophical school, nor is it something we can be taught, but it is *us*; it is ourselves as we search for an understanding of our experience, ourselves as we strive for what is true and good, ourselves as we engage in all aspects of life. Lonergan insists that there is no such animal as a "Lonerganian." His work is a way of challenging human beings "to discover themselves and be themselves" (*Second Collection* 213).[12] Accordingly, in the Introduction to *Insight*, Lonergan says:

> Though I cannot recall to each reader his personal experiences, he can do so for himself and thereby pluck my general phrases from the dim world of thought to set them in the pulsing flow of life. . . . the point here . . . is appropriation; the point is to discover, to identify, to become familiar with, the activities of one's own intelligence . . . (*Insight* 13–14).

As we follow the steps of the generalized empirical method, as we move from one level of human consciousness to another, the *quality* of our consciousness is enlarged. For Lonergan, the data of philosophy (human consciousness) and the methodology used in doing it (intentionality analysis) are coincidental. As questions move us from level to level "it is a fuller self of which we are aware and the awareness itself is different" (*Method* 9). We are conscious, not only that our operations are different, but that *we* are different. In other words, more of ourselves, more of what it is to be human, is at risk as we go from experiencing to understanding to judging to deciding.[13] For example, as a professor correcting examination papers, I find it quite easy to admit that through oversight I missed a student's answer or added up grades incorrectly. As students come to my office to discuss their work, it is a little more difficult to acknowledge that I have misunderstood them, and to concede that I misjudged their motives would necessitate an admission of some personal failure. Finally, to say that I made a mistake and followed a wrong course of action in my dealings with a student is tantamount to confessing to some serious flaw in my very character.

What is significant, for Lonergan, about the movement through the levels of consciousness, then, is not just the growing complexity of the operations involved but the change in ourselves as we move from receptivity, to inquiry, to verification, to decision:

> [As human beings] we are so endowed that we not only ask questions leading to self-transcendence, not only can recognize correct answers constitutive of intentional self-transcendence, but also respond with the stirring of our very being when we glimpse the possibility . . . of oneself as a moral being, the realization that one not only chooses between courses of action but also thereby makes oneself an authentic human being or an unauthentic one (*Method* 38).

But, how do we know that this many-leveled subject really exists? Lonergan, of course, replies that we must answer that question for ourselves. His own answer is unequivocal: "I do not think that the answers are in doubt. . . . There exist subjects that are empirically, intellectually, rationally, morally conscious" (*Collection* 210).[14]

Questions about truth and objectivity are forms of the epistemological question in philosophy. For Lonergan, it is answered, as I hope is becoming clear, by reflecting on the *process* of knowing; i.e., reflecting on the dynamic structure of human consciousness as experiencing, understanding, judging, and deciding.

> If knowing is a conjunction of experience, understanding, and judging, then knowing knowing has to be a conjunction of (1) experiencing experience, understanding and judging, (2) understanding one's experience of experience, understanding, and judging, and (3) judging

Table 5.1

A GUIDE FOR UNDERSTANDING THE SET OF TERMS LONERGAN HAS DEVELOPED IN HIS ANALYSIS OF HUMAN CONSCIOUSNESS				
LEVELS OF CONSCIOUSNESS	**QUESTION**	**TRANSCENDENTAL ACTIVITIES**	**TRANSCENDENTAL PRECEPTS**	**OPEN TO REALITY AS IT IS . . .**
THE LOVING	IS IT LOVABLE?	LOVING/CARING	BE IN LOVE!	LOVABLE
THE RESPONSIBLE	IS IT OF VALUE? OUGHT I TO DO IT?	DECIDING DELIBERATING	BE RESPONSIBLE!	GOOD/OF VALUE WORTHWHILE
THE RATIONAL	IS IT SO?	JUDGING REFLECTING	BE REASONABLE!	TRUE
THE INTELLECTUAL	WHAT IS IT?	UNDERSTANDING INQUIRING CONCEIVING	BE INTELLIGENT!	INTELLIGIBLE
THE EMPIRICAL	NONE (PRIOR TO INQUIRY)	REMEMBERING PERCEIVING SENSING	BE ATTENTIVE!	EXPERIENCED
THE ELEMENTAL	NONE	DREAMING		PRE-CONSCIOUS

one's understanding of experience, understanding, and judging to be correct (*Collection* 208).

Knowing knowing, then, is just a reduplication of Lonergan's basic cognitional structure. The answer to the question 'Why is doing that knowing?' is, simply, 'because *I* know it to be so!'[15] Such reflective knowledge of the framework of human knowing puts us in touch with its very drive or dynamism — human beings by their very nature desire to know. And what is it that we want to know? Like my Orthodox seminarian friend, we want to know *what is* and *what is* is another way of speaking about the 'real' or the 'true'. In philosophical language, human knowing intends *being*. This Lonergan calls "the epistemological theorem" — "namely, that knowledge in the proper sense is knowledge of reality or, more fully, that knowledge is intrinsically objective, that objectivity is the intrinsic relation of knowing to being, and that being and reality are identical" (*Collection* 211).

Intellectual Conversion

In ordinary daily life when we ask someone 'How do you know?' and they respond with a definitive 'Because I saw it!' the issue is normally settled. We often behave as if seeing is knowing (naive realism) or, in a more sophisticated manner, as if the real is what we *know* through sense experience (empiricism). Lonergan does not claim that the empiricist point of view is wrong, only that it is incomplete; it takes just one of the components of knowing (experiencing) and treats it as if it were the whole of knowing. Inquiry, insight, formulation, reflection, judgment, truthfulness, goodness, trust, fidelity, caring, and love cannot be grasped by means of the senses and are therefore pejoratively labeled "subjective" (unreliable) by empiricists, yet these activities are at the very *heart* of the knowing process.

Lonergan asks that we be present to the pattern of our own experiencing, understanding, judging, and deciding as we evaluate his viewpoint. Can we give up the myth that knowing is just taking a "super-look" (*Insight* 658) at the "already-out-there-now-real" (*Second Collection* 272)? Can we discover the intelligible structure of our own dynamic pattern of consciousness, and then affirm the truth about it? To do so, for Lonergan, is to be intellectually converted.

Intellectual conversion is a radical clarification and, consequently, the elimination of an exceedingly stubborn and misleading myth concerning reality, objectivity, and human knowledge. The myth is that knowing is like looking, that objectivity is seeing what is there to be seen and not seeing what is not there, and that the real is what is out there now to be looked at (*Method* 238).

Intellectual conversion, then, is an awakening to the realization that we will only discover what is true when we use our most personal human capacities, when we devote ourselves to experiencing, understanding, and judging with *all* of the resources available to us. Intellectual conversion implies the realization that the personal, interpersonal, and social dimensions of our existence in this world are made up not principally of sense data but by human understandings, judgments, and decisions. The world in which we live is *constituted by human meaning*. Lonergan's claim is that there is a subjective component to *all* knowing and, far from making our knowing suspect, subjectivity is integral to the correct unfolding of the knowing process. In fact, he argues that *all* knowing *is* subjective and in an often quoted phrase points out that "genuine objectivity is the fruit of authentic subjectivity. It is to be attained only by attaining authentic subjectivity" (*Method* 292).

As a simple illustration of what Lonergan means by this significant but perhaps enigmatic expression, consider an x-ray.[16] Knowing what an x-ray means is certainly more than just *looking* at shades of light and dark on a sheet of plastic. A radiologist practicing his/her craft *knows* how to interpret (understand) these shadows and to judge that a certain tiny line on the film *means* that the patient has a fractured rib. The radiologist's trained subjectivity arrives at an objectivity that I, by *looking* at the x-ray, cannot reach. Knowing is not just taking a good look; knowing is an interlocking process of attending (sensing, perceiving, and imagining), understanding (inquiring, gaining insight, and formulating), reflecting and judging. To *know* that this is so and to operate in this way is for Lonergan to be intellectually converted.

At this point in our survey of Lonergan's thought, it may be helpful to recall John Macmurray's remark (chapter 2) that "it is always legitimate to ask, of any theory which claims to be true, what practical difference it would make if we believed it" (*Self* 23). Lonergan may look to you like an ivory-tower philosopher, offering incomprehensible answers to insoluble problems (to borrow a definition I heard somewhere). He was certainly aware that "in the minds of some" he dwelt in a "cocoon of abstractions" (*Transforming* 209). In my opinion, Lonergan *isn't* an abstract, ivory-tower thinker but a prophetic interpreter of our transition from the classical age that is dying, through the modern age, and into the one that is coming to birth. As this summary of his thought unfolds, *you* ought to be able to see the practicality of his approach. As will presently become apparent, Lonergan's analysis bears on significant contemporary questions about the nature of reality.

Metaphysics: What do I know when I have done that?

At least implicitly, we have already answered the metaphysical question. For Lonergan, knowledge is knowledge of *reality*; whatever I can grasp intelligently and affirm as reasonable through the use of the generalized empirical method, is *what is*. Knowing *what is* is knowing the 'real' or 'being,' for *the real* is *what is*.[17]

Note that reality, for Lonergan, is not some *object* totally outside of myself which I know with absolute certitude by use of reason (rationalism) or by taking a good look (naive realism). Nor is reality unknowable (idealism) or merely a matter of opinion (relativism). Lonergan's answer (critical realism) is that *we can know reality* and we do so through the dynamic and conscious process of experiencing, understanding, judging, and deciding.

To see how the critical realist understanding of the dynamic of human consciousness unfolds in a concrete instance, allow me to propose for your consideration the meaning of a recurrent expression from the Hebrew scriptures, describing the Promised Land as "flowing with milk and honey" (Exodus 33:3, Deuteronomy 27:3, et. al.). California has always been my image of a land flowing with milk and honey and so when I visited Israel during the course of my Jesuit formation, I was surprised to discover a landscape quite unlike California. Much of the land of the Bible, bordered on the south by the Sinai Desert and on the east by the vast Arabian Desert, is desert-like wilderness with very little vegetation. Some areas, like Jerusalem itself, are mountainous and at the other geographic extreme we find the lowest point on earth, the lifeless Dead Sea. Except for a relatively small area of productive agricultural land (along the Mediterranean coast and in a few broad valleys), the Bible's "flowing with milk and honey" designation seems hardly appropriate!

In terms of Lonergan's elaboration of the generalized empirical method, this biblical text ("a land flowing with milk and honey") is given to us on the level of experience as a datum to be understood. In my efforts to understand, I consulted the endnotes to various editions of the Bible and found nothing specific. I read several commentaries on scripture which either passed over the expression or said it refers to the fertility of the Promised Land, as compared to the aridity of the desert where the Hebrew people had been wandering for decades. Even though part of Israel is far superior to desert, much of it is, in fact, quite unlike my image of the Promised Land as flowing with California-like "milk and honey." I didn't really understand this "milk and honey" image and I knew that I didn't understand it.

Then, a few years ago I heard a talk on the geography of the Promised Land by a cultural geographer, Dr. James Fleming, from the Hebrew University in Jerusalem. With photographic slides and maps he built up a case for the words "milk" and "honey" as descriptors of two life styles supported by the Promised Land; i.e., the lifestyle of herding in the mountainous areas and on the edges of the deserts (goat's "milk") *and* farming on the broad coast plain and fertile valleys along the Mediterranean (fruit trees give jam or "honey"). The key word in the expression, as it turns out, is the conjunction "and." Peoples living in the areas surrounding the Promised Land were *either* herders *or* farmers. The significance of the Promised Land of "milk *and* honey" is that it is a land supporting *both* herding *and* farming; a very special place indeed!

Based on this scholarly lecture and my own personal experience and study, I made a judgment that Dr. Fleming's explanation of "milk and honey" is the correct one and have even used it in my preaching. Does that mean that this understanding is absolutely certain truth? No! But it is much more than just an opinion, or even a particular scholar's opinion. It represents the accumulated wisdom of many scholars (archaeologists, cultural geographers, climatologists, linguists, anthropologists) and is the consensus of biblical scholarship at the present time. It is a *highly probable explanation*. Note, however, that a highly probable explanation is not *THE* TRUTH (God's Truth) because new evidence from an archaeologist or a textual critic may lead to a somewhat nuanced understanding of the expression which in turn will lead to a slightly different judgment as to its correct interpretation. In more formal terminology, Lonergan says that although the *formally* unconditioned (God's Truth) is beyond our grasp in knowing (*we* cannot know *absolutely*, because *all* possible questions have not been answered), we do reach a *virtually* unconditioned (as much as is humanly possible the relevant questions have been answered). We can make a *reasonable* affirmation as to what is the truth. So, even though what I achieve as a result of the process of experiencing, understanding, judging and deciding is not absolute certainty (classicism) neither am I left with the polar opposite extreme of mere opinion (relativism). What I reach is knowledge of *what is*. It is *truth*. I like to characterize what is known by this transcendental process as being *relatively* absolute!

In addition, truth, for Lonergan, is necessarily *my* truth; truth which *I* arrive at by means of the pattern of human consciousness expanding through empirical, intellectual, *and* rational, and responsible levels. Truth is not something *apart* from me, carved into granite or preserved in an illuminated manuscript, passed down and accepted uncritically by subsequent generations, because, unless I have made it *my* stone or *my* book, it represents the work of another person's mind. *I* do not yet know it as truth (until the stone or manuscript become data I judge with sufficient evidence to be true in light of my own understanding and critical reflection).

Despite the emphasis above on the word *my*, I trust that you can see why Bernard Lonergan is not open to the charge of being a relativist.[18] The choice for Lonergan is not between the *classical* stance supporting eternal, unchanging, absolute truth and what many people take to be the *modern* view that everything is just a matter of opinion or relative. There is, he argues, a third alternative (critical realism); what is absolute or normative in knowing is *not* so much the *object* I am trying to know but the *process I follow* in coming to know. It is the *pattern* of my conscious and intentional operations which forms the "rock" on which I can build truth.

Existential Ethics

How am I to decide what to make of myself?

> The individual grows in experience, understanding, judgment, and so comes to find out for himself that he has to decide for himself what to make of himself (*Method* 79).

At the beginning of this chapter I said that our focus would be on two of Lonergan's works, *Insight* and *Method in Theology*. Our discussion in this section marks the transition from one to the other.

Lonergan's three level description of cognitional activity (empirical, intellectual, rational) governs *Insight* whereas the overarching motif in *Method* is the four level structure which includes responsibility. To this point, our discussion of Bernard Lonergan's achievement has been (like *Insight* itself) highly cognitional. *Method* reflects a decisive shift in his approach in that it emphasizes the central importance of affectivity and love in knowing and doing at the higher levels of conscious intending. "Experience, understanding and judgment without feeling," Lonergan says, "are paper-thin."[19]

Affectivity is at the center of the fourth level of human intending. It is critical to authenticity at this level; it is in feelings that possible values are *first* apprehended and it is largely in negotiating our feelings that deliberation about decision takes place. The addition of the affective dynamics of *heart* to the cognitional dynamics of *mind* leads to a corresponding shift in decision making from doing what is reasonable to acting responsibly.

What is clear in *Method* is that responsible decision making is a level of consciousness quite distinct from experiencing, understanding and judging. Lonergan variously refers to this level of conscious intentionality as the *responsible* level, as existential consciousness, as the level of authenticity or unauthenticity, and the level where "we emerge as persons" and "meet one another in a common concern for values" (*Method* 10).

Lonergan argues (as does Macmurray) that as human beings we are more than mere *knowing* subjects (mind), we are *agent*-subjects imbued with a built-in spontaneous drive to seek congruence between what we know and what we do. So while cognitional theory, epistemology, and metaphysics are *necessary* in understanding human consciousness, they are not *sufficient*: "They have to be subsumed under the higher operations that integrate knowing with feeling and consist in deliberating, evaluating, deciding, acting" (*Second Collection* 204). And how do we arrive at this level? Just as questions calling for understanding move us from the empirical to the intellectual level of consciousness, and questions for reflection move us from the intellectual level to the level of judgment, so questions for deliberation move us from the rational level to the existential level. For Lonergan, there is in us "an internal compass," a fundamental or innate drive, targeted to what is true and worthwhile, and we know when we have arrived there. Because more than mind is involved in our "detached, disinterested, unrestricted desire to know," we are drawn beyond cognition to a fourth level of human consciousness where affectivity (heart) joins with knowledge (head) in responsible decision-making about the values by which we will live (hands and feet).[20] To quote Blaise Pascal, as Lonergan often does, "the heart has its reasons of which reason knows nothing" (*Pensées* 154).[21]

So, as we move beyond the third level of consciousness where we reach a judgment of fact about what is *true* or *real*, we reach a fourth level where we ask about what course of action to follow — 'Is this or that particular project or goal really of value?' In essence, at this level of consciousness we come face to face with the basic ethical question — 'Why be moral at all?' 'Is doing the truth worthwhile?' Lonergan would say that an affirmative answer to this question presupposes "moral conversion,"[22] i.e., presupposes that I desire to put the interests of others ahead of my own, group satisfaction before personal satisfaction. This, of course, leads to further questions: 'Why would I want to do that?' and 'How would I accomplish that even if I wanted to?'

To treat these questions in summary form, Lonergan would answer the *why* question by saying that responsible action is what we human beings, having been created *imago Dei* (in the image of God), are made for; right action is the path to human authenticity. Our choices and actions make us who we are, they are the work of free and responsible agents producing the first and only edition of themselves (*Second Collection* 83). He would answer the *how* question with reference to human beings who have been "grasped by ultimate concern," who have fallen in love, who have surrendered themselves totally to God (*Method* 240). This what Lonergan calls "religious conversion;" it grounds both moral and intellectual conversion.[23]

Moral Conversion

To affirm the existence and structure of *four* levels of consciousness, Lonergan says, is to come to a moral question. Why does he say this? It is because, if the pattern we have been considering is indeed the dynamic method of our consciousness, it is our way to be fully human, and to deliberate about whether to follow its injunctions (conscience) is to deliberate about whether to work and grow as individual human beings and with others. To reject mere personal satisfaction and decide to work for the common good is, for Lonergan, *moral conversion*. Moral conversion involves a shift in the criterion we use for deciding what action we will take; a shift from the criterion of personal satisfaction to that of value (*Method* 240).

The dynamics of human consciousness move us beyond *cognitional* questions of truth to *affective* questions of value, we desire to know because we want to act, and act intelligently. We pay attention to experience and consciousness, inquiry intelligently into the meaning of our experience, and exercise critical judgment, because we want to make responsible decisions, thereby to become *moral* — "to become moral practically, for our decisions affect things; to become moral interpersonally, for our decisions affect other persons; to become moral existentially, for by our decisions we constitute what we are to be" (*Third Collection* 29).[24] The endpoint of the knowing process is ethical, *not* just cognitional. True judgments generate a "peaceful" or "good" conscience and the "uneasy" or "nagging" conscience is the result of false judgment (*Method* 40, *Third Collection* 174). Conscience, for Lonergan is the necessity to make our doing consistent with our knowing.

There is, therefore, a dual creation in our knowing and doing; we not only create objects, we create ourselves (i.e., form character). This critical juncture in our increasing autonomy is where we discover in ourselves and for ourselves that it is ultimately up to ourselves to determine who we are to be (*Third Collection* 230). Lonergan refers to this appreciation as the "existential moment," "the realization that one not only chooses between courses of action but also thereby makes oneself an authentic human being or an unauthentic one" (*Method* 38).[25]

Authenticity, then, involves more than just *knowing* the truth; it is knowledge of truth as oriented towards decision for action, towards *doing* the truth and deciding to live that way habitually. This is a tall order and for Lonergan only possible when we have been "grasped by ultimate concern" (God, for believers). For Christians this "fated acceptance of a vocation to holiness" (*Method* 240) is the experience of God's love having been "poured into our hearts through the Holy Spirit that has been given to us" (Romans 5:5). Lonergan is quick to point out that authenticity is never a permanent, once and for all, achievement:

> Human authenticity is not some pure quality, some serene freedom from all oversights, all misunderstandings, all mistakes, all sins. Rather it consists in a withdrawal from unauthenticity, and the withdrawal is never a permanent achievement. It is ever precarious,

ever to be achieved afresh, ever in great part a matter of uncovering still more oversights, acknowledging still further failures to understand, correcting still more mistakes, repenting more and more deeply hidden sins (*Method* 252).

The path to authenticity, then, is not an easy one and many choose to live unauthentic lives; others "authentically realize unauthenticity." Lonergan explains this, perhaps puzzling phraseology, very well:

> Divers men can ask themselves whether or not they are genuine Catholics or Protestants, Muslims or Buddhists, Platonists or Aristotelians, Kantians or Hegelians, artists or scientists, and so forth. Now they may answer that they are, and their answer may be correct. But they can also answer affirmatively and still be mistaken. In that case . . . what I am is one thing, what a genuine Christian or Buddhist is, is another, and I am unaware of the difference. My unawareness is unexpressed. I have no language to express what I am, so I use the language of the tradition I unauthentically appropriate, and thereby I devaluate, distort, water down, corrupt that language.
>
> Such devaluation, distortion, corruption may occur only in scattered individuals. But it may occur on a more massive scale, and then the words are repeated, but the meaning is gone. The chair was still the chair of Moses, but it was occupied by the scribes and Pharisees. The theology was still scholastic, but the scholasticism was decadent. The religious order still read out the rules, but one wonders whether the home fires were still burning. The sacred name of science may still be invoked but . . . all significant scientific ideals can vanish to be replaced by the conventions of a clique. So the unauthenticity of individuals becomes the unauthenticity of a tradition. Then, in the measure a subject takes the tradition, as it exists, for his standard, in that measure he can do no more than authentically realize unauthenticity" (*Method* 80).

When we have begun the process of self-constitution from a reflective, critical stance on the responsible level of consciousness, Lonergan asserts, we have come to a critical turning point in our lives — the point at which *spiritual* development, properly speaking, begins. Practical reflection moves us from the realm of fact into that of *value* when we deliberate about the goodness of a possible course of action and right action moves us towards community, towards being-in-love. In other words, just as moral conversion takes us beyond intellectual conversion, so "religious conversion" takes us beyond moral conversion.

Love/Community

Religious Conversion

For Lonergan, love is the fundamental basis for all that we do. To affirm love as a *fifth* level of human consciousness (the ultimate good, love, God), in Lonergan's view, requires *religious conversion* which he defines as "being grasped by ultimate concern," as "other-worldly falling in love," as "total and permanent self-surrender without conditions, qualifications, reservations" (*Method* 240). From the viewpoint of causality, Lonergan would say that *first* there is God's freely given gift of love.[26] He was fond of quoting St. Paul's letter to the Romans: "Hope does not disappoint us, because God's love has been poured into our hearts through the Holy Spirit that has been given to us" (Romans 5:5). Religious conversion brings a joy that the things of this world cannot give and its influence is so pervasive that, in the normal course of events, "once it comes and as long as it lasts, it takes over. One no longer is one's own. Moreover, in the measure that this transformation is effective, development becomes not merely from below upwards but more fundamentally from above downwards. There has begun a life in which the heart has reasons which reason does not know" (*Third Collection* 77)

In Lonergan's analysis, because human beings are created in the image of God, human authenticity means being like God. Christianity is authentic to the degree that it is "a love of others that does not shrink from self-sacrifice and suffering" (*Method* 291). Clearly, authenticity, defined in this way, is *only* possible in response to the prior, more fundamental gift of God's love "from above."

Community

Although we have not specifically called attention to it until now, Bernard Lonergan understands the whole process of coming to know as "the work of many," a "group enterprise" (*Second Collection* 87). Even academic research, generally thought of as a solitary, ivory-tower type of activity, he envisages as a *collaborative* enterprise carried out by a *community* of scholars.

In *Insight*, Lonergan writes that human beings have a primordial sympathy for one another. We don't live together mechanically or like ants in an ant hill; we live with feelings for and commitments to other persons. Such community is much more than a number of people living in the same geographic area; it is constituted by means of mutual personal relationships of love.

Lonergan explains mutual love as "the intertwining of two lives" in such a way that an 'I' and 'thou' are transformed into a 'we'; a 'we' "so intimate, so secure, so permanent, that each attends, imagines, thinks, plans, feels, speaks, acts in concern for both" (*Method* 33). Relationships of this kind (respectful, intimate, loving) "bind a community together" whereas relationships characterized by contempt, ignorance, exploitation, and enmity divide a community "into factions, or tear it apart" (*Method* 51).[27]

Because religious experience, however personal and intimate it may be, is not an isolated, solitary experience but a gift given to many, we have the basis for religious *community*. Another way Lonergan looks at community is to see it as a means to "sustain one another in . . . self-transformation" (*Method* 130). Accordingly, he proposes that the Christian church, "the community that results from the outer communication of Christ's message and from the inner gift of God's love" (*Method* 361), ought to have as a primary function the promotion and renewal of community; i.e., the promotion of intellectual, moral, and religious conversion.

When encountered for the first time, this may seem to be strange way to speak about the church. Certainly in times past, the task of the church was understood as enabling believers "to assimilate the available religious meanings, make their own the available religious ideals, [and] participate with their fellows in the customary rituals" (*Third Collection* 59). What has brought about this change in emphasis?

Bernard Lonergan recognized that since the transformation of mathematics, natural science, and philosophy during the enlightenment period, a higher differentiation emerged in human consciousness (the "new learning"), a differentiation which raised new questions about the place of the individual in society. In our own day, he says, those questions have brought about a movement towards "world community" (*Third Collection* 65). Lonergan makes his point with a quotation from the philosopher of religion, Robley E. Whitson:

> Without parallel in the past, contemporary civilization is coming to be centered upon consciousness of man as community: the significance of man in personal relationship — not the isolated individual nor the subordinating society. . . .
>   . . . And an immediate consequent of even the most rudimentary

recognition of human community is the further recognition of human unity . . . as emerging consciousness of what man really is . . .

Yet human unity . . . is still clearly at its beginnings, still mostly dream.[28]

Such developments have, in part, contributed to the ecumenical movement within Christianity and dialogue among world religions.[29] In 1975, as part of an International Symposium on Belief, Lonergan presented a paper on the *emerging* religious consciousness of our time[30] in which he acknowledged (borrowing from Whitson) that the notion of a world community was still a dream but reminded his audience that a dream emerges from our unconscious "as an intimation of a reality to be achieved" (*Third Collection* 66).

Today, in addition to our human relationships, that dream increasingly includes our relationship with the eco-systems of the fragile planet on which we live. According to Bernard Lonergan's analysis, because the knowing process involves both inner and outer aspects, not only do we know and make ourselves we also know and make the world. It is because of this human/earth relationship that we are not only *individually* responsible for the lives we lead but we are also *collectively* responsible for the world in which we lead them (*Second Collection* 93 & 115). Honest concern for the future life of our planet begins, Lonergan says, with self-transcendent moral conversion:

> For to know what is truly good and to effect it calls for a self-transcendence that seeks to benefit not self at the cost of the group, not the group at the cost of mankind, not present mankind at the cost of mankind's future. Concern for the future, if it is not just high-sounding hypocrisy, supposes rare moral attainment. It calls for . . . heroic charity" (*Second Collection* 115–16).

Does such heroism exist? It does for Lonergan because of the Spirit of God "moving the hearts of the many." It is found in those whom "ultimate concern has grasped" (*Second Collection* 116 & *Method* 240). In Christian terms it exists in those who respond to the gift of "God's love [which] has been poured into our hearts through the Holy Spirit that has been given to us" (Romans 5:5). Being-in-love with God, with Other, with others, is a prerequisite for being-in-love with Mother Earth. We need love to create an ecological future: "Being in love is a fact, and it's what you are, it's existential. And your living flows from it. It's the first principle, as long as it lasts"

(*Second Collection* 229). Can that be proven? Lonergan replies that "if you are in love it doesn't need any justification. It's the justification beyond anything else. . . . Love is something that proves itself" (*Second Collection* 230).

Two Ways of Knowing [31]

So far we have principally focused on the four levels of consciousness as moving *upward* (in terms of Lonergan's spatial metaphor) from experience to understanding to judgment to decision. Our discussion of moral and religious conversion surfaced the fact that generally we don't live our lives in this logical order. It was certainly apparent to Bernard Lonergan that the single structure of human consciousness can be traversed in two complementary ways:

> Human development is of two quite different kinds. There is development from below upwards, from experience to growing understanding, from growing understanding to balanced judgment, from balanced judgment to fruitful courses of action, and from fruitful courses of action to the new situations that call forth further understanding, profounder judgment, richer courses of action.
>
> But there also is development from above downwards. There is the transformation of falling in love: the domestic love of the family; the human love of one's tribe, one's city, one's country, mankind; the divine love that orientates man in his cosmos and expresses itself in his worship. Where hatred only sees evil, love reveals values. At once it commands commitment and joyfully carries it out, no matter what the sacrifice involved (*Third Collection* 106).

According to Lonergan, these two ways of appropriating human interiority are inverse but complementary components of a *single structure* of human consciousness. Two examples may help to make the connection between Lonergan's thought and lived experience.

My first illustration goes back to my days in graduate school. For one course I read Neil Postman's *Teaching as a Subversive Activity*[32] which advocates a novel approach to education in the belief that traditional ways of schooling are inadequate for solving modern problems. According to this book, conventional methods of conducting schools shield students from reality, educate for obsolescence, do not develop intelligence, punish creativity and independence, are based on fear, and induce alienation (*Subversive* xi–xv). In terms of Lonergan's elucidation of two kinds of human development, Postman negates what has been handed down in the educational tradition and proposes "subversive" strategies for change which arise out of his analysis of schools.

In drawing attention to *Teaching as a Subversive Activity* I don't mean to imply that I disagree with its criticisms of current educational practices or the solutions it proposes. For the most part I like the book. My point is that it is one-sided, incomplete (honoring and promoting just one way of knowing); surely not *everything* about traditional education is wrong.[33]

The reason why a reference to Postman is included in this section related to Lonergan's understanding of knowing as *both* "from below upwards" *and* "from above downwards," is the interesting fact that, in 1979, he published a second book entitled *Teaching as a Conserving Activity*[34] which was intended to bring balance to the discussion in his earlier work: "Without at least a reminiscence of continuity and tradition, without a place to stand from which to observe change, without a counterargument to the overwhelming thesis of change, we can easily be swept away . . ." (*Conserving* 21). If my understanding of Postman in terms of Lonergan's two ways is correct, *Teaching as a Subversive Activity* is written as an achievement of the creative process of development as from below upwards, whereas *Teaching as a Conserving Activity* is written from the ecological perspective of development as from above downwards, a healing process involving the conservation of and passing on of traditional wisdom. The second book was needed as a corrective to the lack of balance in the first — testimony to the inverse but complementary temper of the two ways of knowing. While it is true that tradition must be submitted to the critique of progress, it is equally true that progress must issue forth from a tradition (*Old & New* 24).[35]

My second example to illustrate Lonergan's two ways of knowing is drawn from the film *Dead Poets Society*.[36] As it opens, a buoyant new English teacher, John Keating, is beginning his career in a fashionable and traditional prep-school. In the first class he tells his students to throw away their textbook article on poetry (written by an authority on the subject) and *learn* about poetry by writing it themselves based on their experience of the world around them. He represents education as a creative achievement (from below upwards). As you might imagine, a conflict arises between his unorthodox ways and the traditional teaching methods advocated by the school. Mr. Keating is no match for the weight of tradition and the film ends as he leaves the school and the august headmaster begins to *teach* the poetry class by appealing to the authority of the very textbook article thrown out earlier! The headmaster, of course, represents the continuity and tradition characteristic of knowing from above downwards.

Lonergan would certainly agree that senior high school students ought to be able to learn à la John Keating, but even as he affirms the creative process, he reminds us that human development is more "fundamentally" and more "importantly" a healing process from above downwards.[37]

What we must keep before us, then, as we reflect on human knowing is that it is not a question of either/or but of both/and — we learn *both* by means of the distinct but interdependent path from below upwards *and* by means of the distinct but interdependent path from above downwards. There are serious limitations inherent in focusing on either way to the neglect of the other. If knowing was *only* conceived classically as preserving and passing on the wisdom of the past (from above downwards), there would be no such thing as progress. Carried to its extreme we would still be starting fire with flint. Yet, if knowing was *only* conceived empirically (from below upwards) there would be constant change and development but there would be no sense of accumulating patrimony or wisdom. In its extreme there would be *nothing* classical; no classical music or art, no classic books or cars. As Lonergan puts it, "just as the creative process, when unaccompanied by healing, is distorted and corrupted by bias, so too the healing process, when unaccompanied by creating, is a soul without a body" (*Third Collection* 107). Elsewhere he clarifies the association of the two ways:

> These two modes of development are interdependent. Both begin from infancy. But only through the second does the first take one beyond the earliest prehistoric stages of human development. Only through the first is there any real assimilation and appropriation of the second.
>
> Such interdependence, as it supposes distinction, so too it opposes separation . . . .[38]

A recognition of the interdependence and balance between the two ways, therefore, is required for authenticity. We receive the traditions and wisdom of our ancestors which we adapt to the needs of our times and places; we live by it, we critique it, we modify it, we add to it, and we pass that on to our descendants.

Lonergan's way of relating to the thought of Thomas Aquinas is an excellent illustration of this balance at work. The generalized empirical method of *Insight* did not drop from heaven but came gradually and with a great deal of effort from Lonergan's study and dialogue with the western philosophical and theological tradition, most significantly with the works of St. Thomas. Having discovered in 1933 that the Angelic Doctor was "not nearly as bad as he is painted" (*Lonergan* 40), Lonergan spent eleven years as an apprentice "reaching up to the mind of Aquinas" (*Insight* 769). This discipleship, combined with his doctoral dissertation on divine grace and human freedom in the thought of St. Thomas might lead you to conclude that Lonergan was a conventional Thomist. Many, in fact, criticized him for being too Catholic and even labeled him a neo-Thomist. In actuality, Lonergan's interpretation of Aquinas was quite unconventional, and dogmatic Thomists were outraged at his unorthodox reappraisal. Lonergan himself has said that:

> The magnitude and brilliance of his [Thomas Aquinas'] achievement permit us to single him out as the example . . . of what was going forward in his day, namely, discovering, working out, thinking through a new mold for the Catholic mind, a mold in which it could remain fully Catholic and yet be at home with all the good things that might be drawn from the cultural heritage of Greeks and Arabs (*Second Collection* 44).

Lonergan's fascination, then, was not with the *answers* Thomas Aquinas gave to theological questions (we have already noted his growing disillusionment with scholasticism) as with his person and the methodology he employed — "the way Aquinas worked and questioned and thought and understood and thought again and judged and wrote" (*Lonergan* 47). In Lonergan's view it was *not* doctrinal content but the intellectual *method* of St. Thomas that was "going forward" (*Second Collection* 160). It was his way of proceeding that shone "as unmistakably as the sun on the noonday summer hills of Italy"[39] and inspired the young Bernard Lonergan to attempt for the twentieth century what Aquinas had done for the thirteenth. "A completely genuine development of the thought of St. Thomas," Lonergan wrote, "will command in all the universities of the modern world the same admiration and respect that St. Thomas himself commanded in the medieval University of Paris."[40] So we see, in Lonergan's engage-

Table 5.2

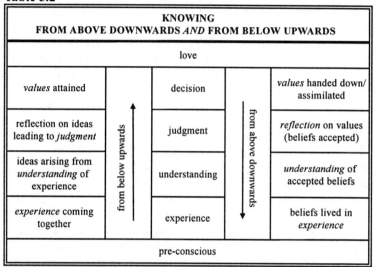

KNOWING FROM ABOVE DOWNWARDS *AND* FROM BELOW UPWARDS				
love				
values attained		decision		*values* handed down/ assimilated
reflection on ideas leading to *judgment*		judgment		*reflection* on values (beliefs accepted)
ideas arising from *understanding* of experience	from below upwards	understanding	from above downwards	*understanding* of accepted beliefs
experience coming together		experience		beliefs lived in *experience*
pre-conscious				

ment with the thought of Thomas Aquinas, new scholarship firmly anchored in the intellectual traditions of the past.

One statement of Lonergan that I often quote reflects this view that one can preserve the best of the old tradition and at the same time be open to the "new learning." Referring to our modern tendency to "brush aside the old questions of cognitional theory, epistemology, [and] metaphysics," Lonergan said, "I have no doubt, I never did doubt, that the old answers were defective" (*Second Collection* 86). Note the balance in this statement; it is not that we have traditionally asked the wrong *questions* (classical science and much that calls itself philosophy today says we did[41]) but that our way of answering them fails to take into account advances (largely in terms of historical consciousness and contemporary scientific approaches) that have been made since the classical answers were carved in stone.[42] Lonergan's "I never did doubt" takes us back to the 1935 letter to his Jesuit Provincial Superior in Canada in which he pointed out inadequacies in current interpretations of Aquinas and his belief that he could show continuity between the medieval synthesis of the Angelic Doctor and ways modern.[43] That he labored almost another fifty years to establish an adequate methodology for the task of recasting philosophy and theology is testimony to his faithfulness to *authentic* tradition![44]

What is important to take away from this discussion is Lonergan's demonstration that authentic human development is dependent upon the successful integration of two seemingly conflictual vector forces; "one from below upwards, creating, the other from above downwards, healing" (*Third Collection* 107–108). The balance and complementarity represented by these two ways of knowing is summarized in Table 5.2.[45]

Method in Theology as Illustrative of the "Two Ways"

Notwithstanding the efforts of Pope Leo XIII (1878–1903) to enshrine Thomas Aquinas as *the* Roman Catholic theologian,[46] Thomism is generally considered passé in our day and "what is going forward in Catholic circles is a disengagement from the forms of classicist culture and a transposition into the forms of modern culture" (*Second Collection* 160). In the decades before and after the Second Vatican Council, scholars worked to construct a "theology of renewal" but, according to Lonergan's analysis, their work of a half century amounted to nothing more than a "scattering of new theological fragments" (*Second Collection* 108). The real task for contemporary Catholic theology, says Lonergan, "is to replace the shattered thoughtforms associated with eternal truths and logical ideals with new thoughtforms that accord with the dynamics of development and the concrete style of method" (*Second Collection* 202). Yet, no new theological *method* appropriate to the contemporary context had been forthcoming. This brings us to a fifth question taken on by Lonergan: "What are we doing when we do theology?" (*Second Collection* 207).

Convinced of the long-term necessity of providing a firmer foundation for the "renewal of theology," Lonergan wrote *Method in Theology*, not really a theological work but a book about the labor of theologians.[47] Specifically, it is an application of the generalized empirical method of *Insight* (called "transcendental method" in *Method*) to the discipline of theology. Described as a "theologian's theologian," Lonergan's entire career was spent developing the *methodology* for this new approach to doing theology.[48]

At the outset, it is important to establish that *Method* does not so much answer theological questions as provide a means for bringing Roman Catholic theology from the thirteenth into the twentieth century.[49] In the medieval world of Thomas Aquinas, theology was conceived *classically* as a universal and permanent achievement. Within our liberal, scientific, historicist, "modern," mindset, theology is conceived *empirically* as an ongoing process in need of adaptation to varying cultures and circumstances. In this contemporary context for theology what is necessary in order to proceed is clarity about methodology. This is Lonergan's contribution:

> Method is not a set of rules to be followed meticulously by a dolt. It is a framework for collaborative creativity. It would outline the various clusters of operations to be performed by theologians when they go about their various tasks. A contemporary method would conceive those tasks in the context of modern science, modern scholarship, modern philosophy, of historicity, collective practicality and coresponsibility (*Method* xi).

Lonergan's methodology for theology focuses on "functional specialization" which "distinguishes and separates successive stages in the process from data to results" (*Method* 126).[50] There are, he says, eight functional specializations, divided into two phases. In phase one, we investigate the past in order to guide our future and in phase two, enlightened by our study of the past, we take our own stand with regards to the problems of our time. These two phases correspond respectively to Lonergan's understanding of human intentionality as unfolding *both* from below upwards *and* from above downwards (*Method* 133–34).

Each of the two phases of theology has its own set of four functions, paralleling the two ways of knowing represented by the dynamic operating through the four levels of human consciousness. The first phase is concerned to retrieve, interpret, narrate, and evaluate what others have said and done in the discipline of theology and what others in the Christian community (in various contextual situations) have said and done. It is the *reporting* phase of theology. To be specific, *research* is concerned to retrieve what has been done; *interpretation* is concerned to interpret what has been retrieved; *history* narrates the interpretation of what has been retrieved; *dialectic* evaluates in an attempt to find out which issues are important and then mediates disputes.

On the basis of what has been achieved in phase one, theologians in the second phase must stand on their own two feet and come to grips with the issues of their day; given the results of phase one, this is what *I* say, what *I* understand, what *I* hold, what *I* want.[51] *Foundations* sets forth the horizon out of which I am working, the basis for holding what I believe to be true; *doctrines* expresses what I hold to be true; *systematics* is my attempt to understand what I hold to be true; *communications* is a sharing of my theology with others, including other theologians and other religious traditions. These eight functional specialties, for Lonergan, are the basic structure of theology.

While the four functions in phase one could be carried out by an unbeliever (any textual scholar can decipher biblical texts, for instance), the second phase is, in Lonergan's view, an explication of the faith of a believer. It is also important to point out that he never intended that this theological method would be the work of one person. Theology, for Lonergan, is understood to be a collaborative enterprise carried out by a *community* of scholars.

To illustrate the dynamics of these two phases in action let us consider the highly public and controversial career of American theologian John Courtney Murray, S.J. (1904–1967).[52]

To put Murray's work in its historical context, recall the longstanding opposition of the Catholic church to the concept of religious liberty. Pope Pius IX's *Syllabus of Errors* (July 26, 1855), for instance, stated the position that "the Catholic religion should be [ideally] . . . the only religion of the state, all other worships whatsoever being excluded" (Error # 77). It was not until one hundred years later, during the papacy of Pius XII, that the Catholic church officially declared that democracy was an appropriate form of government for maintaining human dignity.

In the United States of America, founded on the notion of freedom of religion, the separation of church and state had not hindered the functioning of the Roman Catholic church. In fact, without any help from government, the church in America prospered and grew. This positive American experience made John Courtney Murray credible in proposing the idea that the universal church would be better off if it recognized religious freedom as a basic human right.

In the decades before the Second Vatican Council, Murray researched, evaluated, and wrote on questions dealing with the relationship between Church and State. Believing that theologians are not just to shed light on current church teachings (in Lonergan's schema that is the function of the specialty *interpretation* in phase one) but must be on the leading edge of thought, he zeroed in on the issue of religious liberty and tirelessly affirmed it as a basic human right. Murray deliberately said and wrote things that went against current church teaching. He did so because they were what *he* held to be true and what he believed ought to be the official teaching of his church (*foundations*). He did this at great personal cost (censured in 1955) and for a time was even ordered to stop publishing (which he did). When the ban was lifted, Murray continued to do research and express his unorthodox theological views.

The Second Vatican Council (1962–65) was called by Pope John XXIII to bring the knowledge, wisdom, and experience of the world's bishops and theologians to bear on the great pastoral problems facing both church and world. Although not invited to the first session of the council, Murray served as the personal theologian of Cardinal Spellman of New York during the remaining three sessions where he rose to prominence as America's outstanding theological expert. After much stormy debate, the controversial Vatican II document *Declaration on Religious Freedom* was finally passed towards the end of the council's last session (December 7, 1965). Addressed to the whole world and clearly reflecting the views of John Courtney Murray, it read in part:

> The Vatican Council declares that the human person has a right to religious freedom. Freedom of this kind means that all men should be immune from coercion on the part of individuals, social groups and every human power so that, within due limits, nobody is forced to act against his convictions nor is anyone to be restrained from acting in accordance with his convictions in religious matters in private or in public, alone or in associations with others. The Council further declares that the right to religious freedom is based on the very dignity of the human person as known through the revealed word of God and by reason itself. The right of the human person to religious freedom must be given such recognition in the constitutional order of society as will make it a civil right (# 2).

In this way, Murray's dissenting views on religious freedom became official church teaching. For many, the resolution of this issue, so long resisted by the church, was the climax of the whole council. The Murray Document, as many of the bishops called it, was a great advance in the church's understanding of religious freedom and perhaps *the* major contribution of the American church to Vatican II.[53]

Without going into a further explanation of *Method in Theology*, a largely theological work, it remains to summarize, in chart form (Table 5.3), the relationship between the eight functional specialties essential to theological investigation and Lonergan's generalized em-

Table 5.3

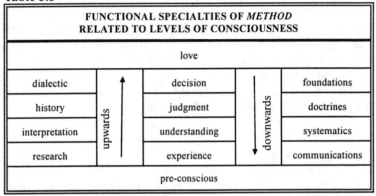

FUNCTIONAL SPECIALTIES OF *METHOD* RELATED TO LEVELS OF CONSCIOUSNESS						
love						
dialectic	upwards	↑	decision	downwards	↓	foundations
history			judgment			doctrines
interpretation			understanding			systematics
research			experience			communications
pre-conscious						

pirical method of human knowing; i.e., the relationship of *Method in Theology* to *Insight*.[54]

From Classicism to Modernity

Lonergan's explication of the significance of modern historical consciousness is entwined with his analysis of the transition from *classicism* to *modernity*. Focusing on his own religious tradition, Lonergan outlines two basic positions:

> One may be named classicist, conservative, traditional; the other may be named modern, liberal, perhaps historicist. . . . The differences between the two are enormous, for they differ in their apprehension of man, in their account of the good, and in the role they ascribe to the Church in the world. . . . For either side really to understand the other is a major achievement and, when such understanding is lacking, the interpretation of Scripture or of other theological sources is most likely to be at cross-purposes (*Second Collection* 2).

The emergence of modern science (Galileo and Newton) and philosophy (Descartes and Kant), changing economic orientations, political freedoms, and a general secularization of modern western society appeared as a threat to the traditional (classical) understanding of religion. Without much success, Christianity tried to reject, avoid, and then understand modernity.[55]

Referring to his efforts to update Roman Catholic philosophy and theology, Lonergan made an observation that is apropos of our discussion here about the relationship that ought to exist between old and new, between classicism and modernity, between tradition and achievement:

> I did not think things wrong because they were classicist; on the contrary, I found a number of things that I thought wrong, and, on putting them together, I found what I have named classicism. Again, I do not think things are right because they are modern, but I did find a number of things I thought right and they are modern at least in the sense that they were overlooked in the nineteenth-century Catholic theological tradition.
>
> Here I should like to stress that our disengagement from classicism and our involvement in modernity must be open-eyed, critical, coherent, sure-footed. If we are not just to throw out what is good in classicism and replace it with contemporary trash, then we have to take the trouble, and it is enormous, to grasp the strength and the weakness, the power and the limitations, the good points and the shortcomings of both classicism and modernity (*Second Collection* 98–99).[56]

Historical Mindedness

The classical emphasis on continuity and permanence ignored obvious variation and change of all kind, in favor of what was seen as the more basic, universal, unchanging component of human nature. Given the assumptions of this worldview, it was natural to assume that the future would be just a continuation of the past (we've always done it this way). History was a repetitive cycle of birth, life, and death presided over by the divine authority of Pope and king who preserved and taught objective, unchanging truth. In contrast with this static view of history we have the modern understanding of historical consciousness.

In the nineteenth century a series of thinkers began to study humankind in its concrete self-realization. In making this shift they recognized not only the givenness of human nature but variability in what we have done with that gift in history: "Man is to be known not only in his nature but also in his historicity, not only philosophically but also historically, not only abstractly but also concretely" (*Third Collection* 179). Historical mindedness is a recognition of the fact that to properly understand human beings and their accomplishments we must study their concrete history. Such historical study reveals "the making of man by man" and in particular is interested to discern, in Lonergan's terminology, what has been "going forward." Accordingly, a modern historian makes a crucial distinction between *data* and *facts*,[57] a distinction Lonergan phrases as between "historical experience" and "historical knowledge" (*Method* chapter 8). An example may help to make the point.

To state that Christopher Columbus sailed westward from Palos, Spain on August 3, 1492, reached land in what we now call the Bahamas on October 12, and returned home to tell about it on March 15, 1493 is a piece of historical data or historical *experience*. But, to say that Columbus *discovered* the New World is a limited Eurocentric interpretation of the data. To say that Columbus was the first person from southern Europe (the Vikings had a settlement in Newfoundland hundreds of years earlier) to encounter the inhabitants of the western hemisphere (the land wasn't *new* to them) is a more accurate interpretation and an example of what Lonergan means by *critical* history leading to historical *knowledge*.[58] I am sure you can see that this approach of modern historians supports Lonergan's illumination of the movement through the levels of conscious intentionality. Their efforts

Table 5.4

COMPARISON OF CLASSICAL AND MODERN WORLDVIEWS[59]		
	classical	**modern**
the real	as what *is*	as *becoming*
truth	as *eternal*: based on immutable principles	as *relative*: based on changing principles
theology	as a permanent achievement	as an ongoing process
science	as rational/certain conceived normatively	experimental/probable conceived empirically
change	as *accidental*	as necessary
history	as *objective* factual	as *subjective* historical consciousness
the world	as *religious*	as *secular*
culture	as *universal* normative	as *particular* empirical
horizon	as *logic*	as *method*

to understand the data of empirical consciousness inexorably move them to critical judgments about the truth or falsity of their reconstruction and interpretation. Moreover, the concerns and questions about objectivity raised earlier in this chapter, are reformulated in this context as a recognition that there are different versions of what happened in the same historical event. This raises the central question as to whether or not there is a such a thing as *objective* history? Lonergan's discussion of *perspectivism* and *horizons*,[60] show that while at times our histories merely represent different (and complementary) perspectives on the same event at other times, in fact, incompatible and irreconcilable histories can and do arise because of historians working from quite different "basic options" (assumptions and value judgments). These histories all may be unauthentic or some may be authentic and others unauthentic. Only a *conversion*, Lonergan asserts, on the part of one or another historian can bring about compatibility.

Before moving on, another example of modern historical consciousness at work may prove helpful. From this vantage point, what we see going forward in European history is an understanding of one expression of culture (Western as it came to us through Greek philosophical categories) as *the* Culture with a capital "C" (*Second Collection* 101). Another way of putting this is that the Christian churches took a Eurocentric understanding of Christianity and made it *the* version. Missionaries traveling to foreign lands inculcated a Western, Eurocentric interpretation of the Christian message but presented it as *the* one and only expression of Christianity.[61]

My own experience supports this. Traveling in India, I discovered that Fort St. George in Madras is virtually identical in design to the Citadel in Halifax, Nova Scotia; each no doubt commissioned by a military engineer in London who gave no thought at all to climatic variations between South India, Nova Scotia and England.[62] In India, I also visited exact reproductions of English country churches and met native Catholic clergy wearing *Roman* collars!

Related to this discussion of historical consciousness is an incident which occurred during my Jesuit Tertianship in South India. When I was asked by some of the Tamil Novices to "speak some Canadian," I thought they meant French. It took me a while to see that they were asking if I knew an aboriginal language. It was only then that I realized that I was not a *native* Canadian in the sense that they were *native* Indians (descendants of the ancient Dravidians).

Bernard Lonergan's Journey

Our biographical sketch of Bernard Lonergan in chapter 4, has, I am sure, stirred up in you an appreciation for the fact that his life and career can be interpreted as the journey of a person *out of* the classicism in which he was nurtured and *into* historical consciousness (*Second Collection* 210).

In the Scholastic tradition which Lonergan grew out of, the focus of theological reflection was on understanding and communicating basic Church doctrine, the truth of which was a given. Without denigrating the genuine achievements of the past, Lonergan sought to elaborate the intellectual justification for a decisive shift in focus, away from the static *doctrines* which express a person's faith, to the spiritual *experience* of the believer who affirms the doctrine; i.e., away from the way of *tradition* to the way of *achievement*. For too long, he argues, we subordinated the realities of the lived Christian faith to seven century old Scholastic doctrinal formulations that had become *the* formulations. We subordinated *living* the faith to *knowing* the truths of the faith, subordinated religious experience to doctrine. Lonergan's approach to theology, beginning as it does from below upwards is to discover in religious existence (the first four functional specialties) the foundation for religious affirmation (the second four functional specialties). So, for Lonergan, a key component in this shift from a classical to a modern worldview is the "recovery of the subject" who experiences, understands, judges, decides, and loves.[63]

It was clear to Bernard Lonergan that an acceptance of this transition demands the complete rethinking of everything, yet (according to his methodology) in a manner that *preserves a continuity* with the genuine achievements of the tradition (let us not throw out the baby with the bath water) and in a manner that enables us to judge precisely what is genuinely going forward from those achievements.[64]

In light of this discussion, the Second Vatican Council can be viewed as an inspired attempt to move Roman Catholicism from an uncritical maintenance of classicism, "the shabby shell of Catholicism" (*Method* 327), to modern historical consciousness and beyond to ecological postmodernism. In fact, Lonergan has said that "the meaning of Vatican II was the acknowledgment of history" and his own work in theology can be understood as an effort to introduce history into that discipline (*Lonergan* 98). However, in some respects, today's institutional Catholic church appears to be carrying on the struggle to preserve its "shabby shell" by silencing theologians and restoring static, culturally specific, "correct formulae" as the key to "the unity of faith."[65] This resistance to historical consciousness and a desperate clinging to "a world that no longer exists" exacerbates efforts to make the pastoral and theological changes appropriate to the emerging ecozoic age.

Bernard Lonergan, S.J.

Wisdom comes
not from watching a parade
(he said),
but from marching consciously,
feeling the rhythm and movement in me.

Theology is not carved lapidary
from the quarry of eternal truth
(he said),
but flashes fresh in each new age,
dancing just beyond the horizon of longing.

He made a deft incision in my mind,
as small and as useful as an episiotomy,
midwifing a less painful birth
for the unthinkable,
cutting the umbilical of fixed assumptions,
the tether of unchanging ideas.

A birth but also a death
of the great fumbling heresy
that faith is blind repetition.

In the end
(he said),
if the Word had not flamed up
and tied himself
to the tree of time and place
there would be no fixed point.

But now there is.

John Kinsella[66]

Notes

1. The first three questions are found often in Lonergan; see, for example, *Second Collection* 203 & 241. In this chapter, we shall also consider a fifth question: 'What are we doing when we do theology?' (*Second Collection* 207).

2. *Insight* speaks of three levels of the generalized empirical method (experience, understanding and judgment) with decision included in judgment as an extension of knowing. Not long after *Insight*, Lonergan began to differentiate decision from judgment as a fourth level of human consciousness. By the mid-1960s, his thinking took a turn (David Tracy, *The Achievement of Bernard Lonergan* [New York: Herder and Herder, 1970]), and Lonergan began to refer to *love* as a fifth level. *Method in Theology* (1972) refers to five levels to the "transcendental method" (Lonergan's new name for "generalized empirical method") and in *A Third Collection* (1985) love is essential to Lonergan's understanding of "method." Michael Vertin, "Lonergan on Consciousness: Is There a Fifth Level?," *Method: Journal of Lonergan Studies* 12, no. 2 (Spring, 1994): 1–36) presents an interesting discussion of the pros and cons of a fifth level. Towards the end of his career, Lonergan put forward the notion that the basic dynamic structure of human knowing is open at both ends. He had uncovered six levels in the generalized empirical method; adding love after decision and inserting dreams before experience. For our purposes in this introduction to his thought we will focus on *experience, understanding, judgment* and *decision*. *Love* and *dreams* will be given brief consideration.

3. Taken together, the first two levels represent *thinking*, not knowing. Our understanding of the world can be mistaken; it is because we can *mis*understand that a third level, judgment, is needed for knowledge. The level of judgment is where we determine how much of our thinking is correct (*Second Collection* 31).

4. The Preface of *Insight* opens with the example of a detective story.

5. Robert M. Doran, S.J. of the Lonergan Research Institute, Toronto, suggested that *Lorenzo's Oil* illustrated Lonergan's transcendental method. A 1992 Universal picture, *Lorenzo's Oil* was directed by George (II) Miller.

6. The two highest levels of consciousness, deliberation about what action to take and the possibility of being-in-love, "sublate" and unify knowing and feeling (*Second Collection* 277). They are the context for the whole knowing project; to use John Macmurray's language, we want to know in order to act responsibly and build a community of love.

7. The reference (*Desires* 25) is to Vernon Gregson, ed., *The Desires of the Human Heart: An Introduction to the Theology of Bernard Lonergan* (Mahwah, NJ: Paulist Press, 1988), 25. Quotations from this work will henceforth be given as here (*Desires* 25).

8. The reference (*Method* 19) is to Bernard Lonergan, *Method in Theology* (Toronto: University of Toronto Press for Lonergan Research Institute, 1990), 19. Quotations from this work will henceforth be given as

here (*Method* 19).

9. The reference in brackets (*Understanding* 143) is to Bernard Lonergan, *Understanding and Being*, vol. 5 in the *Collected Works of Bernard Lonergan*, edited by Elizabeth A. Morelli and Mark D. Morelli, revised and augmented by Frederick E. Crowe with the collaboration of Elizabeth A. Morelli, Mark D. Morelli, Robert M. Doran, and Thomas V. Daly (Toronto: University of Toronto Press, 1990), 143. Quotations from this work will henceforth be indicated as here (*Understanding* 143).

10. I have provided a rather complete answer to the cognitional question. Answers to the epistemological question and the metaphysical question are much more involved philosophically and therefore beyond the scope of this introduction to Lonergan's thought. My treatment of Lonergan's epistemology and metaphysics is merely suggestive of the direction he takes and an invitation to the reader to consult primary sources.

11. At the end of chapter 1 of *Insight*, Lonergan points out that what is important is not the content of the chapter but the experience of our own minds at work as we grappled with that content. See also the Introduction xiii.

12. The reference in brackets (*Second Collection* 213) is to Bernard J. F. Lonergan, S.J., *A Second Collection*, ed. William F. J. Ryan and Bernard Tyrrell (Philadelphia: The Westminster Press, 1974), 213. Quotations from this work will henceforth be indicated as here (*Second Collection* 213).

13. There is a parallel here with John Macmurray's insistence on the primacy of action. It is not *knowing* which is the defining characteristic of being human but right *action* done in congruence with what I know to be true. To know the truth and not to do it is to acknowledge a flaw in our character, i. e., to be less than fully human. This point of congruence in the thought of Lonergan and Macmurray will be developed in chapter 8.

14. The reference in brackets (*Collection* 210) is to Bernard Lonergan, *Collection*, vol. 4 in the *Collected Works of Bernard Lonergan*, ed. Frederick E. Crowe and Robert M. Doran (Toronto: University of Toronto Press, 1988), 210. Quotations from this work will henceforth be indicated as here (*Collection* 210).

15. In using the expression "because *I* say so," I do not in any way mean to imply relativism. *My* truth is not just what is true for *me* but is the best available scholarly conviction which I affirm as mine through experiencing, understanding, judging, and deciding.

16. Bernard Lonergan, *The Way to Nicea: The Dialectical Development of Trinitarian Theology*, a translation by Conn O'Donovan from the first part of *De Deo trino* (London: Darton, Longman & Todd , 1976), viii.

17. *Insight* exhaustively derives what has been summarized here in a few sentences.

18. In chapter 7, as we turn to a consideration of James Fowler's stages of faith development, we will see that this quality of "my-ness," first-hand and not second-hand knowledge of truth, is characteristic of Stage 4 faith.

19. *Time*, April 27, 1970, 11.

20. Lonergan's concern to bring congruence between what we have judged to be true and our decision as to what good action ought to be done, is a significant point of congruence with the philosophy of John Macmurray. The attainment of knowledge is *not* the endpoint for either thinker but is just a step (albeit a crucial step) in the larger process of becoming a full human person capable of good action and love. For Macmurray, as we have seen, knowledge is for the sake of action (and action for friendship). Here Lonergan makes the point that, although knowledge of the truth is the termination of a *cognitional* process, a person is now impelled by further questions to the next level of human consciousness where a decision has to be made about what to do. See chapter 8 for a further discussion of this parallel in the thought of Lonergan and Macmurray.

21. The reference in brackets (*Pensées* 154) is to Blaise Pascal, *Pensées*, trans. A. J. Krailsheimer (London: Penguin Books, 1966), 154. Quotations from this work will henceforth be indicated as here (*Pensées* 154).

22. A perennial question in moral philosophy has to do with justifying the shift from *is* to *ought*. For Lonergan this is the movement from knowing the truth to deciding to do what is good, worthwhile, of value. Moral conversion is required to authentically make the transition.

23. In later writings, Lonergan identifies *deciding* and *being-in-love* as separate levels of consciousness; already hinted at in a 1970 interview in which he stated that "what really reveals values and lets you really see them, is being in love" (*Second Collection* 223).

24. The reference in brackets (*Third Collection* 29) is to Bernard Lonergan, *A Third Collection: Papers by Bernard J. F. Lonergan, S.J.*, ed. Frederick E. Crowe, S.J. (New York: Paulist Press, 1985), 29. Quotations from this work will henceforth be indicated as here (*Third Collection* 29).

25. "In the main it is not by introspection but by reflecting on our living in common with others that we come to know ourselves. What is revealed? It is an original creation. Freely the subject makes himself what he is, never in this life is the making finished, always it is in process, always it is a precarious achievement that can slip and fall and shatter" (*Gregorianum*, 1963 as quoted in *Time*, April 27, 1970, 11).

26. Although the usual order in the conversions is religious, moral, and intellectual, Lonergan preferred to explain them in reverse order as we have done here. See, for example, "Bernard Lonergan Responds," in *Foundations of Theology*, papers from the International Lonergan Congress, 1970, ed. P. McShane (Dublin: Gill and Macmillan Ltd., 1971), 233.

27. "Community coheres or divides, begins or ends, just where the common field of experience, common understanding, common judgment, common commitments begin and end. . . . As it is only within communities that men are conceived and born and reared, so too it is only with respect to the available common meanings that the individual grows in experience, understanding, judgment, and so comes to find out for himself that he has to

decide for himself what to make of himself" (*Method* 79).

28. *Third Collection* 66, quoting Robley Edward Whitson, *The Coming Convergence of World Religions* (New York: Newman, 1971), 17–18.

29. The modern ecumenical movement, with origins in the World Missionary Conference in Edinburgh (1910), took definite shape in 1948 with the founding of the World Council of Churches. Headquartered in Geneva, the WCC is an international association of about 300 Protestant, Anglican, Eastern Orthodox and other Christian traditions committed to the promotion of unity among Christians. In 1960, Roman Catholicism joined the effort as Pope John XXIII established a Secretariat for Christian Unity at the Vatican and subsequently invited "separated brethren" to participate as observers during the Second Vatican Council which produced ground breaking ecumenical documents. More recently, and of great significance in terms of inter-faith dialogue, Pope John Paul II joined leaders of major world religions at Assisi for a day of prayer for peace (October 27, 1986).

30. Bernard Lonergan, "Prolegomena to the Study of the Emerging Religious Consciousness of Our Time," paper presented at the Second International Symposium on Belief, Baden/Vienna, January, 1975. It is reprinted in *Third Collection* 55–73.

31. After *Method*, Lonergan is explicit about there being "two vectors" in the functioning of transcendental method. This is most clearly stated in Bernard Lonergan, "Healing and Creating in History," *Third Collection* 100–109.

32. Neil Postman, and Charles Weingartner, *Teaching as a Subversive Activity* (New York: Dell Publishing Co., Inc., 1969). Quotations from this work will henceforth be given as *Subversive* followed by a page number.

33. I am reminded of a distinction I have heard between "tradition" and "traditionalism" — tradition is the living faith of the dead whereas tradition-alism is the dead faith of the living.

34. Neil Postman, *Teaching as a Conserving Activity* (New York: Delacorte Press, 1979). Quotations from this work will hence forth be given as *Conserving* followed by a page number.

35. The reference in brackets (*Old & New* 24) is to Frederick E. Crowe, S.J., *Old Things and New: A Strategy for Education* (Atlanta: Scholar's Press, 1985), 24. Quotations from this work will henceforth be indicated as here (*Old & New* 24). Moral education is characterized by an ongoing debate as to whether morality is *taught* or *caught*. My sense of Lonergan's two ways of knowing is that the way from above downwards represents morality as *taught* and the way from below upwards represents morality as *caught*. More precisely I would say that, according to the way down, because we love our children we teach them values and the truths on which the way of life implied by those values is predicated. We hope that they will accept what has been given, understand it and put it into practice in their own lives. According to the way up, experiences are given and understanding facilitated, with the hope that students with catch the truth and decide to live in harmony with it.

36. A 1989 film by Touchstone Pictures, *Dead Poets Society* was directed by Peter Weir.

37. *Dead Poets Society* presents us with an either/or choice, the good guy (Keating) versus the bad guy (headmaster); creative and independent thinking versus the boring three Rs. We are left with the impression that there is nothing of value from the past which is worthy of being passed on or made part of the data of experience we work with (reminiscent of the old conflict between science and religion). A critique of the views expressed by the expert on poetry as a prelude to poetry writing, or a critical reading of the article after experience in writing a few poems, represent *balanced* alternatives to the either/or approach reflected in the film.

38. Bernard Lonergan, "Questionnaire on Philosophy," *Method: Journal of Lonergan Studies* 2, no. 2 (October 1984): 10.

39. Bernard Lonergan, *Verbum: Word and Idea in Aquinas*, ed. David B. Burrell (Notre Dame: University of Notre Dame Press, 1967), 219.

40. Bernard Lonergan, *Verbum: Word and Idea in Aquinas*, ed. David B. Burrell (Notre Dame: University of Notre Dame Press, 1967), 220.

41. E. F. Schumacher wrote: "The philosophical maps with which I was supplied . . . failed to show large 'unorthodox' sections of both theory and practice in medicine, agriculture, psychology and the social and political sciences . . . The maps produced by modern materialistic scientism leave all the questions that really matter unanswered. More than that, they do not even show a way to a possible answer: they deny the validity of the questions" (E. F. Schumacher, *A Guide for the Perplexed* [London: Sphere Books Ltd., 1978], 11–12 and 13).

42. I am reminded of a similar comment by the American humanist, Abraham Maslow: "It is increasingly clear that the religious questions themselves . . . are perfectly respectable scientifically, that they are rooted deep in human nature, that they can be studied, described, examined in a scientific way, and that the churches were trying to answer perfectly sound human questions. Though the answers were not acceptable, the questions themselves were and are perfectly acceptable, and perfectly legitimate" (Abraham H. Maslow, *Religions, Values, and Peak-Experiences* [New York: Penguin Books, 1970], 18).

43. In this letter, Lonergan writes: "I can prove out of St. Thomas himself that the current interpretation is absolutely wrong." See chapter 4, note 1.

44. An understanding of the *two ways* of knowing is central to my use of Lonergan's epistemology to shed light on Fowler's faith development theory. Lonergan's *way of tradition* is parallel to Fowler's Stage 3 faith (characteristically *classical*, conservative and based on authority) and his *way of achievement* to Stage 4 faith (characteristically *modern*, liberal, and quite individualistic). As we will see in chapter 7, Fowler's understanding of Stage 5, Conjunctive faith, arises out of a need to bring elements from the two earlier faith patterns together.

45. This chart is adapted from Frederick Crowe's *Old Things and New*, 14. The diagrams and discussion of Lonergan's thought presented in this paper have been simplified to highlight the main upward and downward dynamics of human development. But it is important to recall that the two ways are used in tandem and that there is a horizontal dynamic operating as well. To give just one example from the chart, our reflection on the values that have been handed down to us may lead to the formation of judgments about what we hold to be true.

46. On August 4, 1879, Pope Leo XIII issued the encyclical *Aeterni Patris*, on the restoration of Christian philosophy. It declared that the theology of Thomas Aquinas (Thomism) was to be the standard against which all Catholic philosophy and theology would be judged. The pronouncement gave impetus to the revivals of Neo-Thomism and Neo-Scholasticism. The theology of Thomas Aquinas was foundational in Catholic seminary teaching for eight centuries.

47. "I am writing not theology but method in theology. I am concerned not with the objects that theologians expound but with the operations that theologians perform" (*Method* xii).

48. Answering a question from German theologian Karl Rahner, Lonergan recognized the applicability of *Method* beyond the theological sphere: "Clearly functional specialties as such are not specifically theological. Indeed, the eight specialities we have listed would be relevant to any human studies that investigated a cultural past to guide its future. Again, since the sources to be subjected to research are not specified, they could be the sacred books and traditions of any religion" ("Bernard Lonergan Responds," in *Foundations of Theology*, ed. Philip McShane (Dublin: Gill and Macmillan, 1971), 233. In a later paper, Rahner himself indicated that Lonergan's methodology need not be confined to the theological enterprise but "could be applied to any human science that was fully conscious of itself as depending on the past and looking towards the future" (*Second Collection* 210).

49. *Method in Theology* frankly acknowledges the fact that Roman Catholic theology (i.e., Scholasticism) had not kept pace with humanity's intellectual evolution (*Method* 279 & 311) and takes seriously the shift from classicism to the "new learning" representative of the modern worldview (*Topics* 131).

50. Traditionally, theology has been divided according to departments or subjects (for example, languages of the Near East or Hellenistic history), or in more recent years according to narrow fields or topics. A theologian is no longer an expert in scripture but in the Synoptic gospels, no longer a Patristic scholar but a specialist in the thought of Augustine. In this vein, Lonergan speaks of a specialist as "one who knows more and more about less and less" (*Method* 125).

51. Much of academia holds to the view that scholars are not supposed to (and good scholars don't) enter into the second phase Lonergan describes. It seems clear to me that they do in fact do it; they just don't admit it!

52. In 1992, a two-part conference on John Courtney Murray's thought was held at Notre Dame University, South Bend, Indiana (April 3–5) and Georgetown University, Washington, DC (October 30–November 2). A good selection of Murray's writings can be found in,John Courtney Murray, *Bridging the Sacred and Secular: Selected Writings of John Courtney Murray*, ed. J. Leon Hooper (Washington, DC: Georgetown University Press, 1994).

53. Towards the end of Vatican II, Pope Paul VI quite deliberately invited a group of controversial theologians, John Courtney Murray among them, to concelebrate Mass with him before the assembly of bishops. Branded as rebellious in the decades before the Council, they were vindicated in their own lifetimes!

54. Historical consciousness is a major theme in many of the items in *A Second Collection* (dated between 1966 and the publication of *Method in Theology* in 1973). See, for example, Bernard Lonergan, "The Transition from a Classicist World-View to Historical-Mindedness" (*Second Collection* 1–9); "The Dehellenization of Dogma," *(Second Collection* 11–32) and "Belief: Today's Issue" (*Second Collection* 87–99).

55. This is the process I see occurring during the reigns of Popes in the nineteenth and twentieth centuries. Hostile to modern trends, Gregory XVI (1831–46) banned railways (*chemins de fer* in French) in the Papal States calling them *chemins d'enfer* (roads to Hell). Following the loss of the Papal States in the unification of Italy, Pius IX (1846–78) retired to the Vatican as a "prisoner" from where he proclaimed his Syllabus of Errors (1864) and had Papal Infallibility defined by Vatican I (1869–70). Pius X (1903–14) condemned biblical scholar Alfred Loisy (1857–1940) and "modernism." With *Divino Afflante Spiritu* (1943) Pius XII (1939–58) belatedly allowed Catholic scholars to make use of modern developments in the study of scripture. John XXIII (1958–63) convoked the Second Vatican Council and ushered in *aggiornamento* (updating). John Paul II even pardoned Galileo, albeit three hundred and fifty years after his death!

56. In "The Absence of God in Modern Culture" (*Second Collection* 101–16), Lonergan points out that the *aggiornamento* (bringing up to date) called for by Pope John XXIII "is not desertion of the past but only a discerning and discriminating disengagement from its limitations. *Aggiornamento* is not just acceptance of the present; it is acknowledgment of its evils as well as of its good" (113). The idea that the Roman Catholic Church, indeed the western world, has polarized between two world views is accounted for in Lonergan's analysis of human consciousness. The modern empirical notion of reality rests on his explication of the way from below upwards and, as we have seen, since the birth of scientific methodology, knowing has not been a static permanent achievement but an ongoing, developmental process (*Method* xi). The classicist view is rooted in Lonergan's analysis of human

consciousness as also moving from above downwards. This prior movement in a person and in human history is often considered (notably among religious fundamentalists) to be the *only* way of knowing.

57. An empiricist would identify the facts with the data. An idealist would say that although we can make interconnections in the sense data, we can never really get to the facts. A critical realist (Lonergan) would say with the empiricist that an historian is in immediate contact with real data but would acknowledge the necessity of a prolonged period of reconstruction and thought (first with respect to the authenticity of sources and then with a view to understanding what was going forward) in order to reach the facts. Facts include the interconnections in the data that have been reconstructed.

58. What I think this example makes clear is that we don't know *in our time* what is going forward in our time. What is going forward is a function of intention as well as mistakes and failures; it may be either progress or decline. Only from the perspective of the passage of time do people come to know what was really going forward in time.

59. Many of the terms in this table are found in "The Absence of God in Modern Culture," *A Second Collection*, 101–16.

60. Although a discussion of "perspectivism" and "horizon" are beyond the scope of this book (See *Method*, chapter 9 and *Topics in Education*, chapter 4), I do want to introduce Lonergan's definition of "horizon." There are questions that I can ask and answer (the *known*) and there are questions I can ask but do not yet have answers for (the *known unknown*). Further, there is "the range of questions that I do not raise at all, or that, if they were raised I would not understand, or find significant" (the *unknown unknown*). "Horizon" is the boundary between the *known unknown* and the *unknown unknown* (*Topics* 89).

61. On a visit to the continent during his papacy, Paul VI called, not for a Christian Africa, but for an African Christianity. The Church is no longer to be European but global. It is still Roman Catholic but authentically local. The pertinent question is, 'Who is Jesus Christ for *Africa*?'

62. A few years back a student responded to my defense of the use of English in the liturgy with, "If Latin was good enough for Jesus it is good enough for me."

63. A clear exposition of Lonergan's thought on human subjectivity is found in "The Subject," *Second Collection*, 69–86.

64. C. S. Lewis has said that our uncritical belief that things modern are superior to the past just because they are *new* is "chronological snobbery"(C. S. Lewis, *Surprised by Joy* [London: Collins Fount, 1977], 166).

65. The *Catechism of the Catholic Church*, published in 1992 arises within this viewpoint. According to Lonergan, there can be unity without the uniformity of "correct formulae." Such a unity lies in the structure of our human consciousness as it moves from culturally and situationally limited experience, through insight and conceptualization to judgment, and from judgment on the facts as they are to deliberation and decision making

regarding the real world and the self as they ought to be. For the believer, of course, this also presupposes and demands "being in love with God."

66. *America* 169, no. 6 (September 11, 1993): 13.

James W. Fowler

Chapter 6

James Fowler (b. 1940)

What is there in common between Athens and Jerusalem?
What between the Academy and the Church?
Tertullian

Early Years

James Wiley Fowler III was born October 12, 1940, in Reidsville, North Carolina where his father, James W., Jr., was an ordained Methodist minister (his mother was a Quaker from Indiana). When he was twelve the family moved to Lake Junaluska, in the Great Smoky Mountains of Western North Carolina, because his father has just been named Executive Director of the Methodist Summer Conference Center. This particular corner of God's earth has great significance for Fowler and he continues to maintain a residence there.

With regards to his own faith journey, Fowler recalls that his Christian commitment was "very much a process of gradual formation . . . an ongoing process of growth in grace." In a 1986 interview, he provided a few tantilizing details of this journey:

> I can remember as early as 8 going to a small revival and answering an altar call. This happened again at 15 at a Billy Graham crusade.

I was sitting in the top row of the choir, in front of everyone. Reverend Graham got to the climax of the sermon, gave the invitation, and I stood up before 3,000 people, tears streaming down my face. I spent that night walking, crying, and praying, trying to sort out what this meant, and somehow realizing this didn't finish my business with God."[1]

Newly graduated with a Bachelor of Arts degree from Duke University, he married Lurline P. Locklair on July 7, 1962. They have two grown daughters, Joan and Margaret.

My family is a key commitment and major source of joy in my life. Our two daughters continually pull me out of books and writing, reminding me of the vitality of music, dance, and horseback riding. My wife pursues a career that parallels mine and works with me at the challenging adventure of finding vitality in a lasting marriage. We have a retreat in the mountains of western North Carolina where, with friends, family, and in solitude, we periodically recover the rootedness in Spirit which gives purpose and power to our demanding lives.[2]

Following marriage, Fowler entered Drew Theological Seminary (Madison, New Jersey) from which he graduated (*magna cum laude*) in 1965 with his Bachelor of Divinity degree. He continued his studies (concentration on ethics) at Harvard University Divinity School from which he graduated with a Master's degree in 1968 and was ordained in the United Methodist church of America.

Origins of Faith Development Theory

For nearly two years after completing divinity studies (1968–69) Fowler was Associate Director of Interpreters' House, a Methodist retreat center located above Lake Junaluska in his beloved Great Smoky Mountains. Established by Fowler's friend and mentor, Carlyle Marney (*Becoming* 33),[3] Interpreters' House is "an unusual religious and cultural center . . . a place of conversation — a meeting place where interreligious, interracial, interpersonal engagements of real depth and honesty could occur" (*Stages* 37).[4] Marney took the name of the center from John Bunyan's *Pilgrim's Progress* where the 'house of the interpreter' was a place where pilgrims would break their journey and he spelled it as a possessive plural to indicate that any participant in the conversations, staff or pilgrim, could offer an "interpretation"(*Stages* 37).

The program at Interpreters' House featured interfaith seminars for clergy and laity. A key component of such seminars was an opportunity for pilgrims to share something of their life histories. This faith sharing (and subsequent sorting out of its various dynamics) proved to be a powerful instrument in helping participants, many of whom had reached a point where the struggle and pain of living had become too difficult to handle, begin to put broken lives together again. As these stories unfolded, Fowler, under the tutelage of Marney, learned a great deal about the dynamics of faith. He recalls coming to Marney on one occasion frustrated at not being able to get through to a middle-aged, rigid, and aggressive fundamentalist. Marney's sage advice was to "let him be" because "there are some bales of hay you don't cut the wires on, or you're going to have hay scattered all over the room."[5]

It was at Interpreters' House that faith development theory was born:

> The listening at Interpreters' House usually began with our hearing something of each person's life journey. As I listened to some two hundred men and women that year I began to hear patterns. The particular relationships and events of their lives differed, to be sure, but there did seem to be some important commonalities in the stories. I shall never fully know to what degree my search for and attention to common turning points in life stories were shaped by my immersion in the writings of Erik Erikson. What is certain is that I devoured his work that year, finding him to be an extraordinary teacher and companion as I tried to process the overwhelmingly rich data people shared (*Stages* 38).[6]

Erik Erikson proved to be the major influence on Fowler as faith development theory initially emerged. Although Erikson's theory of eight ages in the life cycle makes no direct appeal to belief in God, he certainly would affirm "the importance and even the necessity" of what Fowler calls *faith* "in the sustaining of lives of meaning and devotion" (*Becoming* 29).[7]

In the fall of 1969, Fowler returned to Harvard Divinity School, Cambridge, Massachusetts, as a doctoral student in theology, at the same time lecturing and serving as the director of continuing education (*Becoming* 98). After successfully defending his dissertation on the thought of the American theologian, H. Richard Niebuhr,[8] Fowler received a Ph.D. from Harvard University in 1971. From 1971–74 he was assistant professor and chairperson of the Department of Church

at Harvard Divinity School and associate professor of applied theology
from 1974–76.[9] He was Director of the Research Project on Moral
and Faith Development (1973–79), funded by a grant from the Joseph
P. Kennedy, Jr., Foundation. This research, conducted first in Boston
and later in Atlanta, involved indepth interviews with almost 400
people (age 4 to 80) representing various religious groups as well as
agnostics and atheists. It provided the basis for his ground-breaking
work in faith development theory, *Stages of Faith*.

It was while teaching applied (pastoral) theology to graduate students at Harvard Divinity School, that Fowler put forward his tentative
theory about something like stages in faith (with echoes of Erikson's
eight ages in the life cycle). At their prompting he began to read the
cognitive development research of Jean Piaget and was introduced to
Lawrence Kohlberg's work in moral development.[10] He spent 1973 in
postdoctoral study at Harvard where he read in the field of pastoral
care while continuing his study of Erik Erikson and the cognitive
developmentalists. During this time too, Lawrence Kohlberg and his
associates helped Fowler to structure his insights from Interpreters'
House into the nature of our growth in faith:

> In my effort to become literate in these new areas I found the
> friendship and colleagueship of Kohlberg. In the circle of associates
> that I met through his work my tourist's approach to developmental
> psychology began to become more systematic and committed. A
> citizen reared in the land of theology began to try to earn dual
> citizenship in the new world of the psychology of human develop-
> ment. . . . I want to communicate some of the immense richness I have
> found in the worlds of Jean Piaget, Lawrence Kohlberg and Erik
> Erikson. I have read and learned from many other theorists of human
> development, but as regards the timbers and foundations of my own
> work these three keep proving most fundamental (*Stages* 38–39).[11]

It was in Boston, too, that Fowler faced a personal faith crisis.
Although he was firm in his belief in God and in God's unconditional
love, the college years had given rise to "real struggles about how God
related to the church and how the church related to Jesus Christ." He
began to see a Jesuit spiritual director and followed the *Spiritual
Exercises of Ignatius of Loyola*,[12] another influence on his subsequent
work. These experiences helped him get his Christology "straightened
out" and introduced him to a form of prayer compatible with what he
understands as Conjunctive (Stage 5) faith:[13]

Not until I was in my thirties, undergoing my first experience of spiritual direction in the tradition of St. Ignatius's *Spiritual Exercises*, did I begin to learn a method of working with scripture that breathed more of the spirit of Stage 5. The Ignatian approach did not require me to give up or negate my critical skills, but it did teach me to supplement them with a method in which I learned to relinquish initiative to the text. Instead of *my reading*, analyzing and extracting the meaning of a Biblical text, in Ignatian contemplative prayer I began to learn how to let the text *read me* and to let it bring my needs and the Spirit's movements within me to consciousness (*Stages* 185–86).

In the fall of 1976, Fowler crossed the Charles River to Boston College, a Jesuit institution in Chestnut Hill, where he was associate professor of theology and human development for one year — for the first time in his career teaching undergraduates. Seventy freshmen and sophomores enrolled in "Faith and the Life Cycle," a theology course Fowler designed to test out some of his ideas relating the faith journey to Erikson's research on the eight ages in the life cycle and Kohlberg's work in cognitive moral development.

My academic career unfolded as I sought to pursue issues that concerned and interested me most. It should not be surprising that interdisciplinary pursuits have claimed me; I was fated by commitment and interest to live in interaction between university and church, and I was inclined by my time, place, and circumstances of birth and early childhood to be one who lives on boundaries.[14]

Emory University

In 1977 Fowler moved to Emory University, Atlanta, Georgia, to establish and direct the Center for Faith Development (renamed in 1988 as the Center for Research in Faith and Moral Development)[15] and teach in the Candler School of Theology:[16]

My chief satisfaction as a teacher and writer has come from the way some early work I did on faith development, based on listening to some two hundred life stories at Interpreters' House, ignited the interests of a wide range of religious and non-religious folk. With some splendid associates across eight years, I have pursued research in this area. To my surprise, the resulting body of theory shows signs of becoming a field of inquiry itself. At Emory University we are founding the Center for Faith Development where this research will continue and where we will expand our work in the direction of experimentation — on behalf of church, education and counseling — with modes of formation and transformation in faith.[17]

In 1979, Fowler was a key participant in a week long International Symposium on Moral and Faith Development. Fittingly scheduled at a conference center in the former twelfth-century Cistercian Abbey of Senanque (southern France), the symposium was a dialogue among distinguished European and North American scholars on the cutting edge of moral and faith development research. The symposium provided a stage on which Fowler was able to present his faith development model to a broad audience. His work was well received.[18]

On a semester's leave from Emory University (1979–80), Fowler drafted a book length manuscript on faith development research and theory. As work on the book proceeded, he was faced with a major career choice between accepting a senior administrative position in a major theology school, or continuing with research, teaching, and completion of the half finished book. It was not an easy decision but Fowler opted to continue along the path opened up for him at Interpreters' House ten years earlier. *Stages of Faith: The Psychology of Human Development and the Quest for Meaning* was one of the impressive results.[19] Other books followed, notably *Becoming Adult, Becoming Christian: Adult Development and Christian Faith* (1984), *Faith Development and Pastoral Care* (1987), and *Weaving the New Creation: Stages of Faith and the Public Church* (1991).

Although Fowler had written articles[20] and conducted workshops[21] on faith development theory in the 1970's, it was not until the publication of *Stages of Faith* in 1981,[22] that the full range of information arising from more than four hundred faith interviews could be systematically presented. Lawrence Kohlberg welcomed *Stages of Faith* as opening up "a whole new area in the study of human development, with wide ranging implications" and acclaimed Christian educator, Thomas Groome, allowed that, "what Piaget and Kohlberg did for cognitive and moral development respectively, Fowler has done for faith development."[23]

Faith Development: Fifteen Years Later

Since its publication in 1981, *Stages of Faith* has undergone six printings (more than 60,000 copies sold) and has been translated into German, Portuguese, and Korean. Summaries of its theory of faith development have appeared in several university textbooks in psychology and psychology of religion[24] and *Stages of Faith* has itself been used as a textbook. To date, four volumes of critical essays on the faith development model have appeared[25] and more than 220 research projects related to the theory have been conducted.[26] The bibliography of secondary literature is growing.[27]

Fowler himself points to several characteristics of faith development theory which help to account for its durability and diverse secular and religious acceptance. Among these are: the definition of "faith as a generic, universal, and dynamically unfolding phenomenon;" the empirical basis of the theory in social science research; its integration of the *development* metaphor from Piaget and Kohlberg and life-cycle research of Erikson; its use as a "comparative and critical hermeneutic theory for studying the reception of traditions;" and its practical use in designing religious education curricula and as a diagnostic tool in counseling.[28]

In my view, Fowler's genius is that he works both as a social scientist and a Christian theologian. His faith development theory is cross-disciplinary, straddling the boundaries between psychology and religion. His application of insights from psycho-social psychology and cognitive developmental approaches to knowing have enriched our understanding of the faith journey. And his inclusion of the affective side of human beings in his concept of rationality allows traditional understandings of religion to be taken seriously by his theory.

New Directions

Two of Fowler's recent books, *Faith Development and Pastoral Care* (1987) and *Weaving the New Creation: Stages of Faith and the Public Church* (1991), as well as a 1994 article, "Keeping Faith with God and Our Children: A Practical Theological Perspective"[29] show less of Fowler the social scientist and more of Fowler the Christian theologian seeking to make a practical contribution to church ministry. His views on the Christian vocation or, more precisely, his "Christian conviction about the *human* vocation" are very much in harmony with the thinking of both John Macmurray and Bernard Lonergan:

From a Christian standpoint, at the heart of what it means to be a human being is the conviction that we are called into being by God for partnership with God. This is . . . a Christian conviction about the *human* vocation.

. . . vocation is the response a person makes with his or her total life to the call of God to partnership. . . .

. . . God does not call us to our vocations in individualistic isolation. God calls us into covenanted relations in community with others. . . . we are called by God into covenant solidarity with all God's children — and more radically, with all of God's creation.[30]

But, because we all fall short of the fullness of that call, Fowler has begun to articulate an outline of a "theory of shame" and its relationship to our sinful condition. The myth of the Western world, he suggests, is that we will *individually* achieve and succeed. Many do, Fowler grants, but the dark side of this myth is shame at not reaching the ideal. For some it may be shame at dropping out of medical school and having to work as a nurse. For another it may be shame at not having a swimming pool in the backyard. For those living in the "permanent underclass" this shame, Fowler argues, moves beyond tolerable limits. Denial and suppression of their deep, pervasive, unacknowledged shame allows them to slip into a shame of apparent shamelessness. In modern "post-Christian" Western society it is young people in particular, he says, who fall into this destructive pattern.

In keeping with his growing conviction that our approach to religious and ethical questions needs to be grounded in a practical theological perspective,[31] Fowler accepted a position as the Human Development Director of the Center for Ethics in Public Policy and the Professions at Emory University (1994). He also continues as the Charles Howard Candler Professor of Theology at Emory.

Notes

1. "Fowler on Faith," in *Christianity Today* (June 13, 1986): 8-1.

2. Some of the biographical material in this account is taken from the entry on Fowler, James W(iley) III in *Contemporary Authors* 104, ed. Frances C. Locher (Detroit: Gale Research Company, 1982), 154.

3. Fowler understands a mentor as "a person usually seven to twenty years older than the one being mentored" who "takes an active interest in the life and dream of the younger adult and develops with him or her a quality of

love relationship that constitutes a special kind of friendship" (*Becoming* 33). This book is dedicated "to James Luther Adams and Carlyle Marney, Mentors and Exemplars in Vocation." In the Acknowledgments (149), Fowler des- cribes Marney as "special beyond words to me from my age seventeen till his death in 1978" at age sixty-one.

4. The reference in brackets (*Stages* 37) is to James W. Fowler, *Stages of Faith: The Psychology of Human Development and the Quest for Meaning* (San Francisco: Harper & Row, Publishers, 1981), 37. Quotations from this work will henceforth be given as here (*Stages* 37).

5. Linda Lawrence, "Stages of Faith," *Psychology Today* 17, no. 11 (November 1983): 56–58.

6. As a divinity student, Fowler had read Erik Erikson's *Young Man Luther: A Study in Psychoanalysis and History* (New York: W. W. Norton & Company, 1958) and with this introduction began an indepth study of his psychosocial theory of development.

7. "It is not the psychologists job to decide whether religion should or should not be confessed and practiced in particular words and rituals. Rather the psychological observer must ask whether or not in any area under observation religion and tradition are living psychological forces creating the kind of faith and conviction which permeates a parent's personality and thus reinforces the child's basic trust in the world's trustworthiness. . . . it seems worth while to speculate on the fact that religion through the centuries has served to restore a sense of trust at regular intervals in the form of faith . . .

Whosoever says he has religion must derive a faith from it which is transmitted to infants in the form of basic trust; whosoever claims that he does not need religion must derive such basic faith from elsewhere" (Erik H. Erikson, *Identity and the Life Cycle* [New York: W. W. Norton & Company, 1980], 66–67).

8. It was published in 1974 as *To See the Kingdom: The Theological Vision of H. Richard Niebuhr* (Nashville: Abingdon Press, 1974) and republished in 1985 by University Press of America, Inc.

9. In 1976, Fowler won the distinguished teaching award from the Associated Alumni of Harvard Divinity School.

10. Fowler says it was 1972 when he "first became seriously aware of Lawrence Kohlberg's structural-developmental research" (*Stages* 270).

11. Fowler "worked closely" with Lawrence Kohlberg and considered him a "good friend." Kohlberg was reported missing on January 17, 1987 and his body was found near Boston's Logan Airport on April 6, 1987. Friends said he took his own life after having suffered many years from a disease caused by an intestinal parasite. In May, 1987, Fowler spoke at a memorial service for Kohlberg. He had occasion to meet Erik Erikson and hear him lecture (*Stages* 41). "I have found it easier to put on paper the influence of Piaget and Kohlberg on our work than I have that of Erikson. I believe this is because Erikson's influence on me has been both more pervasive and more subtle; it has touched me at convictional depths that the

structural developmentalists have not addressed. As unsystematic and unsatisfactory as it may seem, I simply have to say that Erikson's work has become part of the interpretative mind-set I bring to research on faith development" (*Stages* 110).

12. Spiritual experiences at Manresa, Spain (1522–23) provided Ignatius with the essential elements of his *Spiritual Exercises*. If Manresa was the school where Ignatius was taught by God, then the *Spiritual Exercises*, arising out of his mystical experiences, are the school of Ignatius of Loyola. Although the sixteenth century language and form of expression may be somewhat foreign to us, Ignatius' purpose in writing the *Spiritual Exercises* is clear. It is not a book to be read but a practical methodology to be followed by those seeking to discover God's will for their lives and the steps they ought to take to conform their lives to the divine will. A modern English version of the *Spiritual Exercises* is found in D. L. Fleming, S. J., *The Spiritual Exercises of St. Ignatius: A Literal Translation and a Contemporary Reading* (St. Louis: The Institute of Jesuit Sources, 1978). Annually, the Guelph Center of Spirituality (Guelph, Ontario) sponsors a symposium on Ignatian Spirituality. James Fowler will be a presenter during the 1996 symposium on the ministry of the Spiritual Exercises and Ignatian spirituality as we approach the third millenium.

13. Quoted phrases in this paragraph are from "Fowler on Faith," in *Christianity Today* (June 13, 1986): 8-1.

14. *Contemporary Authors* 104, ed. Frances C. Locher (Detroit: Gale Research Company, 1982), 154.

15. In 1988, Dr. John Snarey joined the Center for Faith Development and Emory University. His presence strengthened the Center's research and theory construction work in faith development. Fowler writes that the new name reflects "new levels of engagement and broadened foci in our corporate enterprise" and "the special emphasis which John Snarey's leadership in the Center enables us to advance" (Newsletter of the Center for Research in Faith and Moral Development, no. 7 (January 1989), 1.

16. Fowler has lectured extensively and presented workshops in the United States and abroad. After coming to Emory in 1977 he remained an associate in education at Harvard University. Fowler is a member of the American Academy of Religion, Religious Education Association, and Phi Beta Kappa.

17. *Contemporary Authors* 104, ed. Frances C. Locher (Detroit: Gale Research Company, 1982), 154.

18. The Senanque Papers have been published as *Toward Moral and Religious Maturity* (Morristown, NJ: Silver Burdett Company, 1980). James W. Fowler and Antoine Vergote are senior authors.

19. Fowler describes the complexities of this choice in the Introduction to *Becoming Adult, Becoming Christian*, ix–x.

20. Fowler has contributed chapters to several books addressing faith development theory and his articles and reviews have appeared in various religious magazines and journals, including *Religious Education, Journal of Religion, Christian Century, Religion in Life,* and *Perkins Journal.*

21. My introduction to Fowler and his theory was one such workshop: "Continuing Education Programme," Ewart College, Toronto, Ontario, February, 20–24, 1978.

22. At times, Fowler's style has an almost poetic quality to it, not unusual because he admits to writing blank verse at times (*Stages* 26).

23. "In Praise of *Stages of Faith,*" promotional literature for *Stages of Faith.*

24. Fowler's theory is included in a text I use in my teaching at the University of Manitoba: David M. Wulff, *Psychology of Religion: Classic and Contemporary Views* (New York: John Wiley & Sons, 1991), 399–402.

25. James W. Fowler, Antoine Vergote, et al., *Toward Moral and Religious Maturity* (Morristown, NJ: Silver Burdett, 1980); Craig Dykstra and Sharon Parks, eds., *Faith Development and Fowler* (Birmingham, AL: Religious Education Press, 1986); James W. Fowler, Karl Ernst Nipkow, and Friedrich Schweitzer, eds., *Stages of Faith and Religious Development: Implications for Church, Education, and Society* (New York: The Crossroad Publishing Co., 1991); and Jeff Astley and Leslie Francis, eds., *Christian Perspectives on Faith Development: A Reader* (Grand Rapids, MI: William B. Eerdmans Publishing Company, 1992).

26. Among these is a thesis in the Department of Sociology at the University of Manitoba: Dennis Wayne Hiebert, "Schools of Faith: The Effect of Liberal Arts, Professional, and Religious Education on Faith Development" (Ph.D. diss., University of Manitoba, 1992).

27. Much of this information is summarized in James W. Fowler, "Stages of Faith: Reflections on a Decade of Dialogue," *Christian Education Journal* 13, no. 1 (Autumn 1992): 13.

28. James W. Fowler, "Stages of Faith: Reflections on a Decade of Dialogue," *Christian Education Journal* 13, no. 1 (Autumn 1992): 14–15.

29. James W. Fowler, "Keeping Faith With God and Our Children: A Practical Theological Perspective," *Religious Education* 89, no. 4 (Fall, 1994): 543–60.

30. James W. Fowler, "Keeping Faith With God and Our Children: A Practical Theological Perspective," *Religious Education* 89, no. 4 (Fall, 1994): 546–47.

31. Former U. S. President, Jimmy Carter, a man of deep faith (Fowler has suggested that he may be at Stage 6 in his faith development schema), is partial inspiration for Fowler's effort to articulate a practical theological vision. See "Keeping Faith With God and Our Children," 559–60.

Chapter 7

Fowler's Faith Development Theory

The Lord your God, who goes before you, is the one who will fight
for you, just as he did for you in Egypt before your very eyes, and in
the wilderness, where you saw how the Lord your God carried you,
just as one carries a child, all the way that you traveled until you
reached this place (Deuteronomy 1:30–31).

Introduction

What is faith? What words or images come to mind? As you begin
to read this chapter exploring James Fowler's model of faith development, pause and take a minute to get in touch with your own understanding of faith.

In the previous chapter, we saw that research into the notion of
faith as a developmental process has been done by James Fowler and
associates — at Harvard University in the seventies and more recently
at the Center for Research in Faith and Moral Development, Emory
University, Atlanta. This chapter will begin with an introduction to
Fowler's understanding of faith and then consider how the faith development dynamic typically operates in people's lives.

Faith is a Human Universal

Faith, as Fowler understands it, is a universal human reality, a feature of the lives of all people: "a *human phenomenon, an apparently generic* consequence of the universal human burden of finding or making meaning" (*Stages* 33). Human beings are "creatures who live by faith. We live by forming and being formed in images and dispositions toward the ultimate conditions of our existence" (*Becoming* 50). Fowler's understanding of faith is almost equivalent to our orientation to life, our meaning-making; in fact he refers to the human person as "the meaning-maker."[1] Our faith answers life's deep philosophical questions: Why does the universe exist? Why do human beings exist? Is there a purpose to life? Why is there suffering? What happens when we die? Why do we have deep heartfelt longings and desires?

Faith, then, having "to do with the making, maintenance, and transformation of human meaning,"[2] is our attempt to hold together a coherent vision of the world. According to Fowler, "we do not live long or well without meaning" (*Becoming* 50).[3]

Faith is a Verb

Faith is also an active, dynamic process, involving not just the mind or heart but the whole person. As such, Fowler speaks of faith as more like a *verb* than a noun: "it is an active mode of being and committing, a way of moving into and giving shape to our experiences of life" (*Stages* 16). Fowler's stage theory, drawing as it does on developmental psychology, centers on the *process* by which we come to hold our beliefs and not on the beliefs as such. His primary usage of the term faith, then, is not focused on the *content* of faith but on the *act* of faith; theistic faith is primarily an act of *trusting* God. Accordingly, because faith development theory is not narrowly focused on beliefs but on believers as actively engaged in forming the content of their faith,[4] people holding different theological positions or with no theology at all may share the same faith stage and, conversely, believers who make the same doctrinal affirmation may be at quite different faith stages.

Before proceeding, it is important to point out that, although Fowler understands faith to be a universal human phenomenon and focuses on the process of faith growth (as opposed to specific content), he recognizes that "no person can be religious in general" (*Stages* 292)[5] and does not intend to exclude faith being understood theologically and given a substantive content.[6] In a 1991 work, for instance, Fowler writes that faith development theory, far from denigrating religion, provides religion with an empowering role. He concludes his essay with this thought: "it is appropriate to describe this work, in both its status as a general theory, and in its contribution to practical theology, with the . . . language of Johannes Metz: It *is* a theory of our 'becoming subjects before God.'"[7] Accordingly, we can speak of religious faith as concerned with God[8] and Christian faith with God's self-revelation in Jesus Christ. Our focus in this chapter will be a specific application of Fowler's theory to the Christian tradition.

Faith is "Knowing"

Fowler speaks of faith as a special kind of knowing: "Faith . . . is an active mode of knowing, of composing a felt sense or image of the condition of our lives taken as a whole" (*Stages* 25). Later he adds: "Faith is imagination as it composes a felt image of an ultimate environment" (*Stages* 33). Faith knowing, to recall a maxim of St. Anselm of Canterbury (c. 1033/34–1109), is 'faith seeking understanding;' reflection or thinking about our "relationship of trust and loyalty to the God who promises love and life" (*Passages* 46).[9]

Clearly, when Fowler describes faith as a type of *knowing*, he intends a deeper and more encompassing process than the largely cognitive pattern we normally associate with knowing.[10] Like Lonergan, Fowler would agree with Pascal that "the heart has its reasons of which reason knows nothing" (*Pensées* 154).

Faith is Relational

Central to Fowler's faith development theory is the notion that faith is necessarily relational — "there is always *another* in faith. 'I trust *in* and am loyal *to* . . .'" (*Stages* 16). We do not live lives of faith in a vacuum but in interaction with other people as well as to "centers of value," "images of power," and shared "master stories." Faith is interactive and social: "we are fundamentally social creatures" and "the community of faith, at its best, is an 'ecology of vocations'" (*Becoming* 113 & 126).[11] To have faith is to be related with one's whole being to someone, or something, in a way that one's heart is committed to and one's hope and trust focused on another. For Fowler, this relational quality of faith is *triadic* or *covenantal* in shape, involving self, others, and God[12] (or, for non believers, a transcendent center or centers of meaning and value): "We are not alone. We are created for interdependence and partnership — with each other and with God."[13]

That being fully human is deeply grounded in a relationship to others and a transcendent center of meaning and value is a basic tenet of faith development theory.[14] Fowler uses the following prayer of unknown origin, written on the wall of a Nazi concentration camp, as illustrative of the power of this triadic love relationship with God and neighbor:

> O Lord, when I shall come with glory into your kingdom, do not remember only the men of good will; remember also the men of evil. May they be remembered not only for their acts of cruelty in this camp, the evil they have done to us prisoners, but balance against their cruelty the fruits we have reaped under the stress and in the pain; the comradeship, the courage, the greatness of heart, the humility and patience which have been born in us and become part of our lives, because we have suffered at their hands.
>
> May the memory of us not be a nightmare to them when they stand in judgment. May all that we have suffered be acceptable to you as a ransom for them (*Becoming* 121–22).

Faith is Believing and Trusting

There is a long Christian tradition of distinguishing between two major aspects of faith. In the thirteenth century theology of St. Thomas Aquinas, for example, this distinction was phrased as that between faith as knowledge of revealed truth — 'fides *quae* creditur' (the faith *which* I believe) — and faith as a personal, trusting relationship with God — 'fides *qua* creditur' (the faith *by which* I believe).

Simply put, the distinction is between *believing **in** God* (an activity of the head) and *believing God* (an affective or gut response). A line is drawn, therefore, between the intellectual assent one gives to objective doctrinal propositions about God, Scripture, church, Jesus, for example, and the affective, personal way in which believers encounter and respond to God's mysterious action in their lives. On the one hand, we encourage one another to 'keep the faith' and Roman Catholics even speak of the church as being the guardian of the 'deposit of faith' (the creeds and dogmas which are objective, flat descriptions of that which is believed). On the other hand, in contrast to this formal, intellectual understanding of faith, we find a parallel tradition in which faith is experienced and understood as a personal response to God's freely given grace, a human response to God's self-revelation, measured in terms of love, trust, reliance, loyalty, and commitment.[15]

Past Catholic and Protestant Emphases

In the writings of Saint Cyril of Jerusalem we already see much of the language of faith that is so familiar to older Roman Catholics:

> Since not everyone has both the education and the leisure required to read and know the Scriptures . . . we sum up the whole doctrine of the faith in a few lines. . . . For the present, just listen and memorize the creed as I recite it, and you will receive in due course the proof from Scripture of each of its propositions. . . . Take heed . . . and hold fast to the teachings which are now delivered to you. . . .
>
> Guard them with care else by chance the enemy may despoil those who have grown remiss, or some heretic may pervert the traditions entrusted to you. Faith is like opening a deposit account at the bank . . . keep this faith which is delivered unto you . . .[16]

Since the Protestant Reformation, *the faith which I believe* has been associated with the Roman Catholic tradition. Catechisms,[17] manuals of doctrine usually in a question and answer format, were the main tool used for the moral and religious instructions of Catholics going back to the *Roman Catechism* of the Council of Trent (1566). This *Roman Catechism* served as the model for the *Catechism of the Third Plenary Council of Baltimore*, (first printed in 1885), commonly called the *Baltimore Catechism*. This formal, rather dry and authoritarian, albeit clear and concise, manual was the chief instrument of catechetics among Roman Catholics in North America until the Second Vatican Council. It set forth basic Catholic beliefs (the faith which we believe) which were memorized and given intellectual assent by generations of students. Such training was considered essential so that Roman Catholics would be able to 'defend the faith' in the face of the many hostile critics assumed to be gathered against the church.[18] I recall learning the *Baltimore Catechism* definition: "Faith is the virtue by which we firmly believe all the truths God has revealed, on the word of God revealing them, who can neither deceive nor be deceived."[19]

The second dimension of faith, *the faith by which I believe*, came to be identified with Martin Luther and the Protestant reform movement in Christianity. The emphasis here is not on the objective content of faith (creeds, doctrine, catechisms, confessional statements) but on faith understood as an activity of God. In the words of St. Paul, Christian faith is the work of the Holy Spirit: "no one can say 'Jesus is Lord' except by the Holy Spirit" (1Corinthians 12:3). Martin Luther's commentary on the Third Article of the Apostles' Creed is illustrative of this second movement in faith:

> I believe that I cannot by my own understanding or effort believe in Jesus Christ, my Lord, or come to him. But the Holy Spirit has called me through the Gospel, enlightened me with his gifts, and sanctified and kept me in true faith. In the same way he calls, gathers, enlightens, and sanctifies the whole Christian church on earth, and keeps it united with Jesus Christ in the one true faith (*Passages* 11).

Blaise Pascal (1623–1662), French mathematician, physicist, and renegade religious thinker,[20] also supports Luther's understanding of faith. There are only two kinds of reasonable people, he wrote, those who serve God with all their heart because they know God, and those who seek God with all their heart because they don't know God (*Pensées* 160). To Catholic believers of his day who had substituted a safe and coolly rational faith for the original, radical message of Jesus, Pascal proclaimed that religion is ultimately of the heart, not of the mind:

> And that is why those to whom God has given religion by feeling of the heart are very happy and legitimately persuaded. But to those who have it not [in this way] we cannot give it except by reasoning, while waiting for God to give it them by feeling of the heart, without which faith is only human, and useless for salvation.[21]

It should be emphasized, however, that both aspects of faith (*fides quae* and *fides qua*) are integral to the Christian tradition even though, in the past, Roman Catholics tended to stress the *confessional* dimension of faith and the Reform traditions put the emphasis on faith as *trust* and *commitment*.

Synthesis of Faith as Believing and Trusting

A more complete understanding of faith, then, involves an inter-weaving of these two differing aspects — they cannot really be separated. American philosopher of religion, Paul Tillich, stated the synthesis as follows: "Faith is neither mere *assensus*, nor mere *fiducia*. But in every belief-ful *assensus* there is *fiducia*, and in every belief-ful *fiducia* there is *assensus*."[22]

Aware too of this organic unity of the two aspects of faith, the Second Vatican Council (1962–65), a momentous and profound event in the life of the Roman Catholic Church, sought to reintegrate the intellectual and *cognitive* dimensions of faith; faith as conceptually formulated in belief, doctrine and assent (faith as confession), with the personal[23] and *affective* dimension; faith as existentially realized in trust, fidelity, and love (faith as commitment):

> "The obedience of faith" (Rom. 16:26; cf. Rom. 1:5; 2 Cor. 10:5–6) must be given to God as he reveals himself. By faith man freely commits his entire self to God, making "the full submission of his intellect and will to God who reveals," and willingly assenting to the Revelation given by him. Before this faith can be exercised, man must have the grace of God to move and assist him; he must have the interior helps of the Holy Spirit, who moves the heart and converts it to God, who opens the eyes of the mind and "makes it easy for all to accept and believe the truth."[24]

To draw some conclusions:

a) Religious faith has an *essential* content component of belief, knowledge, and doctrine.

b) It is not that this knowledge, and doctrinal component is not important, it is that it is *not sufficient*! Faith also involves trust, commitment and relationship with God (the most fundamental, prior, sense of faith). Referring to Wilfred Cantwell Smith, Fowler writes: "Faith . . . is the relation of trust in and loyalty to the transcendent about which concepts or propositions — beliefs — are fashioned" (*Stages* 11). Fowler is certainly conscious of the interplay of these two dimensions in faith: "Faith . . . involves rationality and passionality; it involves knowing, valuing and committing" (*Stages* 272).

c) The challenge is for us to effect a synthesis of these two dimensions of faith (form and content) leading to a living out of personal faith in daily life.

Faith is Doing

As is clear in both Macmurray's understanding of what it is to be a person and Lonergan's understanding of the fourth and fifth levels of human consciousness, there is an *actional* element that we must take into account in trying to understand the human faith journey. The performative component of faith, the *deeds* of faith, doing the truth, service to the entire human community, may have been too much neglected in the past but it is integral to a holistic understanding of faith.[25]

We see God as a *doer* in the Exodus event, a foundational experience for the Hebrew people. Yahweh sees the oppression of his chosen people and awakens Moses to his vocation as liberator:

Then the Lord said, "I have observed the misery of my people who are in Egypt; I have heard their cry on account of their taskmasters. Indeed, I know their sufferings, and I have come down to deliver them from the Egyptians . . . I have also seen how the Egyptians oppress them. So come, I will send you to Pharaoh to bring my people, the Israelites, out of Egypt." (Exodus 3:7–10)

In recent years Liberation Theology has reminded Christians that Jesus is the one, par excellence, who works for radical, liberating change:[26]

[Jesus] unrolled the scroll and found the place where it was written: "The Spirit of the Lord is upon me, because he has anointed me to bring good news to the poor. He has sent me to proclaim release to the captives and recovery of sight to the blind, to let the oppressed go free, to proclaim the year of the Lord's favor." (Luke 4:18–19)

Recall, too, that in Matthew's gospel Jesus explains that it is not everyone who professes "Lord, Lord" who enters the kingdom of heaven but only the one who *does* the will of God in heaven (Matthew 7:21). And, of course, the classic New Testament statement on this third dimension of faith is found in the letter of James:

What good is it, my brothers and sisters, if you say you have faith but do not have works? Can faith save you? If a brother or sister is naked and lacks daily food, and one of you says to them, "Go in peace; keep warm and eat your fill," and yet you do not supply their bodily needs, what is the good of that? So faith by itself, if it has no works, is dead. . . . For just as the body without the spirit is dead, so faith without works is also dead. (James 2:14–17, 26)

An often quoted statement from a 1971 Synod of Roman Catholic Bishops, expresses the same faith/action linkage:

Action for the sake of justice and participation in the transformation of the world fully appear to us to be a constitutive element of the preaching of the Gospel, that is, of the mission of the Church for the redemption of the human race and its liberation from every state of oppression.[27]

Faith, then, is more than intellectual assent to beliefs about God and/or heartfelt trust in God; it is a reorientation of the whole person, of one's thoughts, feelings, and actions in the struggle against all forms of injustice and oppression. The following graphic description promotes this actional component of faith:

Daniel Berrigan, always colorful and always deep, had his own way of putting this. Asked in an interview to pin-point faith's deepest seat, he states something to this effect: Where does your faith reside? Your faith is rarely where your head is at. Or your heart. Your faith is where your ass is at! Where are you sitting? What are you involved in? Are you faithful to anything? That will show, or not show, the quality of your faith.[28]

This actional component of faith, the *deeds* of faith, doing the truth, service, is integral to faith. A faith belief or experience which is not lived, which does not express itself, is not really full faith.

Holistic Faith is Believing, Trusting, and Doing

Before moving on, let me offer three additional way of understanding the dimensions that characterize holistic faith, one from the experience of the primitive church and two drawn from the writings of contemporaries.

There is a Syrian catechetical manual, dating from the end of the first century, known as the *Didache* (teaching)[29] which is an early attempt to formalize *the faith which is believed*. The Greek word *koinonia* (companionship), used to describe the faith fellowship in the Holy Spirit of the earliest Christians, is illustrative of *the faith by which they believed.* And we have the Greek word *diakonia* (service) to illustrate the third dimension of faith.

Table 7.1

THREE MOVEMENTS IN FAITH		
HEAD	*HEART*	*HANDS*
fides *quae* creditur	fides *qua* creditur	
content	form/process	
believing *in* God	believing God	doing God's will
intellectual	affective	actional
objective	subjective (personal)	
assensus	*fiducia*	
belief	trust/commitment	deeds
didache	*koinonia*	*diakonia*
conviction	trust	commitment
intellectualist	fiducial	performative
professed	celebrated	lived

Richard McBrien's comprehensive exercise of theology in the post-Vatican II context, *Catholicism*, offers this thought about faith:

> Faith can be understood as *conviction*, as *trust*, and as *commitment*. The first is an *intellectualist* approach; the second a *fiducial* approach; the third a *performative* approach. In the classical tradition, Catholics have tended to emphasize the first, Protestants the second; today both increasingly support the third.[30]

In the same vein, the acclaimed religious educator, Thomas Groome, writes about faith as follows:

> Lived Christian faith has at least three essential activities: believing,

trusting and doing. While they can be distinguished for the sake of clarity, they cannot be separated in the life of the Christian community as if any one of them could exist alone or have priority over the others. . . . As a lived reality, the faith life of the community, and to some extent the faith life of every Christian must include all three activities.[31]

To sum up, then, holistic faith is an interconnected reality involving all three aspects we have considered, the three being so entwined that they cannot be separated. Faith has a cognitive dimension (faith as confessional or as *believing* in doctrinal content), an affective and relational dimension (that *trusting* which enables one to believe), as well as an actional dimension (the concrete *living* out of one's belief and trust in relationship with others in one's daily life). Holistic faith is a movement of the head (*professed*), the heart (*celebrated*), and the hands (*lived*).

This leads us into a final way of looking at faith; as evolving or developing. It is here that Fowler makes an important and unique contribution to our understanding of the journey of life.

Faith is Developing

Until not so long ago, conventional wisdom was that human beings went directly from childhood to adulthood. The works of the great sixteenth century Flemish painter, Pieter Bruegel (c. 1525–1569), for instance, clearly show children as tiny adults (Peasant Dance, Peasant Wedding). I recall learning in primary school that just a century ago children worked ten and twelve hour shifts in the coal mines of England under appalling conditions; a shocking idea to me as a boy but in England at the time it was thought very practical to have short children working under the low ceilings of mines. Cruelty would have been forcing tall adults to work in the mines! It was believed that a child of seven or eight could be taught anything that could be taught to an adult. Smaller, simpler words might have to be used but the concept could still be taught; children were, after all, just miniature adults. Human growth and development was broadly understood as just getting bigger and older.

Until quite recently our image of human development was like putting a jigsaw together; a process of fitting together the pieces of life, completing the puzzle as young adults, and living by the pattern of the completed product for the rest of our days.[32] We more or less held this sort of view until the arrival of the field of developmental psychology in our own century.

Beginning with the cognitive development research of Jean Piaget earlier in this century, and continuing with the work of Lawrence Kohlberg, Erik Erikson, and others, psychology has added substantially to our understanding of the dynamics involved in the ongoing human process of development. According to the developmental view, *all* stages of life hold out the possibility of growth and learning — we are not fully grown-up until we take our last breath. Today, this notion of development across the life span is more or less accepted — we are familiar with adult learning, mid-life crisis,[33] and geriatrics as more than a medical speciality. But, while we accept the notion of development generally, I think it is still unusual to find people who understand their *faith* as *developing*.

Drawing on Erik Erikson's psychosocial theory of development across eight ages in the life cycle, Jean Piaget's cognitive-structural approach to human knowing, Lawrence Kohlberg's theory outlining stages of moral development, Robert Kegan's notion of the "evolving self,"[34] as well as his own study and research, Fowler holds that "faithing" is a dynamic way of perceiving, trusting and valuing that can evolve through seven stages, in concert with other aspects of the whole person, in the maturation process.[35]

Like Piaget and Kohlberg before him, Fowler sees his different faith structures as necessarily sequential, invariant, and hierarchical, each stage building upon and incorporating into its more complex pattern the operations of previous stages:[36]

> We are part of a small but growing field of structural-developmental research and theory building. Jean Piaget is considered the founder of this field. . . . The colleague who has influenced me most is Lawrence Kohlberg . . . but I have also been deeply influenced by Erik Erikson, and through him by the tradition of psychoanalytic ego psychology.[37]

Note, however, that unlike the developmental "myths of becoming" of Piaget and Erikson, movement from one faith stage to another is not automatic or inevitable and not directly age related (*Stages* 50). While biological maturation, chronological and mental age and psychological development are all *necessary* factors in determining a person's readiness[38] to make a faith stage transition, for Fowler they are not sufficient. Movement from one stage to another is not automatic but only occurs when challenges, new information, and crises shake the stability of a given stage and expose its inadequacy. Transition, Fowler points out, is a time when "everything nailed down is coming loose" (*Becoming* 58).[39] The faith development dynamic is both "evolutionary" and "revolutionary" (*Stages* 34).

Consequently, transitions from one stage of faith to another "are often protracted, painful, dislocating and/or abortive" (*Stages* 274). We must let go of old ways of making meaning before we can build a new way of faith knowing; the new rising, as it were, like the mythical phoenix from its own ashes.[40] Because of the distress involved, we often resist the developmental path of faith growth, choosing to hold onto limited ways of faith knowing so as not to "lose" our faith.

A few verses from "Awoken," a poem by Ruth McLean, convey something of the flavor of what is involved in faith stage transition:

> . . . the firm beliefs and solid suppositions
>   that ordered my daily decisions . . .
> had evaporated before my eyes . . .
>
> . . . the props i used
>   to keep me strong
>   now seemed obsolete
> and strangely out of synchronization.
>
>   . . . caught and helpless,
>   uprooted and airborne,
>   i existed . . .
>   dangling in space
>   between the old
>   and the new . . .
>
> one eye was fixed with longing to the past,
>   the other,
>   with an urgent expectancy,
>   to what might lie ahead . . .
>
> one hand was clutching
>   at what had been so easy and certain,
>   the other

Table 7.2

Era and Ages	PIAGET Cognitive Development	ERIKSON Psycho-Social Stages	KOHLBERG Moral Development	FOWLER Faith Development
Infancy (0–1½)	Sensorimotor	Trust v. Mistrust		Primal
Early Childhood (2–6)	Preoperational	Autonomy v. Shame & Doubt Initiative v. Guilt	Pre- conventional *reward/punish*	Intuitive- Projective
Childhood (7–12)	Concrete Operational	Industry v. Inferiority		Mythic-Literal
Adolescence (13–21)	Formal Operational	Identity v. Role Confusion	*reciprocal relativity* Conventional *approval disapproval*	Synthetic- Conventional *ideology borrowed & supported by external authority*
Young Adulthood (21–35)		Intimacy v. Isolation	*law & order* Post- Conventional *social contract*	Individuative- Reflective *construct own rationalized worldview*
Adulthood (35–60)	Post-formal Operational	Generativity v. Stagnation	 *golden rule*	Conjunctive *validity of other systems; paradoxical*
Maturity (60+)		Integrity v. Despair		Universalizing *often prophetic*

grasped at what might fill
the freshly-opened void. . . .[41]

Perhaps you are asking, 'Why bother with the process if it is so painful?' It is because, although the ending of an old way of faith knowing is painful, the possibility of a new, more satisfactory way of living one's faith lies ahead.[42]

Cautions

Before outlining the styles of faith Fowler has discovered, five cautions are in order:[43]

(1) Fowler presents his theory quite tentatively and not as carved in stone or as Gospel! Just as Lonergan speaks of his cognitional structure as not open to revision, Fowler would argue for the normativity of the broad pattern of his faith development schema without claiming infallibility for the specifics.

(2) It is important to keep in mind that Fowler's research is looking at faith from *our* side of the I and Other relationship:

> Faith development theory, focusing resolutely on the human side of the faith relationship, comes up against the fact that the transcendent other with whom we have to do in faith is not confined by the models we build or to the patterns we discern (*Stages* 302).

(3) The movement through the stages is *not* like climbing steps or a ladder. Fowler is much more attracted by Daniel Levinson's metaphor of journeying through "seasons" (*Becoming* 30–33). In fact Fowler diagrams his stages of faith as a "rising spiral movement" where "each successive spiral stage [is] linked to and adding to the previous ones." There is "a movement outward toward individuation, culminating in Stage 4" and then the movement "doubles back, in Stages 5 and 6, toward the participation and oneness of earlier stages" (*Stages* 274).[44] The stages in the process Fowler describes are interwoven like an intricate tapestry and what he offers us are seven windows that look in on particular junctures of the faith journey, that freeze the human person, as it were, in moments of a typical developmental pattern. Accordingly, "Fowler's stage descriptions should not be taken for portrait photographs of a 'still life' but rather as impressionistic paintings of a subject in motion."[45] And the transitions

between stages are at least as important as the equilibrated stages. In the descriptions that follow, keep in mind too that the movement through Fowler's stages is not as mechanical as my presentation which will deliberately exaggerate the distance and differences between the stages for the purpose of explanation.

Table 7.3

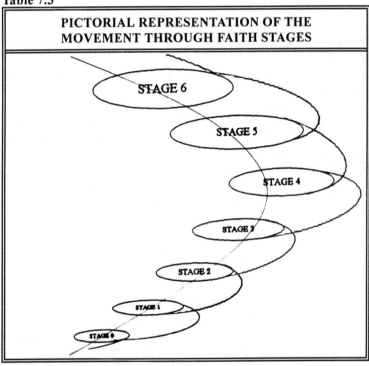

PICTORIAL REPRESENTATION OF THE MOVEMENT THROUGH FAITH STAGES

STAGE 6

STAGE 5

STAGE 4

STAGE 3

STAGE 2

STAGE 1

STAGE 0

(4) In harmony with other developmental stage theories, higher faith stages can be considered "better" in the sense that they offer more encompassing and complex, more differentiated, more "ade-quate," forms of being in faith. Growth in faith cannot add years to one's life but can add life to one's years! It is important to point out however that the higher stages are *not* better in the sense that people living out of higher faith stages are more loving or more open to the "mysterious and unpredictable vector of [God's] extraordinary grace" than those living out of the lower stages (*Stages* 303). To love and self-transcend are *not* characteristics of the faith development process

but characteristics of human authenticity, possible at any faith stage: "Each stage has the potential for wholeness, grace and integrity and for strengths sufficient for either life's blows or blessings" (*Stages* 274).

Theologian Karl Rahner sheds further light on this key point. On the distinction between "steps in the development of the spiritual life" and "grades of perfection," Rahner writes:

> The stages of the spiritual life make sense (and the sense they are actually intended to make) only if it is presupposed that these steps in the development of the spiritual life are actually separate *from one another*, really follow *one after the other*, and that *those* phases which in this theory come *before* another, can also not be skipped over in practice . . . similarly to the way in which the steps of the biological development of a living being follow one another in proper sequence, each clearly having its proper place in the total curve of life, and each later stage essentially presupposing the previous one. The phases of the spiritual life and the grades of perfection of the classes of moral acts are not the same. . . . For it is impossible to see, either in theory or practice, why precisely the higher kind of acts should not be possible on the lower step of the spiritual life . . .[46]

(5) As I write about faith development theory, I tend to refer to Stage 3 *people* or Stage 4 *people*. This is really a shorthand way of saying that the responses in a given Faith Interview (Fowler's way of collecting data)[47] exhibit patterns of thinking, relating, acting, and believing, which can on average be understood to reflect the attributes of a particular stage construct.

Stage 0: Primal Faith

Fowler refers to the faith of the new-born as Stage 0 (not really a stage as such), Primal faith. Primal faith, he suggests, "arises in the roots of confidence that find soil in the ecology of relations, care, and shared meanings that welcome a child and offset our profound primal vulnerability" (*Becoming* 53).

A recent viewing of the birth scene (loving mother and father and caring doctor) in the film *My Life*[48] impressed upon me Fowler's description of this pre-natal and infancy faith stage: "We are bruised and squeezed into life; we gasp our way into community" (*Becoming* 52). Early conscious contact by infants with the world out-there-now is characterized by seeing, hearing, smelling, tasting, and touching things which are immediately present. In Lonergan's terminology the infant lives in a "world of immediate experience" (*Collection* 233).[49]

From this trusting family environment the infant forms a sense of self (strongly affected by its parent's sense of self and life) and the elements from which initial images of God are constructed.

Stage 1: Intuitive-Projective Faith

The transition to Intuitive-Projective faith takes place with the emergence of language and inquiry. A whole new world opens up, one where words have a meaning. The infant's world of immediacy gives way to a world "mediated by meaning" (*Collection* 233). A few minutes in the presence of a five year old child's endless questions brings us up against their exuberant imagination and awakening spirit of wonder. It is this questioning which propels children from the world of immediacy into a world of common meaning.

The most dramatic example I can think of to illustrate this transition is from the life of blind and deaf Helen Keller (1880–1968). During a pivotal incident in her life (at age seven in Tuscumbia, Alabama), she comes to know that Anna Sullivan's touches on her hand (the Manual Alphabet) conveyed the name of the water in which it is immersed. With great rapidity Helen learns the names for things around here (as well as learning that Anna is a teacher!); her introduction to a remarkable career as an author and lecturer in a world mediated by meaning.

Pre-school children at this Intuitive-Projective stage of faith development see God as similar to those with authority in their lives. Their thinking about God, in fact, is largely affected by their relationship to their parents — the biggest most powerful people they know in the world. When taken to church they often point to the clergyperson as God. Their image of Satan (tied in with monsters, ghosts, and scary fairy tales), as one from whom we need to be protected, is also formed during this stage.

Strongly influenced by the stories and images of faith provided by family, children at this stage use their fertile imagination, and sense of fantasy and magic, to construct deep, more or less permanent, faith images and stories. Because we do not leave faith stages behind, these faith images of childhood surface throughout life, especially during times of crisis. There are periods in adulthood when a sense of our own smallness, vulnerability, and powerlessness cause us to turn anew to our childhood image of God's consoling and protective power:

> At such times what we need is a God who is *Abba*, meaning father, a God who is able to be and do what only *Abba* can do. To such a God we can respond not only with trust but also with love and obedience, willing to follow wherever he may lead, no matter how filled with shadows and terrors that way may be (*Passages* 52).

Stage 2: Mythic-Literal

At the Mythic-Literal faith stage, children are far clearer and more logical about their faith experience. They can now distinguish between fantasy and reality, wondering if Santa Claus is "real" and knowing that a clergyperson is not God but God's representative.

Children exhibiting Stage 2 faith are beginning to develop a sense of place, a sense of belonging to a particular family grouping, a neighborhood, a school community, a religious denomination. And they want to know the stories associated with these people, places, and associations. Because they are now able to take the perspective of another person, children can repeat their favorite stories (Stage 1 children may have stories told to them repeatedly but are still unable to retell them).

Stage 2 youngsters have constructed a dependable universe in which God always rewards the good and punishes the bad. Simple stories about good and evil hold a great attraction for children at this stage. I can't help but recall my carefree, childhood Saturday afternoons (in the Regent theater on Main Street in Saint John) cheering on Roy Rogers and The Lone Ranger. In the end, the bad guy always got the punishment he deserved at the hands of the good guy in the white hat. The experience was so satisfying, so right! When I first saw *Star Wars*,[50] I recall the children in the audience cheering for the same reasons that I did as a boy! A parent, teacher or church minister will have great success introducing children to similarly themed bible stories, such as Moses and the Ten Commandments.

The concept of fairness looms large in a person's way of faith knowing at this faith stage: fairness understood, not in any abstract way, but concretely as a way of knowing what to expect from others and as a way of bringing order into one's world. There are times when those around us are not fair and when we ourselves are not being fair but God is seen as always fair. From this it should be obvious why a bible story like the Parable of the Laborers in the Vineyard (Matthew 20:1–16), who all received the same pay even though some worked all day and others only one hour, doesn't meet with much comprehension from Stage 2 people: 'the story is so unfair.'

The absence of 'fairness' in the Vineyard parable helps us to see how some children, coming to a realization that life is not always black and white, can exhibit what Fowler refers to as "11-year-old atheism."[51] Adults who remain fixated at the Mythic-Literal faith stance can develop an exaggerated, unhealthy sense of law and sin. On the one hand they can live in fear of God's judgment condemning them to Hell for one tiny mistake, one weak moment and conversely develop an unhealthy self-righteousness — 'Thank you God that I am not a sinner like the rest of people: I don't smoke or drink, I tithe, I am at church every Sunday morning, I'm saved!'

Stage 3: Synthetic-Conventional

As one reaches adolescence, the ability to think abstractly and reflectively provides a new awareness of oneself in relation to others. A sense of past, present, and future, both as regards the world and people 'out there' and one's own inner self, is also present and one is able to articulate these distinctions.

At Stage 3, I am no longer completely egocentric, no longer living out of a framework where I just want what is good for me, but now I am in touch with other people and their needs, expectations and demands. I have developed the ability to see myself as others see me — a transforming event in interpersonal relations (mutual perspective-taking). I struggle to integrate conflicting self-images into a coherent identity and I seek out a package of beliefs and values to support that identity and connect me emotionally with others.

Stage 3 faith is often characterized as the *conformist* stage because this faith stance is deeply influenced by significant others (individuals and groups) and tends to conform to their expectations and judgments. Fowler has labeled Stage 3, Synthetic-Conventional. Faith development research shows that many adults remain in Stage 3 throughout their lifetime.

Characteristically, at Stage 3, my worldview or meaning-system, my faith, comes from certain trusted others. That authority in my life might be parents, teachers, religious figures, the magisterium of the church, peer group, gang leader, television advertising, or cult guru. It might even be a sacred text like the Bible or Koran. Basic to faith at Stage 3 is the notion that I choose someone or something as my authority, and give that authority unquestioned, uncritical, adherence.[52] In a very real sense, my faith is *second hand*.

We can say, too, that at Stage 3 my identity comes from my relationships: "There is not as yet a self that *has* roles and relations without being fully identical with or fully expressed by them. The self, rather, is a function of its significant social ties" (*Pastoral* 66).[53] At Stage 3, I *am* the Smith boy, I *am* Bill's wife, I *am* the vice president of IBM, I *am* Dr. Jones, I *am* a good Episcopalian. The policeman Javert in the musical, *Les Miserables*, sings "I am the law and the law is not mocked."[54] At Stage 3, I *am* these roles; at Stage 4, I *have* these roles. At this stage of faith development, Fowler says, I am *"embedded* in the interpersonal." To illustrate this quality of embeddedness in faith and lack of critical faculties, Fowler likes to quote a remark of the Spanish-American philosopher George Santayana: "we don't know who first discovered water but we can be sure it wasn't the fish."

In the cohesive society (blending of the secular and religious) of my youth in Eastern Canada, the priests, my teachers, my parents, the druggist, the barber and the family who owned the candy store on the corner all shared the same basic faith consensus. Even my peers all knew the same faith content. A network of significant others (parents, family, neighbors, peers) supported the faith consensus and helped to bolster me/us in Stage 3 faith.[55]

As I reflect on my own Catholic upbringing in light of faith development theory, I think it is fair to say that in the decades before the reforms of the Second Vatican Council the Roman Catholic church reinforced Stage 3 thinking and behavior in its members. The following description of Holy Mother Church is a classic Stage 3 image:

> "Mother Church" . . . is, in many ways, an admirable and dedicated person, deeply concerned about her children, endlessly and tirelessly careful for every detail of their welfare. Her long experience has taught her to understand her family very well. She knows their capabilities and she knows their weakness even better. . . . there are no lengths to which she will not go to help those who turn to her in their need. She is also well able to educate her family. She has a

huge fund of stories, maxims and advice, all of them time-tested, and
usually interesting as well. She is very talented, skilled in creating a
beautiful home for her children; she can show them how to enrich
their lives with the glory of music and art. And there is no doubt that
she loves God, and wishes to guide her children according to his will.

On the other hand, she is extremely inclined to feel that her will
and God's are identical. In her eyes there can be no better, no other,
way than hers. . . . She knows her children's limitations so well that
she will not allow them to outgrow them. . . . she uses her authority
"for their own good" but if it seems to be questioned she is ruthless
in suppressing revolt. She is hugely self-satisfied, and her judgment,
while experienced, is often insensitive and therefore cruel. She is
suspicious of eccentricity and new ideas, since her own are so clearly
effective, and non-conformists get a rough time . . .[56]

Today adolescents and adults at Stage 3, even within the religious
sphere, find themselves surrounded by people whose expectations and
judgments are often very different, making them restless with their
Synthetic-Conventional faith orientation. The result is that as they
grow they can withdraw into a rigid Stage 3 (fundamentalism) or
succumb to the attraction of relativism, one possible interpretation of
Stage 4 faith.

Research has shown that if people stay at Fowler's Stage 3 too
long, then a move to Stage 4 is not a normal evolutionary process but
a real disruption. Joan Chittister, the well known Benedictine prioress
and feminist theologian, spoke of how she moved into the Stage 3-
Stage 4 transition slowly and painfully:

> What was it like when the Order went through renewal? That's
> easy; it was a walk through the outskirts of hell. Absolutely every-
> thing that you had ever been taught, everything you ever saw,
> everything you ever believed, was now up for grabs. . . . The entire
> symbol system had gone . . . so seduced had we been by the symbols
> that we couldn't imagine that you could have the faith without them.[57]

It is important to point out here that Stage 3 faith has substantial
strengths. Potentially, Stage 3 faith can provide a stable and well-
organized meaning system within which one can find equilibrium and
live a productive faith life. Clarity of teaching and solid well-defined
structures are hallmarks of Stage 3 faith. "Tradition," the opening
song in *Fiddler on the Roof*,[58] supurbly conveys this stable sense of
Stage 3 faith.[59] Among us there are Stage 3 voices expressing concern

about the loss of tradition, mystery, and meaning in today's secular and religious culture. These voices need to be heard.

As you might expect, this strong need to obey the letter of the law and/or please significant others can at times place one under what has been called the "tyranny of the *they*."[60] The "Brodie girls" in the film *The Prime of Miss Jean Brodie,* whom she considers the "creme de la creme," are in fact so under her dangerous control that one girl dies senselessly as a result of following Miss Brodie's lead. An example from history of a person rejecting the tyranny of misguided Stage 3 faith is (Saint) Thomas More, executed for high treason on June 6, 1535 because he refused to go against his (Stage 4) conscience and take the required oath about Henry VIII's divorce.

Living out of Stage 3 faith, adult Catholics go to Mass because the third commandment tells them to keep holy the Sabbath day and there is a precept of the church requiring that they "attend Mass on Sundays and holy days of obligation." In the case of youth it is more common to obey some authority figure who tells them they are going to church! I am sure many readers have heard the Stage 3 parental rejoinder, 'As long as you are living in our house you will go to church on Sunday!' And your reaction may have been like one of my student's who said 'they made me *go* but they couldn't make me *pray*!'

The Synthetic Conventional stage of faith, then, exhibits right and wrong as a matter of the expectations of the others, most sophisticatedly in terms of an *uncritical* regard for law and order.[61] In the 1961 film, *Judgment at Nuremberg,*[62] one of the German judge defendants offered the following Stage 3 faith statement in defense of his actions during the Third Reich:

> I have served my country throughout my life and in whatever position I was assigned to; in faithfulness, with a pure heart and without malice. I followed the concept that I believed to be the highest in my profession; the concept that says to sacrifice one's own sense of justice to the authoritative legal order; to ask only what the law is and not to ask whether or not it is also justice. As a judge I could do no other. I believe your honors will find me, and millions of Germans like me who believed they were doing their duty to their country, to be not guilty.[63]

There is a significant limitation to Stage 3 faith. It is that my regard for the authority figure(s) and law is *un*examined, *un*critical. I may have no problem articulating *what* I believe (remember the

Baltimore Catechism) but I have great difficulty offering anything beyond 'because that is what the book says' or "its what my guru teaches' as an answer to *why* I believe what I believe. I can be quite eloquent in expressing what I believe, feel very strongly about those beliefs but still be unable to think *critically* about them. Stage 3 faith remains unexamined.

Reliance on external authority ('the Bible says' or 'my youth pastor says') is needed for the formation and maintenance of my faith. Let me tell you two brief stories to illustrate the point.

As a university professor, I try to give adult answers to my students at this stage, and though they often don't really understand my explanation, I often hear from them a 'thank you Sir/Father;' a puzzling response until I realized that they are not saying thank you for explaining things but thank you (an authority figure) for reassuring me: 'If you're not worried, then I'm not worried.'

A few years ago, I was a resource person at a workshop for advanced spiritual directors at Loyola House, Guelph. During a coffee break one of the participants, a Roman Catholic nun, told me that when she was a novice in her religious order she worked at cleaning a retreat house. After a few months at the task she came to realize that there were better ways to organize the work. Attempting to outline her thinking to her superior, she was stopped short with the rejoinder, "Now, sister, *we* don't think. We leave that to Mother General and her Council."[64]

It is important to remind people at Stage 3, especially if you have hope of sponsoring them towards Stage 4, that something is not wrong because God has given us a commandment against it but because it is inherently wrong God forbids it. The realization of the seemingly subtle difference in this expression is an important step towards appreciating the *intrinsic* moralism which characterizes Stage 4 faith. Enough said about Stage 3 for the moment!

Stage 4: Individuative-Reflective

The question as to whether or not I have an identity apart from the authority I respect or the roles I play initiates the movement towards Stage 4 which Fowler calls Individuative-Reflective faith.

The movement from Stage 3 to Stage 4 is a movement from conformity to individuality, a movement from unexamined faith to critical faith, a movement from being who others want me to be to being who I really am (*Passages* 58).[65] It is an awareness that I and others like me are part of a larger social system, heretofore beyond my horizon. It is an awareness that I must ultimately assume responsibility for making choices of ideology and lifestyle.

It is only in the late teens or early adulthood that I am ready to make the identity I have been given by my socio-cultural milieu my own or ready to begin the process of becoming a new person, i.e., developing a new identity for which I can assume responsibility. I reach a point where I need to know not only what the authority figure or the law says, but the law or authority must correspond to my own experience and be assimilated in a personal way or, alternatively, I need to 'do my own thing.' I need to know who I am for myself, I can't live out of second-hand faith.[66]

In my experience as a professor on a large secular university campus, the move from the shelter of home to the openness of university is often accompanied by a readiness on the part of students to move from Stage 3 to Stage 4 faith.[67] Two brief stories make the point.

A young woman who had come to the noon Mass one day told me that it had not been convenient to get to church on the weekend and so she had decided to attend a weekday Mass. She also said that her mother, clearly Stage 3, told her not to bother because "it won't count" — it's *Sunday* Mass or nothing!

I recall, too, speaking with a student who had appeared at the Sunday Mass on campus for the first time. He told me that although his home in the city was quite near the parish church, he had decided not to go to Mass with his family any more because he was tired of being referred to as so and so's son. He said that he was a person in his own right who was going to Mass as himself, by himself, and for himself and not just because his family insisted upon it. At Stage 4 I go to Mass because *I choose* to go.

On just this point about the qualitative difference between faith Stages 3 and 4, Viktor Frankl's remarks about religion, in *The Unconscious God*, are instructive:

> Being human is not being driven but "deciding what one is going to be."
>
> . . . Authentic existence is present where a self is deciding for himself, but not where an id is driving him (26–27).

> Genuine religiousness has not the character of driven-ness [Stage 3] but rather that of deciding-ness [Stage 4]. Indeed, religiousness stands with its deciding-ness — and falls with its driven-ness (64–65) Religion is genuine only where it is existential, where man is not somehow driven to it, but commits himself to it by freely choosing to be religious (72).

> Unlike an animal, man is no longer told by drives and instincts what he must do. And in contrast to man in former times, he is no longer told by traditions and values what he should do. Now, knowing neither what he must do nor what he should do, he sometimes does not even know what he basically wishes to do. Instead, he wishes to do what other people do — which is conformism — or he does what other people wish him to do — which is totalitarianism (91).[68]

A *critical* attitude toward authority, toward law, emerges as one moves into Stage 4. The term "critical," as Fowler uses it in describing Individuative-Reflective faith, does not necessarily mean negative and harsh judgment but an attitude characterized by careful and exact evaluation. It is as if Santayana's fish develops the ability to jump out of the water and look back at the tank in which it had just been swimming around. An example may help to illustrate what is meant. I am a fan of the Toronto Blue Jays baseball team and as a Jay's fan I am *not* careful and exact in my evaluation of their performance. I readily make excuses for their losses and exaggerate the significance of their wins. My attitude towards them is *uncritical*! But, I do have friends who are more balanced, more careful and realistic, more *critical*, in their evaluation of the team.

Note that the development of this critical faculty does not *necessarily* mean throwing out authority or stability or law or loyalty to institutions. What it does involve, however, is a growing awareness that nothing — no person, no book, no authority — can lift from my own adult shoulders the ultimate responsibility for what I say and do. I must decide for myself who I am, what I believe, and what I am going to do.[69] The following exchange between Jesus and his apostles is an example of the movement from a Stage 3 to a Stage 4 question:

> [Jesus asked] "Who do people say that I am?" And they answered him, "John the Baptist; and others, Elijah; and still others, one of the prophets." He asked them, "But who do you say that I am?" Peter answered him, "You are the Messiah" (Mark 8: 27–29).

Stage 4, therefore, is characterized by *autonomous* faith; i.e., self-directed or *first hand* faith:

> There is a movement from conformity to individuality, from strongly felt but unexamined trust and loyalty to objective reflection on different points of view, from being what others want them to be to being the person they are and can become. This is the shift from Stage 3 to Stage 4 (*Passages* 58).

Further, Stage 4 faith, to borrow Gordon Allport's distinction, is "intrinsic" as opposed to "extrinsic."[70] A doctoral dissertation applying Allport's categories of religious motivation to faith development found that "at Stage 4 and beyond, the incidence of extrinsic motivation . . . virtually disappears."[71]

It is important to point out that in growth from Stage 3 to Stage 4, the *content* of my faith does not necessarily change. My beliefs can remain the same but the reasons I give for holding those beliefs will have changed significantly. Second hand Stage 3 faith gives way to a faith that is becoming my own. This individual responsibility or ownership so characteristic of Stage 4 faith is in sharp contrast to the conformity required of Stage 3 faith.[72] When someone begins to say things following the pattern 'I know that they say . . . but I think . . .' it is likely that such a person is in transition[73] to Stage 4 faith. Another story may help to throw light on the Stage 4 viewpoint on faith.

A few summers ago I had occasion to speak about faith development to a group of young adult counselors at an Anglican church camp. At the end of the day, one young man came up and told me that he appreciated hearing about the difference between the stages and saw himself at Stage 5. He said he was not under the tyranny of any *they* (neither of the church or peer group variety) and he certainly didn't just believe the things he found to his liking (his understanding of the meaning of Stage 4). He said he believed the things that "made sense" to him and went on to illustrate with reference to church doctrine which he accepted and teachings which he didn't think made sense and so were rejected (still Fowler's Stage 4!).

There are limitations however to the Stage 4 faith stance, one being that it is often as much a reaction against Stage 3 as it is a movement towards a new meaning system. Accordingly, a person is likely to see things in terms of polarities — external authority v. personal freedom, church v. conscience, law v. love. Stage 4 people often look down on Stage 3 people (and vice versa) and tension often characterizes these relationships as well as relationships with the wide range of people at Stage 4.

A second limitation of Stage 4 faith is its tendency towards a heroic individualism, the critique of which is a central theme in the work of the thinkers we are considering in this book. If "Tradition," from *Fiddler on the Roof,* captures something of Stage 3, then, Frank Sinatra's song "My Way" is an appropriate theme for Stage 4. Behind "My Way" is "the individualistic assumption that we are or can be *self-grounded persons,*" which Fowler calls "our most serious modern heresy" (*Becoming* 101).[74]

> This assumption means believing that we have within us — and are totally responsible for generating from within us — all the resources out of which to create a fulfilled and self-actualized life (*Becoming* 101–02).

I have heard James Fowler say that the nicest thing that can happen to a person at Stage 4 is that they move on to Stage 5 and his research clearly shows that Stage 4 rational autonomy[75] is not the final goal of faith development but just a rest stop on a longer journey to a paradoxical integration of the best elements of Stages 3 and 4. The following metaphor vividly captures the limitations of both Stage 4 and Stage 3 faith respectively and the consequent need for Stage 5, *conjunctive* faith: "A window stuck open is as useless as a window stuck shut. In either case, you've lost the use of the window."[76]

The move towards Stage 5 faith is stimulated by a restlessness and uncomfortableness with the tough individuality and apparent clarity and coherence of Stage 4 faith ('I know *they* say . . . but *I* think . . .'), coupled with a re-examination of and pull towards the sense of belonging and loyal participation in something bigger than myself characteristic of Stage 3 faith. Fowler see Stage 5 faith as moving beyond the liberal, individualistic assumption underlying the Stage 4 stance to the paradoxical view that "we are called to personhood in relationships:"

> There is no personal fulfillment that is not part of a communal fulfillment. We find ourselves by giving ourselves. We become larger persons by devoting ourselves to the pursuit of a common good. From the standpoint of vocation, fulfillment, self-actualization, and excellence of being are by-products of covenant faithfulness and action in the service of God and the neighbor (*Becoming* 102).

As we saw earlier, one image that Fowler uses to conceptualize the sequence of faith stages is a rising spiral; "each successive spiral stage linked to and adding to the previous ones" (*Stages* 274). At Stage 5, to capture the re-examination of "the participation and oneness of earlier stages," the spiral "doubles back" (*Stages* 274). It is in the tension of this felt need (having achieved an awareness of the limitations of the individuation so characteristic of Stage 4) to double back and recapture something of collective dimension of Stage 3 faith, that the dynamic balance of Stage 5 faith originates.

Stage 5: Conjunctive Faith

Fowler calls Stage 5, Conjunctive Faith.[77] Paradox and the tension of polar opposites, are at the heart of Stage 5 faith.

In *A Guide for the Perplexed*,[78] E. F. Schumacher sought to "look at the world and try and see it whole" (15). His efforts to deal with pairs of opposites (for example, tradition and innovation, stability and change, justice and mercy, freedom and order) reflect, in my view, an awareness of what Fowler means by Stage 5 faith:

> A pair of opposites — like freedom [Stage 4] and order [Stage 3] — are opposites at the level of ordinary life, but they cease to be opposites at the higher level [Stage 5], the really *human* level, where self-awareness plays its proper role. It is then that such higher forces as love and compassion, understanding and empathy, become available . . . as a regular and reliable resource. Opposites cease to be opposites; they lie down together peacefully like the lion and the lamb . . . (146)

To take an example from religion, many people see the contradiction between their commitment to a religious tradition that has been handed down through the centuries (Stage 3) and openness to the experience of others who are not part of that tradition (Stage 4) as too great to be bridged (Stage 5). Some resolve the tension by keeping the world at a distance and living in safe situations (the Catholic church before Vatican II encouraged this Stage 3 form of Catholicism), others by abandoning the "illusion" (Sigmund Freud) of religion and God and choosing to live in the real (i.e., secular, scientific) Stage 4 world. But Stage 5 is a third, more encompassing, alternative. In the words of Parker Palmer:

There is a third way to respond. A way beyond choosing either this pole or that. Let us call it "living the contradictions." Here we refuse to flee from tension but allow that tension to occupy the center of our lives. And why would anyone walk this difficult path? Because by doing so we may receive one of the great gifts of the spiritual life — *the transformation of contradiction into paradox*. The poles of either/or, the choices we thought we had to make, may become signs of a larger truth than we had ever dreamed. And in that truth, our lives may become larger than we had ever imagined possible! (*Promise* 19).[79]

A contradiction is a statement containing components logically at variance with one another, whereas a paradox is a statement which *seems* self-contradictory but on investigation may prove to be essentially true. The character of paradox then is that both poles (Stages 3 and 4 in faith development theory) are true. When either extreme is taken alone, the reality of what it is to be a full adult human being is distorted. Only when the poles are held in creative tension with each other is the fullness of humanity adequately expressed. In the words of the psalmist, we are made "a little lower than God" and "crowned . . . with glory and honor" (Psalm 8:5) but we are also "like the animals that perish" (Psalm 49:12) In Isaiah we hear God say: "I form light and create darkness, I make weal and create woe" (Isaiah 45:7). Jesus said "Those who find their life will lose it, and those who lose their life for my sake will find it." (Matthew 10:39)

At faith Stages 3 or 4, people discussing a controversial point in religion are likely to end up in an argument, each one convinced that his or her viewpoint is the only correct one. At Stage 3 their conflicting views as to the truth (with a capital 'T') can be thought of (from the Stage 5 faith stance) as fundamentalist and sectarian. The liberalism and relativism which can characterize Stage 4 faith (there is no such thing as truth with a capital 'T') would produce at best an answer like 'You hold on to what you think is true and I'll hold on to what I think is true and we'll still be friends.' Two Stage 5 people in the same discussion are able to *dialogue*; there is real interchange, real listening, even openness to change of heart; certainly an expectation of learning something new from the exchange.[80] A person must have great confidence in his or her faith stance in order to freely and openly engage in such dialogue.

One of the purposes of our thinking is to provide us with a map — call it an image or a picture — of what we experience. So it is also in our faith-thinking. . . .

Stage 5 persons discover that their maps are not only incomplete and limited in capturing the depth and beauty of the landscape, but they also sense that something in addition to maps is needed to put one in touch with the fullness of what has been revealed. . . .
Imagine an encounter between two Stage 5 persons who have mapped the territory of faith experiences. As distinguished from a person at Stage 4, they will be ready to compare their maps without prejudgments, will make corrections where these seem warranted, and may even withhold final judgment where there seems to be irreconcilable differences between the maps (*Passages* 60–61).

As you might expect, Stage 5 faith is characterized by an openness to genuine dialogue with communities and traditions quite different from our own:

Truth is more multiform and complex than most of the clear, either-or categories of the Individuative stage can properly grasp. In its richness, ambiguity, and multidimensionality, truth must be approached from at least two or more angles of vision simultaneously (*Becoming* 65).

Fowler goes on to say that what he means by conjunctive faith is analogous to the discovery in physics of the necessity for two different and unreconcilable models (packets of energy and wave theory) to adequately explain the behavior of light. Related to this, Abraham Maslow comments: "Isolating two interrelated parts of a whole from each other, parts that need each other, parts that are truly 'parts' and not wholes, distorts them both, sickens and contaminates them".[81]
To live Stage 5 faith, then, means that we hold onto the gains of independence, autonomy, and personal responsibility made at Stage 4 but take a fresh look at Stage 3 — at the stability, at the loyalty, at the respect for law and authority, and ask whether it has to be either/or — can't it be both/and? We now try to live in the creative tension between those polarities, i.e., with paradox.[82] Fowler doesn't think we reach Stage 5 until at least age thirty.[83]
Three concrete examples of the Stage 5 faith phenomenon may help to clarify the way in which it is an advance over faith Stages 3 and 4.
My first example is taken from Paul's letter to the Galatians in the Christian scriptures. The following passage conveys something of the shift from the Stage 3 authoritarian faith stance to the inclusive and

paradoxical faith of Stage 5:

> Now before faith came, we were imprisoned and guarded under the law until faith would be revealed. Therefore the law was our disciplinarian until Christ came, so that we might be justified by faith. But now that faith has come, we are no longer subject to a disciplinarian, for in Christ Jesus you are all children of God through faith. As many of you as were baptised into Christ have clothed yourselves with Christ. There is no longer slave or free, there is no longer male and female; for all of you are one in Christ Jesus. And if you belong to Christ then you are Abraham's offspring, heirs according to the promise (Galatians 3:23–29).

A second example of the movement from Stage 3 to Stage 5 faith is found in Ari Goldman's *The Search for God at Harvard*.[84] A religion writer with *The New York Times*, Goldman spent a year at Harvard Divinity School studying comparative religions. Raised "in a warm cocoon of Orthodox [Jewish] observance" (6), Goldman feared "the threat of the pagan and Christian worlds" (4) and imagined that his tenure at Harvard might lead to religious conversion or even abandonment of religion. He did not convert; in fact his Orthodox Jewish identity was strenghtened. What he experienced in Fowler's terminology was a transition from Stage 3 faith through to Stage 5.

> No, I did not convert. . . . But what did happen was an extraordinary dialogue, one between the religious ideas that I encountered and the Jewish ideas within myself. The dialogue continued every day in the classroom, in the words of the New Testament, the Koran, the Upanishads and in fellowship at my own Sabbath table, around which I assembled people of various faiths. As a result of these encounteres, I learned how others experience their faith. But more important, I developed a richer and fuller understanding of myself and my own Judaism (8).

It was five years after his Harvard experience that Goldman wrote *The Search for God at Harvard*. It concludes with a Fowler Stage 5 expression of his renewed faith:

> Today, when I go on assignment to a church, synagogue, mosque or temple, I no longer go as a stranger, an outsider. The ideas preached and the rituals practiced are familiar, unthreatening and, ultimately, enriching to me. The amazing dialogue that began at Harvard between the Judaism within me and other faiths I encountered continues

at St. Paul Community Baptist Church in a black section of Brooklyn, at St. Patrick's Cathedral on Fifth Avenue, at a Reform temple in Cincinnati, at a Zen retreat center in Los Angeles, at a Sunni mosque in Detroit.

. . . In each case I leave as a Jew, rooted in the richness of my own faith but nourished by the faith of others (282–83).

My third and final illustration of the journey to Stage 5 faith is Trappist monk, Thomas Merton (1915–1968).[85] In light of Fowler's finding that Stage 5 is rare before age thirty, what impresses me about Merton's faith journey is the contrast between his early writing and later works. *The Seven Story Mountain,*[86] an autobiographical work describing the process of his conversion, shows Merton as a narrow and somewhat self-satisfied Catholic, intolerant of other Christian churches and overly self-righteous about his Trappist vocation as the most authentic form of Christianity. A few years later, in the Prologue to *The Sign of Jonas,* Merton has changed. He writes, "The life of every . . . Christian is signed with the sign of Jonas . . . but I feel that my own life is especially sealed with this great sign . . . because like Jonas himself I find myself traveling toward my destiny in the belly of a paradox."[87] And still later in life Merton satirizes and distances himself from the pious "modern [Saint] Jerome" image he painted in *The Seven Story Mountain* speaking of himself as a "man in the modern world:"

This is simply the voice of a self-questioning human person who . . . struggles to cope with turbulent, mysterious, demanding, exciting, frustrating, confused existence in which almost nothing is really predictable, in which most definitions, explanations and justifications become incredible even before they are uttered, in which people suffer together and are sometimes utterly beautiful, at other times impossibly pathetic. In which there is much that is frightening, in which almost everything public is patently phoney, and in which there is at the same time an immense ground of personal authenticity that is right there and so obvious that no one can talk about it and most cannot even believe that it is there.[88]

At the time of his death, Merton was building ecumenical bridges between the great religious traditions of both East and West referring to a "hidden wholeness" in inner experience where "we are already one."[89] Merton's writings themselves document the journey of "a very public hermit" (itself a paradoxical expression) from Stage 3 to Stage

5 faith. That he was aware of this paradoxical character of his faith journey is clear from the following reflection:

> I . . . accept the fact that my life is almost totally paradoxical. . . . It is in the paradox itself, the paradox which was and is still a source of insecurity, that I have come to find the greatest security. I have become convinced that the very contradictions in my life are in some ways signs of God's mercy to me . . . (*Promise* 17).

Thomas Merton, Ari Goldman, and Paul of Tarsus illustrate Fowler's conviction that the capacity to accept paradoxical but complementary thought patterns is a hallmark of this stage of faith development. Further, at Stage 5, faith knowing is more open to the numinous and an affective sense of the world which takes us to levels of awareness well beyond the capacity of our intellect. To recall again an often quoted phrase from Blaise Pascal's *Penseés*, at Stage 5 "the heart has its reasons of which reason knows nothing" (*Penseés* 154). Unusual before full adulthood, Conjunctive faith is born of "the sacrament of defeat and the reality of irrevocable commitments and acts."[90]

We do not give up the individuality and intellectual gains of Stage 4 but instead can consolidate them in a rich paradoxical, affective, personal, other-directed experience of the world and the elements of mystery and paradox inherent in it. Stage 5 faith is a realization that I am not able to do everything on my own. I need others, I need the Other, in order to realize my own full human potential:[91]

> A Christian view of the human vocation suggests that partnership with the action of God may be the single most fruitful way of finding a principle to orchestrate our changing adult life structures (*Becoming* 105).[92]

As Fowler's friend and mentor, Carlyle Marney said (quoting Martin Luther): "We serve God, we love God, we serve and love our neighbors *in commune per vocatione — in community, through vocation*" (*Becoming* 93).

Fowler's research has shown that only 7% of the adult population attain Stage 5 faith and fewer than 1% can be categorized as Stage 6. Accordingly it has been argued that practically and realistically Stage 5 is the normative endpoint of Fowler's faith development theory (*Becoming* 72–73). In our discussion of Fowler's theory in the concluding chapter, we will focus on faith Stages 3 through 5, the stages that typically characterize adults. My reading of Fowler has led me to diagram and highlight the relationship between faith Stages 3, 4 and 5 as in Table 7.4.

Table 7.4

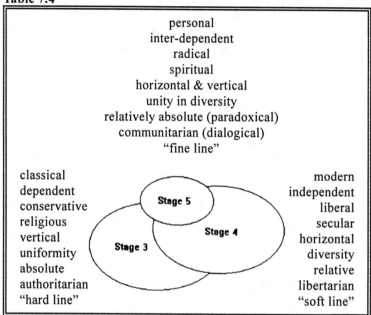

personal
inter-dependent
radical
spiritual
horizontal & vertical
unity in diversity
relatively absolute (paradoxical)
communitarian (dialogical)
"fine line"

classical　　　　　　　　　　　　　　　modern
dependent　　　　　　　　　　　　independent
conservative　　　Stage 5　　　　　　liberal
religious　　　　　　　　　　　　　　secular
vertical　　　　　　　　Stage 4　　　horizontal
uniformity　　Stage 3　　　　　　　diversity
absolute　　　　　　　　　　　　　relative
authoritarian　　　　　　　　　　libertarian
"hard line"　　　　　　　　　　　"soft line"

Stage 6: Universalizing Faith

If the movement through faith Stages 0–5 can be seen as a *natural* process of development, the movement to Stage 6 Universalizing faith introduces a new factor to the developmental process which Fowler identifies as "grace." The movement from Conjunctive faith to Universalizing faith is a radical leap made only by a few (there is practically no empirical data on Stage 6) and, as Fowler understands it, this leap seems to require a religious, if not theistic, orientation (*Becoming* 72–74).

The words "I have a dream," from Martin Luther King, Jr's famous speech, delivered from the steps of the Lincoln Memorial in Washington, D.C. at the height of the civil rights movement, conjure up one image of Stage 6 faith. The speech focused the thoughts and feelings of a nation which was slowly, and often painfully, coming to realize the evils of racial discrimination. They are powerful words just because they are spoken by Martin Luther King, Jr., a living symbol of the peace, justice, unity and love for which he gave his life. It is the Christian doctrine of the cross, the condition of true discipleship. In the words of Jesus: "If any want to become my followers, let them deny themselves and take up their cross daily and follow me. For those who want to save their life will lose it, and those who lose their life for my sake will save it" (Luke 9:23–24).

Mahatma Gandhi, Abraham Heschel, Dag Hammarskjold, and Archbishop Oscar Romero were also such people. But you don't have to be a great leader and/or a saint to be a candidate for Stage 6, *Universalizing* faith. One can be less than perfect (as were Martin Luther King, Jr. and Mahatma Gandhi, for example) and one can also at times regress to lower stages of thinking and behaving (especially in situations that one feels one cannot handle). What shines forth, though, in the Stage 6 person is a special grace that makes them a living, breathing representation of the God who is always at work transforming the world and people's lives. Brief excerpts from the writings of Mohandas K. Gandhi and Martin Luther King, Jr. provide a sense of Stage 6 faith:

> To see the universal and all-pervading spirit of Truth face to face one must be able to love the meanest of creation as oneself. And a man who aspires after that cannot afford to keep out of any field of life.[93]

> The old law of an eye for an eye leaves everybody blind. It is immoral because it seeks to humiliate the opponent rather than win his understanding; it seeks to annihilate rather than to convert. Violence is immoral because it thrives on hatred rather than love. It destroys community and makes brotherhood impossible. It leaves society in monologue rather than dialogue. Violence ends by defeating itself. It creates bitterness in the survivors and brutality in the destroyers.[94]

Faith development theory claims[95] that the normative end point to the faith development process is not the individualistic autonomy so characteristic of Western society but an inclusive universal human community living in harmony with the earth. "Pioneers in the commonwealth of love and justice" is one way Fowler describes those visionaries in our midst who live out of universalizing, Stage 6, faith.[96]

Notes

1. James W. Fowler, Karl Ernst Nipkow, and Friedrich Schweitzer, eds., *Stages of Faith and Religious Development: Implications for Church, Education, and Society* (New York: The Crossroad Publishing Company, 1991), 92; referring to "Commonalities of Faith in Religious Pluralism: An Encounter with Wilfred Cantwell Smith," Unpublished Paper, 1987.

2. James W. Fowler, "Faith and the Structuring of Meaning," in *Toward Moral and Religious Maturity*, J. Fowler and A. Vergote , eds. (Morristown, NJ: Silver Burdett, 1980), 53. Fowler understands that "God has prepotentiated us for faith" (*Stages* 22). See also *Faith Development and Pastoral Care* 54.

3. This statement reminds me of Rollo May's view that *true* religion "is essential to a healthy personality." Every genuine atheist with whom he had worked, he says, had shown "unmistakable neurotic tendencies," for each lacked an integrating sense of purpose and direction (David M. Wulff, *Psychology of Religion* [New York: John Wiley & Sons, 1991], 619–20).

4. Ideally, the content of our faith does not come to us passively but we are *agents* (John Macmurray) in the process. Bernard Lonergan's understanding of what it is to move towards authentic adulthood is that of an agent subject knowing for oneself that one has to decide for oneself what one is going to make of oneself.

5. He is quoting the Spanish-American philosopher George Santayana (1863–1952). Fowler says: "As a theologian I never lost sight of the crucial importance of the 'contents' of faith — the realities, values, powers and communities on and in which persons 'rest their hearts'" (*Stages* 273). *Stages of Faith* seriously addresses the "interplay of structure and content in the life of faith" (*Stages* 273).

6. Fowler's understanding of faith, in fact, owes much to the theological tradition represented by Paul Tillich (1886–1965) and H. Richard Niebuhr (1894–1962). Historian of religion, Wilfred Cantwell Smith, helped him to distinguish between *faith, belief,* and *religion* in formulating his understanding of the universality of faith. It is important to highlight the fact that Fowler does not intend to exclude religious content from his faith development theory. This is made quite clear in the opening sentences of the final section of *Stages of Faith*, "On Grace—Ordinary and Extraordinary:" "There is a limit to how much one can talk about faith and development in faith without acknowledging that the question of whether there will be faith on earth is finally God's business. Faith development theory, focusing resolutely on the human side of the faith relationship comes up against the fact that the transcendent other with whom we have to do in faith is not confined by the models we build or to the patterns we discern. . . . God is recognized as sovereign reality — as creator, ruler, and as redeemer of *all* being" (*Stages* 302).

7. James W. Fowler, "The Vocation of Faith Development Theory," in James W. Fowler, Karl Ernst Nipkow, and Friedrich Schweitzer, eds., *Stages of Faith and Religious Development: Implications for Church, Education, and Society* (New York: The Crossroad Publishing Company, 1991), 36.

8. Religious faith, in the language of American theologian Paul Tillich, is concerned with *the* Ultimate Environment; God defined by Tillich as "our ultimate, unconditional concern." Faith, therefore, is universal among humans (i.e., everybody has faith) and everybody even holds to a *religious* faith if we accept Tillich's definition. Such a broad definition prompted Abraham Maslow to ask: "If, as actually happened on one platform, Paul Tillich defined religion as 'concern with ultimate concerns' and I then defined humanistic psychology in the same way, then what is the difference between a supernaturalist and a humanist?" (Abraham H. Maslow, *Religions, Values, and Peak-Experiences* [New York: Penguin Books, 1976], 45).

9. The reference in brackets (*Passages* 46) is to Thomas A. Droege, *Faith Passages and Patterns* (Philadelphia: Fortress Press, 1983), 46. Quotations from this work will henceforth be given as here (*Passages* 46).

10. It seems to me that Lonergan's understanding of the role of feelings in human cognition and decision making is helpful in understanding what Fowler intends by saying that faith knowing involves the *whole* person, not just the intellect. Also pertinent to this discussion is a quotation attributed to American author Evelyn Scott (1893–1963) — "I realized a long time ago that a belief which does not spring from a conviction in the emotions is no belief at all."

11. "Covenant existence" is discussed in *Stages* 33 and *Becoming* 110.

12. Here Fowler is drawing on American theologian H. Richard Niebuhr, the subject of his own doctoral dissertation (1974). See James W. Fowler, *To See the Kingdom: The Theological Vision of H. Richard Niebuhr* (Lanham, MD: University Press of America, 1985), 207–08.

13. Linda Lawrence, "Stages of Faith," *Psychology Today* 17, no. 11 (November 1983): 61.

14. "The covenantal structure of our significant human relations is often made visible as much by our betrayals and failures of 'good faith' as by the times when we are mutually loyal and faithful" (*Stages* 33). A footnote to the quotation tells us that Fowler explores this idea in chapter 5 of *To See the Kingdom*.

15. John Macmurray's study of scripture led him to conclude that *faith*, which he contrasts with *fear*, might "be better translated, 'Trust'" (*The Philosophy of Jesus*, a pamphlet published by the London Friends Home Service Committee in 1973, 5).

16. *The Works of Saint Cyril of Jerusalem*, vol. 1, trans. Leo P. McCauley, S.J. and Anthony A. Stephenson (Washington, DC: The Catholic University of America Press, 1968), 146–47. These lines are from a catechetical instruction by the fourth century bishop.

17. Ironically, Martin Luther's was perhaps the first!

18. "How does a Catholic sin against faith? A Catholic sins against faith by not believing what God has revealed, and by taking part in non-Catholic worship" (*The New Saint Joseph Baltimore Catechism* [New York: Catholic Book Publishing Co., 1964], 79).

19. This is the answer to question 122 in the Baltimore Catechism asking, "What is faith?" (*The New Saint Joseph Baltimore Catechism*, no. 2 [New York: Catholic Book Publishing Co., 1969], 64). In *Evangelization and Catechesis*, Johannes Hofinger, S.J., a well-known Catholic educator, defined faith as "the divine virtue by which we assent to the truths revealed by God, since God cannot deceive or be deceived" (New York: Paulist Press, 1976, 17).

20. Already at age nineteen, Pascal had invented a calculating machine that worked and his research into hydrodynamics and fluid mechanics is preserved in Pascal's Law which is the basis for hydraulics. His religious thought, which emphasized the reasons of the heart over those of rationalism or empiricism, is found in *Pensées* (*Thoughts*) published posthumously by his friends. He felt that metaphysical proofs for God's existence had very little impact on people. "Pascal's wager" (*Pensées* 149–53) recommends that we bet on God because if we win we win everything and if we lose we really lose nothing because religious people are happier anyway.

21. Quoted by Robert Coles in *Irony in the Mind's Life: Essays on Novels by James Agee, Elizabeth Bowen, and George Eliot* (New York: New Directions, 1974), 25. See Bruce A. Ronda, *Intellect and Spirit: The Life and Work of Robert Coles* (New York: The Continuum Publishing Company, 1989), 24.

22. Paul Tillich, *What is Religion?* (New York: Harper Torchbooks, 1973), 76.

23. Vatican II saw *personal* faith as complementary to purely *intellectual* faith. Macmurray's use of the term personal is inclusive of both meanings.

24. *Dogmatic Constitution on Divine Revelation* (*Dei Verbum*), November 18, 1965, chapter 1, # 5. The *Dei Verbum* quotation is taken from Austin Flannery, ed., *Vatican Council II: The Conciliar and Post Conciliar Documents*, New Revised Edition (Boston: St. Paul Books and Media, 1992), 752.

25. For several years I have presented Fowler's understanding of faith as involving the three components of head, heart and hands. I am not sure that the third (action) is as explicit in his work as I will make it seem here.

26. Fowler tells the moving story of a twelve year old boy's "pure and strongly held theism" which reflected an understanding of God as Liberator and Redeemer. "We will never know," the boy said, "how much God *does* [emphasis mine] every day to keep our world working as well as it does" (*Becoming* 88).

27. The quotation is from the document *Justice in the World*, # 5, produced by the Second ordinary World Synod of [Roman Catholic] Bishops meeting in Rome in the fall of 1971. For a discussion of this specific passage, see Charles M. Murphy, "Action for Justice as Constitutive of the

preaching of the Gospel: What did the 1971 Synod Mean?" in *Theological Studies* 44, no. 2 (June 1983): 298–311.

28. Ronald Rolheiser, "Chronicle," *Catholic Herald* (London: Herald House, June 3, 1994): 10.

29. Literally, *didache* means "a teaching." This document is also called the "Teaching of the Twelve Apostles."

30. Richard P. McBrien, *Catholicism*, Study Edition (San Francisco: Harper & Row, 1981), 967.

31. Thomas H. Groome, *Christian Religious Education* (San Francisco: Harper & Row, 1980), 65–66.

32. My puzzle image comes from the fact that on holidays I enjoy working on jigsaw puzzles. Fowler speaks of the "teepee model" which he attributes to his late friend and mentor, Carlyle Marney. The poles represent education, profession, associations, religion, state of life, life style, and so on. In our mid-twenties, we tie the poles together at the top, wrap a skin around them, and crawl inside to spend the rest of our lives (*Becoming* 11–13).

33. Once, I spoke to a group of professional men and women over breakfast at the Carleton Club in Winnipeg. During the meal, and before my talk, a few of them were discussing a new board game called Midlife Crisis.

34. Robert Kegan, *The Evolving Self: Problem and Process in Human Development* (Cambridge, MA: Harvard University Press, 1982).

35. Fowler's faith development model makes use of seven facets of faith that provide insight into the form of faith at a given stage. Briefly, they deal with the way we think (Jean Piaget), perspective taking (Robert Selman), moral judgment (Lawrence Kohlberg), our sense of faith community, authorities, worldview, and use of symbols. Fowler is both a social scientist and a Christian theologian. His faith development theory is cross-disciplinary, straddling the boundaries between developmental psychology and pastoral theology. Here, for instance, it is Fowler's inclusion of the affective side of human beings in his concept of rationality that allows traditional understandings of religion to be taken seriously by faith development theory.

36. See *Stages* 98–105. There has not been enough cross-cultural research completed to claim "universality" for the faith stages (James W. Fowler, Karl Ernst Nipkow, and Friedrich Schweitzer, eds., *Stages of Faith and Religious Development* [New York: Crossroad Publishing Company, 1991], 10).

37. Linda Lawrence, "Stages of Faith," *Psychology Today* 17, no.11 (November 1983): 62.

38. "Readiness" is the term favored by Ronald Goldman in conjunction with stage transition; see Ronald Goldman, *Readiness for Religion: A Basis for Developmental Religious Education* (London: Routledge & Kegan Paul, 1965).

39. Here Fowler is quoting a character in *Green Pastures* by Mark Connelly. John Macmurray wrote a Postscript to the 1963 edition of *Green Pastures* (published in London by Delisle). It occurs to me that "Dark

Nights of the Soul" as described in the writings of Spanish mystic St. John of the Cross (1542–1591) correspond to the transitions between Fowler's higher faith stages.

40. The phoenix is a legendary bird (according to Herodotus only one existed at a time, living for five hundred years) which built its own funeral pyre out of aromatic materials. The dying phoenix was consumed by fire and from its ashes a new bird arose. In early Christian art and writings the phoenix is a symbol for resurrection and immortality.

41. A poem by Ruth McLean as quoted by John A. Veltri S.J., *Orientations: A Collection of Helps for Prayer*, vol. 1 revised (Guelph, ON: Loyola House, 1993), 21–22. Orientations can be found on the Internet at *http://www.oise.on.ca/~rboys/veltri.html*. This poem reminds me of an image of stage transition as like jumping from a cliff without wings trusting that you'll be able to grow them before you hit the ground; wings that will take you to new heights far above the top of the cliff from which you jumped.

42. This process might be referred to as one of "positive disintegration." Khalil Gibran is quoted as saying: "Your joy is your sorrow unmasked. The self-same well from which your laughter rises was sometimes filled with tears" (*Celebration*, January 1991 [Epiphany]: 19). I am reminded of Fowler's remark that the Chinese ideogram for *crisis* is a combination of the characters for *danger* and *opportunity* (*Pastoral* 103). *Global Brain* by Peter Russell (London: Routledge & Kegan Paul, 1982) also makes use of this image.

43. Constructive critiques of Fowler's theory have helped clarify the issues involved. I have found the work of Mary Ford-Grabowsky particularly helpful. See "The Concept of Christian Faith in the Light of Hildegard of Bingen and C. G. Jung: A Critical Alternative to Fowler" (Ph.D. diss., Princeton University, 1985); "What Developmental Phenomenon is Fowler Studying?", *Journal of Psychology & Christianity* 5, no. 3 (1986): 5–13; "The Fullness of the Christian Faith Experience: Dimensions Missing in Faith Development Theory," *Journal of Pastoral Care* 41, no. 1 (1987): 39–41; "Flaws in Faith Development Theory," *Religious Education* 82, no. 1 (1987): 80–93; and "The Journey of a Pilgrim: An Alternative to Fowler," *The Living Light* 24, no. 3 (March 1988): 242–254.

44. This description reminds me of a sentence from T.S. Eliot's poem *Little Gidding*:

> We shall not cease from exploration
> And the end of all our exploring
> Will be to arrive where we started
> And know the place for the first time.

T. S. Eliot, *Collected Poems: 1909–1962* (London: Faber and Faber, 1963), 222.

45. *How Faith Grows: Faith Development and Christian Education*, A Report to the General Synod [Church of England]. London: National Society/Church House Publishing, 1991), 17. What I see as a major contribution

of Fowler is his organization of the order or pattern in which the developmental features of faith appear.

46. Karl Rahner, *Theological Investigations*, vol. 3, The Theology of the Spiritual Life (London: Darton, Longman & Todd, 1967), 13–14.

47. For detailed information on the administration and analysis of faith development interviews, see Romney M. Moseley, David Jarvis, and James W. Fowler, *Manual for Faith Development Research* (Atlanta: Center for Research in Faith and Moral Development, Emory University, 1986).

48. A 1993 film by Columbia Pictures, *My Life* was directed by Bruce Joel Rubin.

49. For adults, beyond the world "we know about, there is the further world we make," the "larger world mediated by meaning" (*Collection* 233).

50. A 1977 Twentieth Century Fox film, *Star Wars* was directed by George Lucas.

51. "Fowler on Faith," *Christianity Today* (June, 1986): 7-I-8-I.

52. A 1968 Twentieth Century Fox film (directed by Robert Neame), *The Prime of Miss Jean Brodie* shows some students, at least at the outset, uncritically accepting Miss Brodie's worldview. In the title role, Maggie Smith won the 1969 academy award as best actress.

53. The reference in brackets (*Pastoral* 66) is to James W. Fowler, *Faith Development and Pastoral Care* (Philadelphia: Fortress Press, 1987), 66. Quotations from this work will henceforth be as here (*Pastoral* 66).

54. Based on the novel by Victor Hugo, *Les Misérables* is a musical by Alain Boublil and Claude-Michel Schönberg. It opened at the Palais des Sports in Paris in 1980.

55. The television serials, *Little House on the Prairie* and *The Waltons* are examples of positive Stage 3 faith culture.

56. Rosemary Haughton, *The Catholic Thing* (Springfield, IL: Templegate Publishers, 1979), 9.

57. Peter Occhiogrosso, *Once A Catholic* (New York: Ballantine Books, 1987), 12–13.

58. The Broadway musical *Fiddler on the Roof* was written by Jospeh Stein.

59. The musical also conveys the limitation of Stage 3 faith in that it portrays two parallel but conflicting religious world views in the same village (Judaism and Ukrainian Orthodoxy).

60. Sharon Parks, *The Critical Years* (San Francisco: Harper & Row, 1986), 76. Fowler first quotes her in *Stages* 154.

61. In terms of Lawrence Kohlberg's stages of moral development, a person living out of Stage 3 faith exhibits Stage 4 "conventional" morality.

62. *Judgment at Nuremberg* is a 1961 film from MGM, directed by Stanley Kramer.

63. This quotation is transcribed from a videotape of the film. The statement is made just before the judges retire to deliberate on the verdict and sentencing.

64. Teaching faith development theory in classes and workshops, I have been struck by how often the interest of participants and their questions arise, not out of their professional involvements, but from the depths of their own faith journey. This ability of faith development theory to "engage its readers' own memories, convictions, and core intuitions" (James W. Fowler, "Stages of Faith: Reflections on a Decade of Dialogue," *Christian Education Journal* 13, no. 1 [Autumn 1992]: 16.) is also reminiscent of the personal involvement and self-appropriation called for by John Macmurray and Bernard Lonergan.

65. If we stay at Fowler's Stage 3 too long, the move to Stage 4 is not a normal evolutionary process but a real disruption. An example comes to mind. Many Jesuits left the Order in the years following the Second Vatican Council (1962–65). Personally, I suspect that a number of them identified the prevailing Stage 3 form of the Jesuit vocation (characterized by a strict hierarchical governance structure and rigid rules of dress and behavior) as *the* Jesuit life. When the reforms of the Council urged us forward in faith, their identity was so tied to externals like clerical dress and conformist behavior that, as these fell away, they found it quite easy to leave the community. More than once in my early days as a member of the Society of Jesus I heard variations on the theme, 'I didn't leave the Jesuits, the Jesuits left me.'

66. In *Becoming Adult, Becoming Christian*, Fowler uses the image of Protean Man ("fluid, flexible, and frequently ready to change fundamental convictions and outlooks") as illustrative of faith at this stage (13–15).

67. Not many young adult Catholics living in a university residential setting continue to go to Mass. Generally, the few who do attend see their understanding of why they go to Mass shift from conformity to external pressures to go to church to self-appropriation of their attendance at Mass. This is one of the conclusions of the *Young Adult Faith Study* conducted by the Jesuit Center for Faith Development and Values at St. Paul's College, University of Manitoba. A report on the findings of this four year (1988–92) investigation into the faith development of young adults as they move from high school through a university undergraduate program is found in David G. Creamer, "Faith Development in Young Adult Catholics," *Insight*, no. 4. Ottawa: Canadian Conference of Catholic Bishops (1991): 56–73.

68. The page references are to Viktor Frankl, *The Unconscious God* (New York: Washington Square Press, 1985).

69. The transition to Fowler's Stage 4 faith is, in my view, more or less equivalent to what Lonergan means by moral conversion — ". . . what are we to choose to be? What are we to choose to make of ourselves? In our lives there . . . comes the moment of existential crisis when we find out for ourselves that we have to decide for ourselves what we by our own choices and decisions are to make of ourselves . . ." (*Collection* 243). For a similar quotation see chapter 5, note 25.

70. Perhaps Allport's major contribution to the empirical study of religion is his distinction between two orientations to (or types of) religion; intrinsic [I] and extrinsic [E], which he views as the two ends of a continuum.

Intrinsic religion is a "religion that is lived." "Such religion does not exist to serve the person; rather the person is committed to serve it"(Will Herberg, *Protestant-Catholic-Jew* (Garden City, NY: Doubleday, 1960), 132). Extrinsic religion is "religion that is used." Those having this orientation find religion useful in a number of ways and emphasize its rewards over its demands (Robert W. Crapps, *An Introduction to Psychology of Religion* [Macon, GA: Mercer University Press, 1986], 156).

71. John Chirban, "Intrinsic and Extrinsic Religious Motivation and Stages of Faith" (Th.D. diss., Harvard Divinity School, 1980). This research is reported in *Stages* 300–301.

72. If the Roman Catholic church prior to the Second Vatican Council saw Stage 3 faith as the ideal, then to move beyond that put one on dangerous ground as Martin Luther found out on April 18, 1521, at the Diet of Worms. The remark "Here I stand, I can do no other," attributed to him, is a characteristically Stage 4 remark.

73. The term *transition* is used to refer to the process of growing *out of* one way of living faith preparatory to growing *into* the next.

74. The 1965 Vatican II document, *Gaudium et Spes* (Pastoral Constitution on the Church in the Modern World), points out that the modern world tends to privatize religion (Fowler's Stage 4), a tendency that it calls one of "the gravest errors of our time" (# 43).

75. Many of the descriptors of Stage 4 can be traced to Enlightenment ideals, in large measure the nucleus of our modern worldview.

76. Linda Lawrence, "Stages of Faith," *Psychology Today* 17, no. 11 (November, 1983): 58. The metaphor is attributed to Carlyle Marney.

77. *Conjunctive Faith* is a name Fowler traces to creation-centered medieval mystic Nicholas of Cusa (1401–1464) who put forward the notion of God as "the coincidence of opposites" (*coincidentia oppositorum*). This notion was altered by Carl Jung to "conjunction of opposites" (*Becoming* 64).

78. E. F. Schumacher, *A Guide for the Perplexed* (London: Sphere Books Ltd, 1977). Page numbers are given in brackets.

79. The reference in brackets (*Promise* 19) is to Parker Palmer, *The Promise of Paradox: A Celebration of Contradictions in the Christian Life* (Notre Dame, IN: Ave Maria Press, 1980), 19. Quotations from *The Promise of Paradox* will henceforth be indicated as here (*Promise* 19).

80. I think that my own Roman Catholic tradition needs a lot of Stage 5 people these days to make peace between the 4s and the 3s. Stage 5 adult Catholics understand that the magisterium of the Church is a very important cornerstone in the moral decision-making process but further understand that they can be loyal to the church without abdicating personal responsibility to church authorities, even the Pope. If people have been operating at the conventional level of moral decision-making for a long time, this faith transition can be difficult.

81. Abraham H. Maslow, *Religions, Values, and Peak-Experiences* (New York: Penguin Books, 1970), 13.

82. The notion of Stage 5 as existing in dynamic tension between the extremes of Stage 3 and Stage 4 reminds me of the position of the Earth (life giving water as solid, liquid, and gas) as in tension between the extremes of climate represented by Mars (lifeless rock) and Venus (veiled in poisonous gases). This is one of the reasons why I diagram Stage 5 as balanced between Stages 3 and 4.

83. Not long ago I met a 29 year old man who was embarking on a two year volunteer committment in a communal setting. He was a succcessful professional but unhappy with his lonely, individualistic lifestyle (Stage 4). It was a longing for the "team-work" that characterized his years in the scouting movement (Stage 3) that brought him to the volunteer program (Stage 5).

84. Ari L. Goldman, *The Search for God at Harvard* (New York: Times Books, 1991). In the discussion of Goldman's faith journey, the numbers in brackets refer to page numbers in his book.

85. Twenty-five years after his death (December 10, 1968), articles on Merton appeared in several journals. To name just two: Thomas P. Rausch, "Thomas Merton: Twenty-five Years After," *America* 170, no. 1 (January 1–8, 1994): 6–12; and Jim Forest, "A Very Public Hermit," *The Tablet* (December 25, 1993/January 1, 1994): 1685.

86. Thomas Merton, *The Seven Story Mountain* (New York: Harcourt, Brace and Company, 1948).

87. Thomas Merton, *The Sign of Jonas* (New York: Harcourt, Brace and Company, 1953), 11.

88. Thomas Merton, "Is the World a Problem?," *Commonweal* 84, no. 11 (June 3, 1966): 305.

89. Jim Forest, "A Very Public Hermit," *The Tablet* (December 25, 1993/January 1, 1994): 1685.

90. James W. Fowler, "Faith and the Structuring of Meaning" in *Toward Moral and Religious Maturity: The First International Conference on Moral and Religious Development* (Morristown, NJ: Silver Burdett, 1980), 73.

91. There are obvious parallels with John Macmurray's "mutuality of the personal" and Martin Buber's "I and Thou."

92. If Stage 3 faith interprets human action in the face of transcendental reality and Stage 4 faith interprets transcendental action in the face of human contingencies, then Stage 5 faith is concerned with interpreting the relational structure between the human and the transcendent. If Stage 3 faith can be characterized as tribal (dependent) and Stage 4 as individualistic (independent), then Stage 5 can be understood as communal (interdependent).

93. M. K. Gandhi, *My Autobiography* (Boston: Beacon Press, 1957), 504.

94. Coretta Scott King, ed., *The Words of Martin Luther King, Jr.* (New York: Newmarket Press, 1983), 73.

95. Fowler rationalizes this claim and discusses the objections to it in *Becoming* 71–75. See also the "character of the last stages" in developmental theories (*Becoming* 20).

96. James W. Fowler, "Stages of Faith: Reflections on a Decade of Dialogue," *Christian Education Journal* 13, no. 1 (Autumn 1992): 15.

Chapter 8

A Summing Up

There is, then, a road which all profoundly "serious," "ultimately concerned" people of good will can travel together for a very long distance. Only when they come almost to its end does the road fork so that they must part in disagreement. Practically everything that, for example, Rudolf Otto defines as characteristic of the religious experience — the holy; the sacred; creature feeling; humility; gratitude and oblation; thanksgiving; awe before the *mysterium tremendum*; the sense of the divine, the ineffable; the sense of littleness before mystery; the quality of exaltedness and sublimity; the awareness of limits and even powerlessness; the impulse to surrender and to kneel; a sense of the eternal and of fusion with the whole of the universe; even the experience of heaven and hell — all of these experiences can be accepted as real by clergymen and atheists alike. And so it is also possible for all of them to accept in principle the empirical spirit and empirical methods and to humbly admit that knowledge is not complete, that it must grow, that it is in time and space, in history and in culture, and that, though it is relative to man's powers and to his limits, it can yet come closer and closer to "The Truth" that is not dependent on man.

This road can be travelled together by all who are not afraid of truth. (Abraham Maslow)[1]

Introduction

John Macmurray, Bernard Lonergan and James Fowler represent different eras, places, and traditions. Yet, as I read Lonergan, I hear resonances with Macmurray and Fowler. As I teach Fowler's faith development theory I find myself using Lonergan and Macmurray to explain aspects of the faith stages. It is my position that the thought of Macmurray, Lonergan, and Fowler is congruent in ways which those of us journeying in these last years of the twentieth century need to take to heart. The very fact that they enter into the discussion of human meaning making and authentic living through different doors only to arrive at views which converge around a common normative endpoint (friendship, being in love, citizenship in a commonwealth of love and justice) is, in my view, most significant. It is this commonality that we will explore here. In turn we will consider Macmurray and Lonergan, Lonergan and Fowler, and conclude with a section on the three together.

Macmurray and Lonergan

Methodology

John Macmurray's philosophical summary, "All meaningful knowledge is for the sake of action, and all meaningful action for the sake of friendship" (*Self* 15) is, in my view, consistent with Bernard Lonergan's insight that as we move in consciousness from a judgment as to truth (meaningful knowledge), to a decision to act responsibly (meaningful action), to falling in love (friendship), we are engaged in progressively more human activity. Further, Macmurray's use of the adjective *meaningful*, in my view, expresses something of what Lonergan intends by *conversion*. *Meaningful* knowledge of truth (the result of intellectual conversion) brings us to the existential decision about what to do. A decision to do the good and to put others before ourselves, *meaningful* action in Macmurray's terminology, is only possible as a result of what Lonergan describes as moral conversion. And as meaningful action is "for the sake of friendship," so religious conversion takes us beyond intellectual and moral conversion to love (*Second Collection* 228). I chart this relationship between Macmurray and Lonergan as in Table 8.1.

Table 8.1

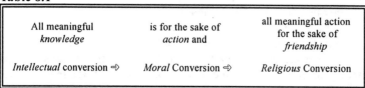

All meaningful *knowledge*	is for the sake of *action* and	all meaningful action for the sake of *friendship*
Intellectual conversion ⇨	*Moral* Conversion ⇨	*Religious* Conversion

John Macmurray's insistence on the primacy of action over thinking parallels Lonergan's view that the end point of the transcendental method is not knowledge of truth but right *action* done in harmony with what I know to be true. The dynamics of human consciousness move us beyond questions of truth to questions of value; we need to know because we want to act responsibly. We pay attention to experience and consciousness, we probe intelligently into the meaning of our experience, and we exercise critical judgment, so that we can act as befits our human dignity. To know the truth and not to do it is to acknowledge that we are living at less than our full human potential.[2]

According to Lonergan, when we begin the process of self-constitution from a reflective, critical stance on the responsible level of consciousness, we arrive at a crucial turning point in our lives — the point at which spiritual development really begins. Why does he say this? I think it is because spirituality implies a way of life and not just a system of ideas. Practical reflection moves us from the realm of fact into that of *value* where we deliberate about a possible course of action, and right action (done for the common good) moves us towards community, towards being-in-love, towards what Macmurray calls friendship. For both Macmurray and Lonergan the goal of knowing points far beyond cognition; the endpoint of the process is ethical and religious. Their central insight is that we are not mere *thinking things* but *moral agents*, capable of acting out of friendship or love. Our humanity, Macmurray and Lonergan would say, is more evident in our creations than in our ideas, and most evident in our loving relationships.

Community

In times past, both figuratively and concretely, the peoples of the earth built walls around themselves, the 6000 year old Great Wall of China being the most dramatic example. Whatever happened outside the wall had no bearing on life within. In fifth century B.C. Greece, to be a civilized human being was to live in a Greek *polis* (city-state); all other peoples were barbarians (i.e., non-Greek and by implication not fully human) and their activity was of no consequence to Greek citizens. With the age of discovery and growth of world trade beginning in the sixteenth century, there was a need to regulate relationships among different peoples and nation states but this was more or less done along utilitarian lines, some notion of justice as fairness serving as the highest operative morality (I might need to *trade* with them but I don't have to *live* with them). Less than a century ago on our North American continent, within the confines of the extended family living on 'Walton's Mountain' or in the 'Little House on the Prairie' there was no need to be concerned about anybody or anything beyond perhaps the nearest town. Within my own religious tradition, the image I have of Roman Catholicism in the decades before the Second Vatican Council is of an institution with an ideological wall around itself.[3]

However, at this time in earth's story, in whatever sphere of life we may want to consider, retreating behind a wall or fortifying oneself on a mountain doesn't afford much protection or isolation. The world, to use Marshall McLuhan's (1911–1980) much overworked phrase, has shrunk to become a "global village."[4] After the Chernobyl nuclear disaster in the Ukraine, friends of mine in Paris were concerned about contamination in the milk their children were drinking and radiation levels had risen halfway around the globe in Manitoba. Like it or not, we all breathe the same air, drink the same water and live under the ultraviolet protection of the same shrinking ozone layer. Our need to achieve community today is on a global scale. Such was the vision of John Macmurray and Bernard Lonergan. What we are just coming to appreciate as we near the end of the millennium is that movement in this direction is not just an option, but a necessity. To continue to live in the old way is to condemn ourselves and the earth to extinction. What we *do* in the next decade or so will determine whether life as we know it on this planet continues or not:

> The changes presently taking place in human and earthly affairs are beyond any parallel with historical change or cultural modification as these have occurred in the past. This is not like the transition from the classical period to the medieval period or from the medieval period to the modern period. This change reaches far beyond the civilizational process itself, beyond even the human process into the biosystems and even the geological systems of the Earth itself.[5]

To save ourselves and the planet is a daunting task requiring cooperation on a scale heretofore never imagined. But the nagging question remains: 'If up until this moment we have not been too concerned about our children's children and the world they will inherit, why will we start now?' The answer, if we accept what Macmurray and Lonergan have to say, is because a new consciousness of what it is to be a fully authentic human person is forming; we human beings are discovering that we, as a species, are fashioned to live cooperatively and in friendship, that we exist because of and for love. As *human* creatures we are not designed to work together like the parts of a clock, nor are we genetically programmed to live like ants in an ant hill; we are imprinted with feelings and the ability to make commitments in order to live communally. Community, Macmurray has shown, is constituted by means of mutual personal relationships of friendship. Lonergan writes that we human beings have a "primordial sympathy" for one another (*Insight* 237).

Reminiscent of John Macmurray's "mutuality of the personal," Bernard Lonergan explains mutual love as an "intertwining of two lives" in such a way that an 'I' and 'thou' are transformed into a "'we' so intimate, so secure, so permanent, that each attends, imagines, thinks, plans, feels, speaks, acts in concern for both" (*Method* 33). Relationships of this kind (respectful, intimate, loving) which "bind a community together" (*Method* 51) are required to bring us into the Ecozoic Age:

> The Ecozoic Era can only be brought into being by the integral life community itself. If other periods have been designated by such names as the Reptilian or the Mammalian periods, this Ecozoic Period must be identified as the Era of the Integral Life Community. For this to emerge there are special conditions on the part of the human, for although this period cannot be an anthropocentric life period, it can come into being only under certain conditions that dominantly concern human understanding, choice, and action.[6]

In one of his last published essays, *The Philosophy of Jesus*, John Macmurray identifies the mission of Jesus Christ as most fundamentally that of a social reformer concerned about the salvation of *this* world: "A religion which despairs of this world, and takes for its task to prepare men in this life for a blessed future in another world is not the religion of Jesus."[7] Thus, he characterizes the early faith community which gathered around Jesus as "a way of life on earth" and "an instrument for the salvation of a world gone wrong." The church of Christ which succeeded it he understands to be a "brotherhood," existing "for the sake of the world outside it."[8] In the same vein, Bernard Lonergan describes the Christian church as "the community that results from the outer communication of Christ's message and from the inner gift of God's love" (*Method* 361) and claims that it ought to have as a primary function the promotion and renewal of community; i.e., the promotion of intellectual, moral, and religious conversion. At this point, allow me to add that we might even dare to think of the emerging Ecozoic era as contiguous with the continual inbreaking of the reign of God so central to Hebrew scriptures and the life and mission of Jesus.[9]

> In days to come . . . they shall beat their swords into plowshares, and their spears into pruning hooks; nation shall not lift up sword against nation, neither shall they learn war anymore (Isaiah 2:2–4).

> The wolf shall live with the lamb, the leopard shall lie down with the kid: . . . The nursing child shall play over the hole of the asp, and the weaned child shall put its hand on the adder's den. They will not hurt or destroy on all my holy mountain for the earth will be full of the knowledge of the Lord . . . (Isaiah 11:6–9).

> All who believed were together and had all things in common; they would sell their possessions and goods and distribute the proceeds to all, as any had need. (Acts 2:44–45)

Lonergan and Fowler

Because Lonergan and Fowler are each concerned with the process of human meaning-making, it is reasonable to assume that they may be describing different facets of the same human developmental pattern. As near as I can tell, what Bernard Lonergan discovered through self-appropriation of human consciousness, James Fowler uncovered by means of empirical research. In a sentence, the point of this discussion of Lonergan and Fowler is to argue that Lonergan's way of tradition (from above downwards ↓), way of achievement (from below upwards ↑), and the totality of development as an integration of the two ways (↑↓) illuminate what Fowler describes as faith Stages 3, 4 and 5 respectively. Further, I will argue that the transitions between faith Stages 3 through 6 parallel Lonergan's intellectual, moral, and religious conversion.

Telling Us What We Already Knew

Both Lonergan and Fowler understand human beings to be natural meaning-makers and each puts forward a model for elucidating the dynamics of the meaning making process. Both would agree that they are not offering us something *new* but making explicit something that we already *knew* and can verify by critical reflection on our life experience. The introduction to a series of essays on Fowler's model proposes that:

> Fowler's theory is more than just one of any number of interesting and potentially useful academic analyses. It is an expression of a wider cultural and intellectual mood. It is a consolidation and crystallization of a whole way of seeing things that is already in some sense "out there." Fowler, we think, tells many of his readers, but in a way that they could not have put it themselves, what they in some sense already "knew" to be the case.[10]

Similarly, Lonergan's epistemological framework can be understood as something *out there* that in some sense we already *knew*. The generalized empirical method is not something that we learn or are taught but is a process of self-appropriation — it is ourselves maturing in experience, growing in understanding, and searching for what is true and good and lovable.

Roman Catholicism and Faith Development Theory

Fowler's Stage 3 faith, as we have seen, is characterized by conformity to the expectations of others and an uncritical regard for authority. At Stage 3 one is "embedded" in one's faith outlook; "I *am* my relationships; I *am* my roles" (*Pastoral* 66). Research has shown that this faith stage is the life stance of a large percentage of adults. In my view, it is coincidental with the classical understanding of religious faith and parallels what Lonergan calls the traditional way of knowing as from above downwards.

As we have seen, Stage 3 was *the* faith understanding of the majority of Roman Catholics until developments in our own century, culminating in the reforms of the Second Vatican Council. The Scholastic tradition in theology, best exemplified by Thomas Aquinas, was the only acceptable expression of the basic doctrine of Catholicism for eight centuries. To question the authority of Thomism was to question one's very (Stage 3) faith. This was the church milieu in which Bernard Lonergan studied and did most of his teaching and writing. That he suffered as a teacher and author because of this limited understanding of faith is clear. In terms of Fowler's stage theory, Lonergan's life and career can be seen initially as an effort to extricate himself (remember that he studied Thomistic theology and began to teach and write in Latin!) and his religious tradition from embeddedness in the Stage 3 faith perspective.

Lonergan's elaboration of the way of achievement from below upwards as complementary to the way of tradition (from above downwards) provides an intellectual justification for the shift from Fowler's Stage 3 (*they say*) to Stage 4 (*I think*) faith. For Lonergan, part of the shift from a pre-modern to a modern worldview, from Stage 3 to Stage 4 faith, involves the "recovery of the subject," a focusing on the human subject searching for truth.[11] In terms of Lonergan's levels of consciousness, the way of development from below upwards is integral to faith growth and in mature *adult* faith it assumes priority.

Lonergan's notion that the way from above downwards (Fowler's Stage 3 faith) is not the only way that human beings come to knowledge but needs to be complemented by the way from below upwards (Fowler's Stage 4 faith) was not readily accepted within the church or the academy.[12] The insight of both Lonergan and Fowler is that full human maturity moves one beyond the either/or Stage 3/Stage 4 polarity to an awareness of the strengths and limitations of each way and the need to replace the old adversarial view with a *complementary* view of meaning-making.

If the ideal of the pre-modern Roman Catholic church was Fowler's Stage 3 faith (Lonergan's way of tradition), then the Second Vatican Council can be viewed as an attempt to move Catholicism through modern, historical, consciousness (Fowler Stage 4) to Conjunctive faith characterized by a promulgation of religious liberty and genuine dialogue with other Christian churches and religious traditions (Fowler Stage 5). Fowler's research has shown that the transition from Stage 3 to Stage 4 faith (if it happens at all) is often long and protracted. Speaking in 1970 about his own post-Vatican II faith community, Lonergan was aware of this difficulty as is clear in this astute observation:

Ours is a time that criticizes and debunks the past. . . .
It also is a time of confusion, for there are many voices, many of
them shrill, most of them contradictory. . . .
To confusion there are easily added disorientation, disillusionment,
crisis, surrender, unbelief. But . . . from the present situation Catholics are suffering more keenly than others, not indeed because their
plight is worse, but because up to Vatican II they were sheltered
against the modern world and since Vatican II they have been
exposed more and more to the chill winds of modernity (*Second
Collection* 93).

Cardinal G. Emmett Carter, retired Archbishop of Toronto, offers
a perspective on the two extreme positions characteristic of the church
in our time:

We must not fall into the trap of ultramontanism, a truly doubtful
position which makes the Pope sort of the centre and fount of all
wisdom and authority in the Church, or into the opposite excess, . . .
namely that authority of the Church is almost uniquely from popular
opinion.[13]

It seems to me that Cardinal Carter's view can be rephrased in
terms of Fowler's stages of faith development. "Ultramontanism" is
Stage 3 because of the certainty it offers; "popular opinion" is Stage
4. "True loyalty" (Stage 5), Cardinal Carter goes on to say, is not
"blind obedience," nor is it intent on destroying everything handed
down; it is "one thing to adjust and it is another thing to destroy."[14]

Bernard Lonergan and Faith Development Theory

Lonergan, I think, admirably represents the balance which characterizes "true loyalty." In his own life, he passed from the absolute-
ness of classical Catholicism, through a period characterized by the
individuality of Stage 4 ("*I* can prove out of St. Thomas himself that
the current interpretation is absolutely wrong"), and into the Conjunctive faith of Stage 5 ("I have no doubt, I never did doubt, that the old
answers were defective"). It is not that we have traditionally been
asking the wrong *questions* but our way of answering them failed to
take into account modern scientific methodology and the dynamic of
historical consciousness which characterize Stage 4 faith. The old
questions were good (↓) but they need the best of current creativity (↑)

Table 8.2

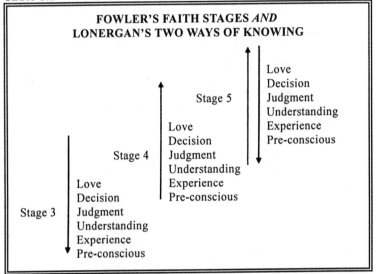

FOWLER'S FAITH STAGES *AND*
LONERGAN'S TWO WAYS OF KNOWING

Stage 5

Love
Decision
Judgment
Understanding
Experience
Pre-conscious

Stage 4

Love
Decision
Judgment
Understanding
Experience
Pre-conscious

Stage 3

Love
Decision
Judgment
Understanding
Experience
Pre-conscious

to achieve the most accurate and helpful formulation of truth for our day (↑↓).

Lonergan was well aware of the limitations inherent in just passively receiving a tradition from the past (Stage 3) and also of the limitations rooted in ignoring the accumulated wisdom of the ages (Stage 4). He fought for the complementarity and integration of the two ways in adult development to produce creative agents of a new and improved tradition (Stage 5). His work is a philosophical foundation for the conjunctive meaning-making that Fowler calls Stage 5 faith. Cognizant of the power and grace of the conjunctive faith stance, Fowler says that the best thing that can happen to a person living Stage 4 faith is that they grow into Stage 5. Sadly, his research shows that only 7% of adults attain this level of faith consciousness.

There is an extraordinary *balance* between old and new, as I am sure is becoming apparent, in Lonergan's two ways of development (↑↓) and Fowler's conjunctive Stage 5 faith; a posture which is unacceptable to the majority of people who live their faith according to either the classicism of Stage 3 or the modernism of Stage 4. Remember that Bernard Lonergan's thought on Aquinas was attacked from both sides; as unorthodox by doctrinaire Thomists (Stage 3) and as holding onto a relic from the middle ages (scholastic thought) by liberal thinkers (Stage 4).

Lonerganian, Vernon Gregson, sums up the polarity in the critiques of Lonergan's position and their blindness to his "higher synthesis:"

> . . . If one finds oneself firmly planted on one side or the other of the various dichotomies that Lonergan manages to transcend by a higher synthesis, if one belongs to one or other of the various groups that achieve ascendancy and then are supplanted in the shorter cycle, whether in the academy, the Church, or the wider society, will one not resent and reject a thought that would relativize one's own position by sublating it into a higher viewpoint, a viewpoint that brings forward what is to be brought forward and leaves behind what is to be left behind? Lonergan's thought meets with resistance from the advocates of both the old and the new, the right and the left, the reactionary, the liberal, and the Marxist. And the resistance is not due to the fact that, transcending these oppositions, he stands for nothing at all, but is rather the manifestation of an all too human tendency to oppose moving beyond the limitations of one's own position . . . (*Desires* 12).

It is precisely because of his lifelong effort to move "beyond the narrow confines of less inclusive viewpoints" and put forward the thinking consistent with Fowler's conjunctive and universalizing faith descriptions that Lonergan's work on methodology can be described as a remarkable achievement. Reaching up to the mind of Bernard Lonergan, just as Lonergan described his early work as reaching up to the mind of Thomas Aquinas, "will transform our own approach to every serious issue with which we attempt to come to terms; and precisely that transformation will be the most important ingredient that we can bring to the resolution of the issues with which we must be concerned today" (*Desires* 13).

That Bernard Lonergan was well aware of the tensions between what Fowler describes as Stage 3 and Stage 4 faith and also of the need to move to the integrated Stage 5 position is poignantly clear in a 1965 lecture at Marquette University, Milwaukee. At the time, the Second Vatican Council was preparing for its fourth (and last) session. In his concluding remarks, Lonergan offered this analysis of what would unfold within Roman Catholicism following the enthusiasm of the Council:

> Classical culture cannot be jettisoned without being replaced; and what replaces it cannot but run counter to classical expectations.

There is bound to be formed a solid right that is determined to live in a world that no longer exists. There is bound to be formed a scattered left, captivated by now this, now that new development, exploring now this and now that new possibility. But what will count is a perhaps not numerous center, big enough to be at home in both the old and the new, painstaking enough to work out one by one the transitions to be made, strong enough to refuse half-measures and insist on complete solutions even though it has to wait (*Collection* 245).

In a recent paper, Frederick Crowe characterized Lonergan's legacy as "a direction and momentum for others" to follow in working out the "transitions to be made."[15] For Lonergan the "center" was a position endowed with the best of the old tradition and the best of the new creativity. If I understand Fowler correctly, Lonergan's center is Conjunctive faith; a philosophical stance that includes an appreciation of both Stage 3 (traditional faith) and Stage 4 (autonomous faith).

Lonergan's "Conversions" and Fowler's Stage "Transitions"

I have argued that the parallel between Lonergan and Fowler is that Lonergan's way of tradition (from above downwards ↓), way of achievement (from below upwards ↑), and the totality of development as an integration of the two ways (↑↓) illuminate what Fowler describes as faith Stages 3, 4 and 5 respectively. At this point in our discussion I would like to go further in drawing a parallel between Lonergan and Fowler and suggest that the transitions between faith Stages 3 through 6 correspond to what Lonergan understands by intellectual, moral, and religious conversion.[16]

For Lonergan, intellectual conversion has to do with embracing and appropriating *for oneself* the dynamism that is foundational to the human search for meaning and truth. This *for oneself* is at the core of intellectual conversion (*meaningful* knowledge for Macmurray) — "one needs to know for oneself . . ." The move from Stage 3 faith to Stage 4 faith involves a similar *conversion*. Fowler states the case as follows:

> For a genuine move to Stage 4 to occur there must be an interruption of reliance on external sources of authority. The "tyranny of the they" — or the potential for it — must be undermined. In addition to . . . critical reflection on one's previous assumptive or tacit system of values . . . there must be, for Stage 4, a relocation of

Table 8.3

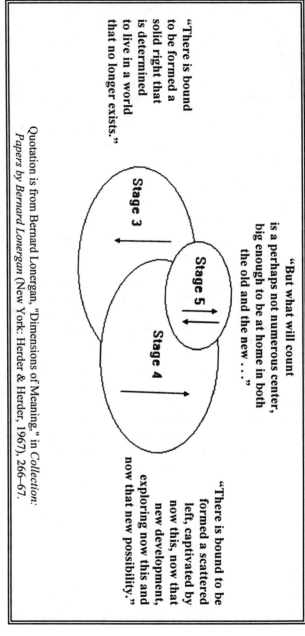

"There is bound
to be formed a
solid right that
is determined
to live in a world
that no longer exists."

"But what will count
is a perhaps not numerous center,
big enough to be at home in both
the old and the new . . ."

"There is bound to be
formed a scattered
left, captivated by
now this, now that
new development,
exploring now this and
now that new possibility."

Stage 3

Stage 5

Stage 4

Quotation is from Bernard Lonergan, "Dimensions of Meaning," in *Collection: Papers by Bernard Lonergan* (New York: Herder & Herder, 1967), 266–67.

authority within the self. While others and their judgments will remain important . . . their expectations, advice and counsel will be submitted to an internal panel of experts who reserve the right to choose and who are prepared to take responsibility for their choices (*Stages* 179).

Moral conversion, for Lonergan, requires a shift in the criterion one uses for making decisions from personal satisfaction (what is good for me) to communal values (what is good for others). Affirming and appropriating for myself that my decisions about what to do are not based on personal whim or satisfaction but on what is truly good or worthwhile is key to a proper understanding of Lonergan's notion of moral conversion.

Similarly, the movement from Fowler's Stage 4 to Stage 5 faith involves a realization that autonomous individuality and freedom have their limitations. I am part of a larger whole that needs to be taken into account for my actions to be just (or "meaningful" in Macmurray's terminology). Fowler writes:

> . . . commitment to justice is freed from the confines of tribe, class, religious community or nation. And with the seriousness that can arise when life is more than half over, this stage [Stage 5] is ready to spend and be spent for the cause of conserving and cultivating the possibility of others' generating identity and meaning (*Stages* 198).

Lonergan's religious conversion arises out of intellectual and moral conversion (*Method* 101) and, in the full critical sense is an ideal which is rarely realized. Fowler, interestingly enough, has identified only 0.5% of his inteviewees as at Stage 6 Universalizing faith. Significant too is the fact that the movement from Conjunctive faith to Universalizing faith, as many commentators on faith development theory have noted, necessitates the introduction of "a particular 'content' — a particular image" having to do with God and religion:

> This image is Fowler's concept as a Christian theologian of the Jewish-Christian vision of the Kingdom of God as the fulfillment of faith. And this image determines a particular behavior — the capacity for "radical commitment to justice and love and . . . selfless passion for a transformed world."[17]

The connection between Fowler's understanding of the strengths required for Stage 6 faith and Lonergan's understanding of religious conversion seems obvious, especially when we recall that Fowler's rare examples of Universalizing faith are generally well known religious personages.

All of this leads me to diagram another connection between Lonergan and Fowler as in Table 8.4.

Table 8.4

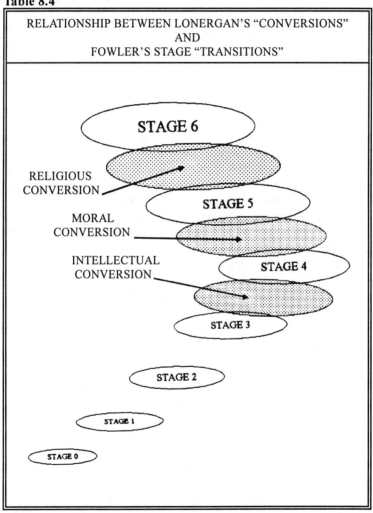

RELATIONSHIP BETWEEN LONERGAN'S "CONVERSIONS"
AND
FOWLER'S STAGE "TRANSITIONS"

STAGE 6

RELIGIOUS
CONVERSION

STAGE 5

MORAL
CONVERSION

INTELLECTUAL
CONVERSION

STAGE 4

STAGE 3

STAGE 2

STAGE 1

STAGE 0

Conclusion

This section in no way pretends to be a well worked out description of the similarities between Bernard Lonergan's epistemological model and James Fowler's faith development theory. What it does intend to propose, however, is that Lonergan's work provides a strong philosophical foundation for Fowler's empirical research and Fowler's research provides scientific verification of the dynamics of human consciousness which Lonergan has elucidated. If this proposal provokes reflection and dialogue about the dynamics of the ways human beings engage life, its purpose will have been achieved.

Macmurray, Lonergan, and Fowler

One of the things that excites me about all three thinkers under study is that their creative work is in continuity with what has gone before. They honor authentic tradition but at the same time don't accept it *uncritically.* What has been received must be investigated under both modernity's telescope and microscope and, in turn, subjected to a postmodern critique before it can be judged worthy. I am attracted by their concern to bring forward the best of our intellectual and faith traditions while at the same time not being blind to the searching questions generated in our present secular and scientific reality. With this thought in mind I want to use this final section to summarize my thoughts about Macmurray, Lonergan and Fowler under two headings; science and religion, and community.

Science and Religion

In Dayton, Tennessee, on July 21, 1925, John Scopes, a high school biology teacher, was found guilty of breaking state law by teaching Charles Darwins evolutionary *theory.* The so-called "monkey trial" featured celebrated criminal lawyer Clarence Darrow for the defense and three-time populist presidential candidate William Jennings Bryan as an assistant to the prosecution. The trial was later dramatized in *Inherit the Wind*, a Broadway play loosely based on the trial.[18] In a climactic scene from the stage play Darrow (Drummond) calls Bryan (Brady) to the stand as an expert in the bible and proceeds to use modern science to demolish his literal interpretation of scripture. In the minds of the liberal populus, allied with Freud's understanding of religion as "illusion," Darrow had demolished not just fundamentalist interpretations of the bible but *religion*. An excerpt from *Inherit the Wind* captures the animosity existing between the camps of science and religion in the early part of this century:

DRUMMOND Now tell me. Do you feel that every word that's written in this book should be taken literally?

BRADY Everything in the Bible should be accepted, exactly as it is given there.

DRUMMOND (*Leafing through the Bible*) Now take this place where the whale swallows Jonah. Do you figure that actually happened? . . .

BRADY I believe in a God who can make a whale and who can make a man and make both do what he pleases! . . .

DRUMMOND . . . I recollect a story about Joshua, making the sun stand still. Now as an expert, you tell me that's as true as the Jonah business. Right? (BRADY *nods, blandly*) That's a pretty neat trick. . . .

BRADY I have faith in the Bible!

DRUMMOND You don't have faith in the solar system.

BRADY (*Doggedly*) The sun stopped.

DRUMMOND Good (*Level and direct*) Now if what you say factually happened — if Joshua halted the sun in the sky — that means the earth stopped spinning on its axis; continents toppled over each other, mountains flew out into space. And the earth, arrested in its orbit, shriveled to a cinder and crashed into the sun (Turning) How come they missed *this* tidbit of news.

BRADY They missed it because it didn't happen.

DRUMMOND It must've happened. According to natural law. Or don't you believe in natural law, Colonel [Brady]? Would you like to ban Copernicus from the classroom along with Charles Darwin? Pass a law to wipe out all the scientific development since Joshua. Revelations — period!

BRADY (*Calmly, as if instructing a child*) Natural law was born in the mind of the Heavenly Father. He can change it, cancel it, use it as He pleases. . . .[19]

To show that the adverserial relationship between science and religion as dramatized in the "monkey trial" are not dead, I would like to offer two stories that shed light on this issue of the relationship between science and religion, one from the conservative right represented by fundamentalist religion and one from the liberal left of naive science.

A few years ago I had a student in my 'Psychology of Religion' class who was studying for the ministry in a conservative christian church. He found the first few months of the course quite difficult, particularly Freud's attack on religion and Skinner's behaviorist explanation of human living, but he persisted. Over time, he began to see that there were both strengths and weaknesses in the various theorists we encountered and even came to see elements of truth in Freud and Skinner. During a visit home for the winter vacation, his father saw the course text book[20] and told his son that it was 'written by the devil.' The son countered that he didn't agree with everything in the text but it did contain some significant truth and if that truth could not be integrated with his divinity studies then he would need to look for another church.

My second story recalls a brief exchange among participants in a seminar during my graduate studies in education. One of the members made reference to Bernard Lonergan during the discussion and another participant asked who Lonergan was. Having been informed that he was a "Canadian philosopher and theologian," he remarked, "I don't think I can learn anything from a theologian." Then, still another participant voiced my sentiments: "How sad."

I share these stories because one way to interpret the interest of Macmurray and Lonergan and Fowler in both science and religion as well as other fields is that they recognized the need for interdisciplinary work in attempting to resolve life's ultimate questions. Neither my student's father nor the new professor in graduate school could see beyond their own narrow horizons. All three of the thinkers we have been considering are aware that philosophy is just one brand of knowledge and philosophical answers must be integrated with those of the physical and biological scientists, social scientists, writers, poets and shamans.[21]

Macmurray, as we have seen, characterized himself as a Christian in that he stood "in the contemporary world for and with the movement that Jesus originated" but "outside all the Churches" because they "do not stand in and with that movement."[22] His boyhood attraction to science was reflected in his early articles and lifelong effort to conceive of science and religion as partners, not adversaries. Lonergan, a Catholic philosopher and theologian, offers a model of human knowing that shows how the so-called scientific method is really the way human beings know, period.[23] And Fowler, a theologian from the reform tradition, takes a seemingly religious concept, faith, and gratefully draws on insights from developmental psychology to analyze its "human side."

" Their work echoes Abraham Maslow's thesis that "it is because both science and religion have been too narrowly conceived, and have been too exclusively dichotomized and separated from each other, that they have been seen to be two mutually exclusive worlds."[24] Spiritual values are not the exclusive possession of organized churches, but the general heritage of humankind.[25] Any important question worthy of consideration is a human question that can only be adequately answered cooperatively.

Community

To pick up on Fowler's understanding of faith as a verb and not a noun, we can characterize community as a verb; not as something that *is* but as something that people *do*. Let me illustrate this point with a story.

In July 1993 I was in Denver, Colorado, for a workshop on community building sponsored by the Foundation for Community Encouragement (FCE) begun by Dr. M. Scott Peck.[26] The focus of the five days was the building and maintaining of community according to the stage model Peck sets forth in *The Different Drum*.[27] On the last afternoon of the workshop one of the participants shared a dream that has stayed with me ever since and is relevant here. The central feature of the dream was a large workshop full of tiny little clay figures all busily working together at various tasks (a kind of Santa's workshop full of elves was the image that came to mind). The dreamer saw herself as above and apart from the scene looking down, conscious that the apparently disjointed activity in the workshop was being directed by some higher power. Her interpretation was that the scene represented the whole earth and that, just as Denver was a community building workshop for 175 participants from around the continent, the earth was the Creator's community building workshop. It had taken a great deal of work, pain and time before our Denver group blossomed forth in community, she shared, and it would take a little more time for the significantly larger and more complex earth community to achieve its glory.

In my opinion, the direction we must take in our search for a "personal" vision of community is expressed in the thought of John Macmurray, Bernard Lonergan, and James W. Fowler. Macmurray's ideal is a world of persons relating in "friendship." For Lonergan "being in love" is the crowning level of human consciousness. And Fowler's highest stage is reserved for those willing to be "pioneers in the commonwealth of love and justice."

Today, of course, community includes our relationship not only with one another but with the fragile blue planet with which we live. First Galileo and Newton and more recently astronauts viewing the earth from space have forever changed the way we human beings conceive of our place in the universe. Dethroned from our exaggerated feeling of self-importance as the center of things, we now know ourselves to be inhabitants of a small, fragile planet circling an ordinary star at the edge of the Milky Way, one of more than one hundred billion galaxies. And the awareness is growing that our destiny is one with the destiny of that blue-green sphere thrown against the blackness of space. In the words of Scottish-American naturalist, John Muir (1838–1914), "when we try to pick out anything by itself, we find it hitched to everything else in the universe."[28]

Macmurray, Lonergan, and Fowler tell us that the most *real* world we live in is the world of relationship with our fellow human beings, with the Other and with Mother Earth. Without all of them, we experience a sense of enormous emptiness because our humanness is made in our relationships. We are gradually coming to full consciousness of the fact that we live in a participatory universe.

I often think of Bernard Lonergan's acknowledgement that while world community is still a "dream," dreams do in fact emerge from our unconscious "as an intimation of a reality to be achieved" (*Third Collection* 66).[29] I humbly suggest that the ecozoic "dream" of cultural historian and "geologian," Thomas Berry, and physicist and cosmologist, Brian Swimme, is such an intimation of a reality that *must* be achieved:

> As industrial humans multiplied into the billions to become the most numerous of all of Earth's complex organisms, as they decisively inserted themselves into the ecosystemic communities throughout the planet, drastically reducing earth's diversity and channeling the majority of the Gross Earth Product into human social systems, a momentous change in human consciousness was in process. Humans discovered that the universe itself is a developing community of beings. Humans discovered by empirical investigation that they were participants in this fifteen-billion-year sequence of transformations that had eventuated into the complex functioning Earth. A sustained and even violent assault by western intelligence upon the universe . . . had brought forth a radically new understanding of the universe,

not simply as a cosmos, but as a cosmogenesis, a developing community, one with an important role for the human in the midst of the process. . . .

    The future of earth's community rests in significant ways upon the decisions to be made by the humans who have inserted themselves so deeply into even the genetic codes of earth's process. This future will be worked out in the tensions between those committed to the technozoic, a future of increased exploitation of Earth as resource, all for the benefit of humans, and those committed to the Ecozoic, a new mode of human-earth relations, one where the well-being of the entire Earth community is the primary concern.[30]

As a species, then, we are facing a problem of an order of magnitude never encountered by human beings on the planet before — the issue now is survival, ours and the planet's. In these pages we have grappled with three congruent philosophical models of *becoming*. The world today Macmurray says "has reached the borders of Utopia,"[31] yet Fowler's research shows that only 7% of adults (Lonergan's "not numerous center") seemed to have crossed over. More of us need to move into this new ecozoic consciousness to achieve a new humanity living in harmony with Mother Earth.

In the Book of Deuteronomy, Moses sets forth the fundamental option before the people: "I call heaven and earth to witness against you today that I have set before you life and death, blessings and curses. Choose life so that you and your descendants may live . . ." (Deuteronomy 30:19). What we learn from Macmurray, Lonergan, and Fowler is that we have before us a choice between a continuation of old ways of being which are now shutting down the very life systems of the planet and a new communal consciousness inviting us to a new partnership in an Earth community. To engage you in a process of thought leading to action in this regard is why I have written this book!

Notes

1. Abraham H. Maslow, *Religions, Values, and Peak-Experiences* (New York: Penguin Books, 1970), 54–55.

2. I am reminded of an expression I heard somewhere: "impression without expression leads to depression," which I take to mean that truth (impression) which is not acted upon (expressed) makes us less than human (depressed).

3. From 1870, when the Italian forces of unification marched into Rome, until 1929, when Mussolini and Pope Pius XI reached a settlement of the Roman Question, the Popes considered themselves prisoners in the Vatican, literally living behind a wall on 14.7 acres.

4. Marshall McLuhan, *The Gutenberg Galaxy* (Toronto: University of Toronto Press, 1962), 31.

5. Thomas Berry, "The Ecozoic Era," a paper presented as part of the E. F. Schumacher Society Lectures (October 19, 1991), 1.

6. Thomas Berry, "The Ecozoic Era," a paper presented as part of the E. F. Schumacher Society Lectures (October 19, 1991), 1.

7. John Macmurray, *The Philosophy of Jesus* (London: The Society of Friends, 1973), 3.

8. John Macmurray, *The Philosophy of Jesus* (London: The Society of Friends, 1973), 9.

9. The central image Fowler uses to describe people characterized by Stage 6 faith is that of "colonists in the Kingdom of God" or, as he phrases the same image today, "pioneers in the commonwealth of love and justice."

10. Craig Dykstra and Sharon Parks, eds., *Faith Development and Fowler* (Birmingham, AL: Religious Education Press, 1986), 2.

11. In Lonergan's model, the subject systematically searches for truth through empirical, intellectual, reasonable, and responsible levels of consciousness. It is this systematic aspect of the search by means of *two* ways of knowing which places Lonergan's work in the context of Fowler's Stage 5 faith, avoiding the dogmatism of Stage 3 and the relativism of Stage 4. It is my contention that all three of the thinkers discussed in this book write from a conjunctive (Fowler Stage 5) faith stance.

12. The great either/or debate which raged for centuries (and continues in some domains), can be characterized in the terminology of Fowler and Lonergan as a debate between Stage 3 faith and the traditional understanding of religion as from above downwards, on the one hand, and Stage 4 faith and the traditional understanding of science as from below upwards, on the other hand.

13. "Address by His Eminence Gerald Cardinal Carter, July 30, 1991," is printed in *Companions of Jesus, Pilgrims with Ignatius: Congress '91* (Toronto: Canadian Institute of Jesuit Studies, 1991), 32.

14. It seems to me that this is the rationale for the concept of the "loyal opposition" in the British parliamentary tradition — "loyal" is characteristic of Fowler's Stage 3 faith, "opposition" of Stage 4, wherreas the paradoxical phrase "loyal opposition" strikes me as compatible with Stage 5 faith.

15. Frederick E. Crowe, "An Expansion of Lonergan's Notion of Value," a paper presented at the twelfth annual Lonergan Workshop, Boston College, June 17–21, 1985. It is reprinted in Michael Vertin, ed., *Appropriating the Lonergan Idea* (Washington: The Catholic University of America Press, 1989), 344–59.

16. A similar suggestion is found in Brendan Carmody, S.J., "Faith Development: Fowler and Lonergan," *The Irish Theological Quarterly* 54, no. 2 (1988), 93–106.

17. Craig Dykstra and Sharon parks, eds., *Faith Development and Fowler* (Birmingham, AL: Religious Education Press, 1986), 144. The quotation within the quotation is from *Stages* 201.

18. Jerome Lawrence and Robert E. Lee, *Inherit the Wind* in Cy Groves *Plays on a Human Theme* (Toronto: McGraw-Hill Ryerson Limited, 1967). It opened at the National Theatre, New York, in 1955.

19. Jerome Lawrence and Robert E. Lee, Act 2 of *Inherit the Wind* in Cy Groves *Plays on a Human Theme* (Toronto: McGraw-Hill Ryerson Limited, 1967), 177–78.

20. David M. Wulff, *Psychology of Religion: Classic and Contemporary Views* (New York: John Wiley & Sons, 1991).

21. Macmurray, Lonergan and Fowler were positive in their evaluation of science and scientific methods. At the same time, all three recognized that, just as the seventeenth century world of René Descartes was sceptical about the revelations of religion, there is a great deal of scepticism in our twentieth century world but now it is with science!

22. John Macmurray, "Here I Stand," a somewhat autobiographical talk found in the John Macmurray Collection, Regis College, University of Toronto, Canada. It is undated.

23. The Vatican II document *Gaudium et Spes* states that there can be no conflict between the wisdom derived from honest research and the truth of the Christian faith because both come from God: "We cannot but deplore certain attitudes (not unknown among Christians) deriving from a shortsighted view of the rightful autonomy of science; they have occasioned conflict and controversy and have misled many into opposing faith and science" (# 36).

24. Abraham H. Maslow, *Religions, Values, and Peak-Experiences* (New York: Penguin Books, 1970), 11.

25. *Gaudium et Spes* (December 7, 1965), considered by many scholars to be the most advanced document of the Second Vatican Council, is a good example of expansive religion, a Stage 5 faith formulation influenced by Lonergan's work during the council. *Gaudium et Spes* speaks of the willingness of the Catholic church to work cooperatively with others (even non-Christians and atheists) to solve the many problems which threaten peaceful living and impede the progress that is God's will for the human family on this fragile planet: "The joy and hope, the grief and anguish of the men of our time, are the joy and hope, the grief and anguish of the followers of Christ as well. Nothing that is genuinely human fails to find an echo in their hearts . . ." (# 1). The document speaks of the "basic equality" of all people and reminds us of our responsibility to participate in the struggle for justice for our brothers and sisters everywhere as "moulders of a new humanity" (# 30). It is an extraordinary example of the dramatic and unprecedented changes in Roman Catholic practice and attitude mandated by Vatican II.

26. The FCE Mission Statement reads, in part: "FCE encourages people, in a fragmented world, to discover new and better ways of being together. Living, learning, and teaching the principles of community, we serve as a catalyst for individuals, groups and organizations . . ." The Foundation for Community Encouragement can be reached at 109 Danbury Road, Suite 8, Ridgefield, CT, 06877.

27. M. Scott Peck, *The Different Drum: Community-Making and Peace* (New York: Simon & Schuster, 1987).

28. Charlene Spretnak, *States of Grace: The Recovery of Meaning in the Postmodern Age* (San Francisco: HarperCollins, 1991), 30.

29. Bernard Lonergan, "Prolegomena to the Study of the Emerging Religious Consciousness of Our Time," in a paper on the *emerging* religious consciousness of our time presented at the Second International Symposium on Belief, Baden/Vienna, January, 1975. It is reprinted in *A Third Collection* 55–73.

30. Brian Swimme and Thomas Berry, *The Universe Story* (New York: Harper Collins Publishers, 1992), 14–15.

31. John Macmurray, *To Save From Fear*, a BBC Lenten talk (London: Friends Home Service Committee, 1964), 13.

GLOSSARY

Action: John Macmurray understands action as technically descriptive of human beings: "In the strict sense of the term only a person can 'act,' or in the proper sense 'do' anything" (*Self* 88-89). He adds that "action is activity in terms of the distinction between 'right' and 'wrong'." It is "knowledge-imbued activity" (*Self* 88-89).

Aquinas: In his *Summa Theologica*, Dominican friar Thomas Aquinas (1225-1274) provided the medieval, pre-modern world with a synthesis of Greek philosophy (Aristotle) and Christian thought (Augustine). This synthesis accepted the Aristotelian concept that science deals with *necessity*. With the birth of the modern world, an understanding that science is empirical and contingent replaced the Aristotelian notion of science as *necessary* and made the Thomistic synthesis obsolete. Within Roman Catholicism, Thomism was *the* theology until well into the twentieth century.

Aristotle: Aristotle (384–322 B.C.) studied in Athens under Plato who was his mentor and friend for twenty years (he eulogized Plato as "one who showed in his life and teachings how to be happy and good at the same time"). From 343–336 B.C., Aristotle served the king of Macedonia as tutor to his son Alexander (the Great). Later, in Athens, Aristotle founded a school (Lyceum) and came into his own as an empirical observer or scientist. He was the last and most influential of the classical Greek philosophers. Aristotelianism is not the opposite of Platonism but a development of that body of philosophic thought, correcting Plato's 'theory of forms' and his dualistic psychology. Aristotle begins his *Metaphysics* with the optimistic statement: "All men by nature desire to know." Elsewhere Aristotle defines the human being as a "rational animal." His understanding of what it is to be human has had a tremendous influence on subsequent thought in the Western World. For Aristotle, there are different degrees of knowledge; "mere experience," *techne* (technical knowledge), and *sophia* (wisdom). Wisdom is not utilitarian but aims to apprehend the first principles or first causes of reality; knowledge is for its own sake. Aristotle places the person who seeks for wisdom (knowledge for its own sake) higher than the person who seeks for technical knowledge with a view to bringing about some practical effect.

Baltimore Catechism: Catechisms are manuals of doctrine in a question and answer format; one of the first was Martin Luther's. The *Roman Catechism* of the Council of Trent (1566) served as the model for the *Catechism of the Third Plenary Council of Baltimore*, commonly called the *Baltimore Catechism*, first printed in 1885.

Behaviorism: Behaviorism is the philosophy (psychology) that strictly limits itself to the study of objective observable behavior. During his life, B.F. Skinner (1904–1990) was the standard-bearer of the behaviorist school of psychology. The following quotation from his autobiography makes his position clear: "I am sometimes asked, 'Do you think of yourself as you think of the organisms you study?' The answer is yes. So far as I know, my behavior at any given moment has been nothing more than the product of my genetic endowment, my personal history, and the current setting. . . . I have tried to *interpret* my life in the light of what I have learned from my research. . . . I do not believe that my life shows a type of personality à la Freud, an archetypal pattern à la Jung, or a schedule of development à la Erikson. There are a few abiding themes, but they can be traced to environmental sources rather than to traits of character. They became part of my life as I lived it; they were not there at the beginning to determine its course" (B. F. Skinner, *A Matter of Consequences*, Epilogue).

Buber: Martin Buber (1878–1965) was an influential Jewish philosopher whose central philosophical concept is "I-Thou" as descriptive of the relationship that ought to exist among human beings and between humanity and God. "Next to being the children of God," he wrote, "our greatest privilege is being the brothers [and sisters] of each other" (Martin Buber as quoted by Seymour Siegel in *Martin Buber: An Appreciation of His Life and Thought* [New York: American Friends of the Hebrew University, 1965], 6). Macmurray writes: "As a philosopher I could not see the Hegelian system as the summing up of all philosophy. . . . I found myself in these things much closer to the prophetic insight of one of the very greatest of modern thinkers, Martin Buber" (*Search* 24). For a comparison of the two, see Gerald A. Largo, "Two Prophetic Voices: Macmurray and Buber," *America* 129 (March 31, 1973): 283–86.

Cartesian: Adjective referring to the rationalist philosophy (and mathematics) of René Descartes [See **Descartes**].

Classicism: This term is more or less synonymous with the terms premodern, traditional, and feudal [See also **Scholasticism**].

Cognitional Theory: Cognitional (Latin *cogito*, I think) theory is about the process by which knowledge is acquired [See **Epistemology**].

Consciousness: Consciousness is inner awareness of myself and my activities.

Copernicus: Nicholas Copernicus (1473–1543), a polish Canon (a priest with the right to vote for a new Bishop), proposed in *The Revolution of the Terrestrial Orbs* (published in 1543 and dedicated to the reigning Pope!) that the sun is at the center of our planetary system and the earth (which turns on itself) and the other planets revolve around it. The Inquisition condemned Copernicus and heliocentrism in 1616 and his work was put on the Index of Forbidden Books "until such time as it is corrected." The German atheistic philosopher, Ludwig Feuerbach, called Copernicus the "first revolutionary of modern times" (Hans Kung, *Freud and the Problem of God* [New Haven: Yale University Press, 1990], 3.

Critical Realist: Bernard Lonergan's position on knowing is that of a critical realist. He writes, "Only the critical realist can acknowledge the facts of human knowing and pronounce the world mediated by meaning to be the real world; and he can do so only inasmuch as he shows that the process of experiencing, understanding, and judging is a process of self-transcendence" (*Method* 239).

Crowe: Fr. Frederick Crowe, S.J. (b. 1915) has been a student, friend, co-worker, and interpreter of Lonergan for more than forty years. He is the co-founder (with Robert M. Doran, S.J.) of the Lonergan Research Institute of Regis College, Toronto and co-editor of the *Collected Works of Bernard Lonergan*, projected to be twenty-two volumes. A theologian in his own right, he is recognized as one of the leading experts in Lonergan's thought.

Darwin: Charles Darwin (1809–1882) is best known for his *Origin of Species* (1859) which proposed the theory of evolution and the idea that only the fittest living species survive. In 1871, Darwin published *The Descent of Man* which argued that human beings were not the product of an immediate creation as Genesis records but the result of a long evolutionary process. This was the origin of conflict in the early twentieth century between the *facts* of science and *revelation* of scripture. Teilhard de Chardin (1881–1955), a Jesuit priest-scientist, argued that the discoveries of science, far from threatening faith, show forth more deeply the glories of God's creation.

Descartes: René Descartes (1596–1650) was educated at the famous Jesuit College of La Fleche, France. Descartes soon rejected what he had been taught, passed through a period of scepticism and eventually sought certainty in his own rational powers. Impressed by the certainty and precision of mathematics, he invented co-ordinate geometry (Cartesian co-ordinate system). In philosophy, following the four rules of "doubt," he arrived at one indubitable principle, *cogito ergo sum* (I think, therefore, I am), upon which he built his philosophy. Considered the "father of modern philosophy," Descartes' two most important works are *Discourse on Method* (1637) and the *Meditations* (1642) [See also **Cartesian**].

Determinism: Determinists hold that all events, including human actions and choices, are fully determined by preceding events and states of affairs, making freedom of choice illusory.

Dialectic/al: Dialectic is the name Bernard Lonergan gives to the fourth functional specialty in his theological method. Dialectic, he acknowledges, is a term that is used with a variety of meanings but his use of the term "has to do with the concrete, the dynamic, and the contradictory . . . in the history of Christian movements. . . . The materials of dialectic, then, are primarily the conflicts centering in Christian movements" (*Method* 129). Dialectical, as used to describe Fowler's Stage 5 faith, refers to the characteristic of Conjunctive faith as seeking to resolve differences between opposing views as opposed to establishing one of the other as true.

Ecozoic: Ecozoic is a "biological term that can be used to indicate the integral *functioning* of life systems in their mutually enhancing relations." Ecozoic is a broader term than ecological (eco-logos "refers to an *understanding* of the interaction of things") (Thomas Berry, "The Ecozoic Era," a paper presented as part of the E. F. Schumacher Society Lectures (October 19, 1991), 9).

Empiricism: A philosophical viewpoint which holds that the 'real' is only what can be known through the senses [See **Hume**].

Epistemology: Epistemology [Greek *episteme*, knowledge] is more than just cognitional theory. Whereas cognitional theory is satisifed with a phenomenology of knowing, epistemology is concerned with the *validity* of our knowing [See **Cognitional Theory**].

Erikson: Erik H. Erikson (1902–1994) trained with Freud in Vienna before becoming Boston's first child psychoanalyst in 1933. He is recognized as one of the founders of the field of *life-span* development. His assertion (1963) that personality development does not end with the achievement of physical maturity but continues over the entire life span (eight ages in the life cycle) is one of his major contributions to psychology. More than a psychologist, Erikson is also an ethicist and supporter of religion, credited with having introduced the concept of the human spirit through the back door of psychoanalytic theory.

Ethics: In philosophy, ethics is the study of moral principles. The term comes from the Greek word *ethos* which in the plural means 'character'.

Existentialism: The existentialist maxim is "existence precedes essence"

(Jean-Paul Sartre). The point is that we are what we make of ourselves and we are also responsible for the self we create. Existentialism is in harmony with the approach to philosophy of both Macmurray and Lonergan. Existentialists can be divided roughly into theistic and atheist wings, understanding the critical problem of twentieth century philosophy in the alternatives *God* or *nothing*. The *nothing* alternative has been argued passionately by Karl Marx, Sigmund Freud, and others.

Form: The pre-Socratic philosophers in sixth century B.C. Greece were the first thinkers concerned to discover the basic 'stuff' or substance found in all things. According to the ancient Greek philosophers, things needed to be 'formed' to be 'real'. In Macmurray's terminology, their philosophical question was the 'form' of the material.

Fowler: James Fowler (b. 1940) and associates have done the ground breaking work on the application of developmental psychology to an understanding of faith (meaning-making) as developing.

Galileo: Galileo Galilei (1564–1642) was an Italian mathematician and physicist who discovered the laws of falling bodies. He used the newly invented telescope to prove the truth of Copernicus's theory that the earth and other planets revolve around the sun. His work brought him into conflict with the church. His influential Jesuit friend, Cardinal Robert Bellarmine (1542–1621), refused to look into his telescope because he said Galileo's proposition couldn't be so because it would contradict the Bible. In his defense, Galileo argued that in the Bible "the intention of the Holy Spirit is not to show us how the heavens move but how we get to heaven." Galileo was condemned by the Inquisition in 1633 and ended his days under house arrest. On October 31, 1992, Pope John Paul II accepted a report by the Pontifical Academy of Sciences which acknowledged that Galileo was correct!

Gifford Lectures: The Gifford Lectures on Natural Religion were inaugurated in 1888 with an endowment from Lord Adam Gifford, a Scottish jurist. They alternate between Glasgow and Edinburgh. *Varieties of Religious Experience* by William James represents his Gifford Lectures at the turn of the century. Physicist, A. S. Eddington presented the lectures for 1927 on the topic "The Nature of the Physical World." American philosopher of education, John Dewey, was a Gifford lecturer on the topic "The Quest for Certainty" (1929). Other lecturers include A. J. Ayer, Karl Barth, Henri Bergson, Rudolf Bultmann, and Alfred North Whitehead.

Hegel: Georg Friedrich Hegel (1770–1831) was a German Idealist philosopher whose thought had a major influence on nineteenth and twentieth century thought and history [See **Idealism/Idealist**].

Hooke: Robert Hooke (1653–1703), a physicist, invented the compound microscope which enabled us to see that the human body far from being a kind of complicated machine is a complex living *organism*.

Hume: David Hume (1711–1776) was the most important and influential of the British empiricists (knowledge is derived from sense experience). The sceptical approach of his most important philosophical work, *A Treatise of Human Nature*, established the limits of empiricism's claims to knowledge. On Hume, Lonergan writes: "Hume thought the human mind to be a matter of impressions linked together by custom. But Hume's own mind was quite original. Therefore, Hume's own mind was not what Hume considered the human mind to be" (*Method* 21) [See **Empiricism**].

Idealism/Idealist: This is the name applied to philosophies which in some way or other affirm that it is the mind (not the senses) which give us whatever knowledge we have of truth [See **Kant** and **Hegel**].

Intentionality: "Intentional," for Lonergan, does *not* mean deliberate. By intentionality he means that the operations of experiencing, understanding, judging, and deciding, in their very operation, *intend* objects; i.e., when I open my eyes, seeing is an *intentional* operation.

Jesuit: Jesuit is a shorthand designation for a member of the Society of Jesus, a religious order within the Roman Catholic church, founded in the mid-sixteenth century by Ignatius of Loyola. The initial two year formation period for Jesuits is the *Novitiate*. Those following the program are called Novices. In traditional Jesuit formation, the *Juniorate* refers to two years (following the Novitiate) devoted to the study of classics, literature, history, and modern languages. The term *Regency* is used to describe that period in Jesuit formation, which normally involves teaching in a Jesuit high school or college for two or three years, falling between the completion of philosophical studies and the beginning of theology. *Tertianship* is the final stage of Jesuit formation; a kind of second Novitiate following ordination to the priesthood.

Kant: In philosophical terms, Immanuel Kant (1724–1804) was a German idealist. Kant's three great critiques, *Critique of Pure Reason*, *Critique of Practical Reason*, and *Critique of Judgment*, provided a synthesis and new direction for philosophy. His major contribution was an attempt to synthesize empiricism and rationalism. The process of knowing was unified; without raw sense experience we would not become aware of any object but without understanding we would not be able to form an intelligible concept of it (See **Empiricism**, **Idealism**, and **Rationalism**).

Kierkegaard: Soren Kierkegaard (1813–1855) was a Danish religious philosopher. He is perhaps best known for his view that a "leap of faith" is required to take us from the ethical to the religious point of view. His thought is viewed as a precursor to existentialism [See **Existentialism**].

Kohlberg: Lawrence Kohlberg (1927–1987) was an American moral philosopher and educator. He is best known for his stage theory of cognitive moral development which was an addition to and elaboration of the work of Jean Piaget [See **Piaget**].

Lonergan: Bernard Lonergan (1904–1984) was critical of both traditional and modern ideas about knowing. Most of his life was devoted to developing an integrated and generalized method of inquiry which he saw as able to overcome modern divisions and fragmentation in knowledge.

Macmurray: Personalist philosopher John Macmurray (1891–1976) has been called "'the best-kept secret of British philosophy in the twentieth century.' He was frequently misunderstood; and when it seemed he was being understood, he was frequently rejected" (John Costello, in the Introduction to John Macmurray, *Reason and Emotion* [Atlantic Highlands, NJ: Humanities Press International, Inc., 1992], vii).

Metaphysics: Metaphysics (Greek *meta* means beyond and *physics* refers to the physical world) is the branch of philosophy which deals with the fundamental questions about existence, the nature of reality, cause and effect, being, and God.

Method: For Lonergan, "a method is a normative pattern of recurrent and related operations yielding cumulative and progressive results" (*Method* 4). In *Insight* Lonergan usually calls this structured process the "generalized empirical method" and in *Method* the "transcendental method." He also refers to it as the "rock" and "common ground" (*Insight* 19–20), "normative source of meaning" (*Third Collection*176), and often just as "method."

Modernism/Modernity: The intellectual foundations of the modern world were conceived in the Renaissance and born in the Enlightenment. In the late nineteenth and early twentieth centuries "modernism" was a term applied to the movement within Christian theology seeking to align itself with modernist trends in philosophy, literature, history, and science. As regards the interpretation of scripture, Modernists embraced liberal views. Using the work of liberal Protestant bible scholars, Catholic scholars, like Alfred Loisy (1857–1940) and George Tyrrell (1861–1909), hoped to close the growing gap between the Catholic Church and the modern world. Their working principle was that the discoveries of modern science had made much of the traditional language of Catholic belief obsolete and even ridiculous at times. Critics argued that their use of the historical-critical method of interpretation emptied church doctrine of its traditional meaning and content. Modernism was condemned by Pope Pius X in his encyclical *Pascendi Dominici Gregis* (September, 8, 1907) which made it quite clear than any new idea in theology, church history or scripture study was suspect. Modernism was described as "the synthesis of all heresies" intent on "the destruction not of the Catholic religion alone but of all religion." The "remedies" Pius X proposed included the study of scholastic philosophy and theology, church censorship of publications, and "diocesan watch committees." Many respected Catholic scholars felt the Pope's fury; Loisy and Tyrrell were excommunicated when they refused to reconsider their "modernist" positions [See **Classicism**, its opposite].

Naive Realism: A philosophical viewpoint which identifies knowing with seeing.

Newton: British mathematician and thinker, Sir Isaac Newton (1642–1726), is best known for his theory of universal gravitation. His mathematical representation of nature became the paradigm for modern science.

Normative: To say that there is a normative pattern in the unfolding of the generalized empirical method is to say that the dynamic structure of human consciousness cannot change or be revised. Although revision of the structure is not possible, a more adequate account of the structure is always possible and Lonergan gave a progressively more adequate account of the structure over his career. Normativity does not mean that the structure cannot be violated; as free agents we can choose to be inattentive, imperceptive, unreasonable and irresponsible.

Pascal: Blaise Pascal (1623–1662) was a French mathematician, physicist, and religious thinker. Already at age nineteen he had invented a calculating machine that worked and his research into hydrodynamics and fluid mechanics is preserved in Pascal's Law which is the basis for hydraulics. His religious thought which emphasized the reasons of the heart over those of rationalism or empiricism is found in his *Pensées* (*Thoughts*) published posthumously by his friends. He felt that metaphysical proofs for God's existence had very little impact on people. "Pascal's wager" (*Pensées* 149–153) recommends that we bet on God because if we win we win everything and if we lose we really lose nothing because religious people are happier anyway. Elsewhere (*Pensées* 155–163), Pascal says that there are only two kinds of reasonable people; those who serve God with all their heart because they know God, and those who seek God with all their heart because they don't know God.

Personal: John Macmurray writes: "The unit of personal existence is not the individual, but two persons in personal relation. . . . we are persons not by individual right, but in virtue of our relation to one another. The personal is constituted by personal relatedness. The unit of the personal is not the 'I', but the 'You and I'" (*Persons* 61).

Personalism/ist: Both John Macmurray and Bernard Lonergan are personalist philosophers in that their central understanding of humanness is not as "thinking thing" but as human subject, as moral "agent," even as capable of relating personally out of "friendship" (love). In philosophy, the term personalism generally refers to a movement originating in the nineteenth century (usually theistic and stressing the value of the free, responsible human person) as a reaction to the prevelant materialism (Hegel), evolutionaism (Darwin), and idealism (Kant).

Piaget: Jean Piaget (1896–1980) dedicated his life to the "biological explanation of knowledge" and the relationship between this knowledge and religion. He published more than sixty books and is ranked as one of the greatest geniuses of the twentieth century and this century's foremost theorist in human intellectual development. Before Piaget, most educators thought intelligence (fixed at birth) was measured according to the amount of knowledge acquired over time. Piaget demonstrated that growth in intelligence takes place in stages. It is not more knowledge that is added from stage to stage but transformations of mind. A good metaphor for the process Piaget uncovered is the metamorphosis of a caterpillar into a butterfly.

Plato: Plato (c. 427–347 B.C.) was a student of Socrates. One of his most notorious and often quoted remarks is: "I thank God that I have been born a Greek and not a barbarian, a free man and not a slave, a man and not a woman; but above all that I have been born in the age of Socrates." Plato's Academy in Athens can be thought of as the first European University. His distinction between soul (*psyche*) and body (or mind and matter) and his emphasis on rational thought has had a significant impact on the Western philosophical tradition. Neo-Platonism exercised a great influence on Christianity (Augustine was a neo-Platonist) and Plato has been called the most influential philosopher of the early Christian Church even though he died about 350 years before the birth of Jesus! In *Process and Reality*, Alfred North Whitehead wrote: "The safest general characterization of the European philosophical tradition is that it consists of a series of footnotes to Plato."

Positivism: Positivists admire the procedures of natural science and disdain intuitive or speculative approaches to knowledge.

Postmodern: This term first appeared in the 1930's as descriptive of new form of architecture. Broadly, it means that which takes us beyond the failed assumptions of modernity. As I am using the term it refers to a sense that the "modern" is in need of reconception; a revisioning along holistic lines. "Constructive," "deconstructive," or "ecological" postmodernism "recognizes not only that all beings are structurally related through our cosmological lineage, but also that all beings are internally constituted by relations with others, even at the molecular level" (Charlene Spretnak, *States of Grace* [San Francisco: HarperCollins, 1993], 20). As used in this book, "postmodern" is more or less synonomous with John Macmurray's understanding of the "personal" [See also **Ecozoic, Personal** and **Personalism/ist**].

Quaker: A Quaker is a member of the Society of Friends, a "church" founded in seventeenth century England by George Fox. Quakers reject the organization of traditional churches and dogmatic creeds. They are known for their pacifism and humanitarian works. With no formal creed or clergy they put their faith in the "inward light" of God's guidance. Persecuted in England, many Quakers emigrated to America where they have prospered and today have their largest concentration of members (c. 130,000).

Rationalism: Rationalism is the philosophical position that reality has a logical structure that can be known by means of deductive reasoning. Descartes is a rationalist. By the nineteenth century, rationalism, allied with liberalism, was understood as hostile to religion. In defense of Christianity, John Henry Newman wrote: "Rationalism is a certain abuse of Reason; that is, a use of it for purposes for which it was never intended, and is unfitted. To rationalize in matters of Revelation is to make our reason the standard and measure of the doctrine revealed. . . . The Rationalist makes himself his own center, not his Maker . . ." (John Henry Newman, *Essays Critical and Historical* [London: Longmans, Green, & Co., 1895], 31) [See **Descartes**].

Relativism: Relativists hold that all knowledge is relative to the historical and personal context in which it is formulated and interpreted.

Romanticism: The "Romantic" period in Western cultural history covers the eighteenth and nineteenth centuries. Romantic thinkers saw *reason* solely as that within us which enables us to produce science. *Faith*, which really mattered, was our capacity for aesthetic experience. The Romantics substituted the artist's standpoint for the scientist's as the basis of our knowledge of the real. Their concerns were ideas about the 'true,' the 'good,' the 'beautiful' (the Romantic poet Keats wrote, "Beauty is truth"). The productive spontaneity of the imagination (an artistic activity, consisting in combining the elements of experience in a way that is not given in experience) underlies all experience, and particularly all cognition (knowing). This is an activity of synthesis. It is the source of knowledge. Therefore, all knowledge is synthetic [See **Rousseau**].

Rousseau: Jean-Jacques Rousseau (1712–1778) argued for *feeling* rather than *reason* as the basis for philosophy. He argued in *Discourse on the Arts and Sciences* that the arts and science had "degraded" human beings and that before the development of civilization human beings were perhaps "rude" but "natural." His political theory (Social Contract) played a major influence during the French Revolution and continued through the period of the German Enlightenment (*Self* 32) [See **Romanticism**].

Scholasticism: In the Collins English Dictionary (1986), scholasticism is defined as "the system of philosophy, theology, and teaching that dominated medieval western Europe and was based on the writings of the Church fathers and (from the twelfth century) Aristotle" [See **Classicism**].

Second Vatican Council: The twenty-first ecumenical council of the Catholic church, the second such council held in the Vatican, took place between 1962 and 1965. Vatican II has been called the most important event in the history of the Church since the Protestant Reformation. Karl Rahner said that "with the Second Vatican Council, the Church . . . has expressly and consciously become a world Church. . . . The Second Vatican Council is the first council of a World Church that really wants to be a World Church and not a Church with European exports to all parts of the world. . . . This Council also brought to an end . . . a neo-scholastic period of theology" (Karl Rahner, *I Remember: An Autobiographical Interview*, 88– 89). It is fair to say that most of the laity, clergy and religious were not prepared for the cultural and religious revolution that Vatican II unleased in the Catholic church.

Self-Appropriation: Self-appropriation, self-affirmation, self-knowledge is central to the thought of Bernard Lonergan. It is on the basis of our knowledge and appropriation of our own interior consciousness that we come to appreciate who we are as human beings and what is true and good.

Self-Transcendence: As John Macmurray and Bernard Lonergan use the term they mean it to refer to pointing beyond oneself.

Society of Friends: [See **Quaker**].

Transcendent/Transcendental: Transcendent refers to God. Transcendental (outside of oneself) is used by Lonergan to refer to a type of knowledge, a method for achieving knowledge. It is because the levels of consciousness are so foundational that Lonergan calls them "transcendental."

They transcend all other methods and are operative in all other methods.   One first uses the method which one is (the transcendental method is no mere technique or procedure, it is ourselves, the dynamic structure of our creativity) to establish any other technique or procedure, or method, one will use.   For example, to decide on the technique to be used in building a bridge or the procedure for filling out the income tax form, one first gathers data, seeks to understand the data, makes judgments about truth and takes decisions about what is the right way to proceed.

Transcendental Precepts: The transcendental precepts or "transcendental imperatives" are, for Lonergan, "native spontaneities and inevitabilities."

Ultramontanism: Literally the word means "on the other side of the mountains" (Alps).   It refers to a movement within Roman Catholicism favoring strong centralized authority under the pope.

Vatican II: [See **Second Vatican Council**].

BIBLIOGRAPHY

Astley, Jeff, and Leslie Francis, eds. *Christian Perspectives on Faith Development: A Reader.* Grand Rapids, MI: William B. Eerdmans Publishing Company, 1992.

Bach, George R. and Ronald M. Deutsch. *Pairing: How to Achieve Genuine Intimacy.* New York: Avon Books, 1971.

Barnes, Kenneth C. *Energy Unbound: The Story of Wennington School.* York, England: Williams Sessions Ltd., 1980.

Barnes, Kenneth, Kathleen Lonsdale, and John Macmurray. *Quakers Talk to Sixth Formers: A Series of Broadcasts.* London: Friends Home Service Committee, 1970.

Baur, M. "A Conversation with Hans-Georg Gadamer," *Method: Journal of Lonergan Studies* 8, no. 1 (March 1990): 1–13.

Bellah, Robert N., et al. *Habits of the Heart.* Berkeley: University of California Press, 1985.

Berry, Thomas. *The Dream of the Earth.* San Francisco: Sierra Club Books, 1988.

———. "The Ecozoic Era," a paper presented as part of the E. F. Schumacher Society Lectures, October 19, 1991.

Bibby, Reginald W. *Fragmented Gods: The Poverty and Potential of Religion in Canada.* Toronto: Irwin Publishing, 1987.

———. *Unknown Gods: The Ongoing Story of Religion in Canada.* Toronto: Stoddart Publishing Co. Limited, 1993.

Buber, Martin. *I and Thou.* Translated by Ronald Gregor Smith. New York: Charles Scribner's Sons, 1958.

Burnham, Frederic B., ed. *Postmodern Theology: Christian Faith in a Pluralist World.* San Francisco: Harper & Row, Publishers, 1989.

Carey, John J. *Carlyle Marney: A Pilgrim's Progress.* Macon, GA: Mercer University Press, 1980.

Carson, Harry A. "Macmurray's Prophetic Voice," *America* 129, no. 7 (September 15, 1973): 172–74.

Carter, Gerald Emmett. "Address by His Eminence Gerald Emmett Cardinal Carter," July 30, 1991, in *Companions of Jesus: Pilgrims with Ignatius.* Toronto: Canadian Institute of Jesuit Studies, 1991: 26–34.

Catechism of the Catholic Church. Ottawa: Canadian Conference of Catholic Bishops, 1994.

Chiban, John. "Intrinsic and Extrinsic Religious Motivation and Stages of Faith." Th.D. dissertation, Harvard Divinity School, 1980.

Coles, Robert. *Walker Perry: An American Search.* Boston: Little, Brown & Company, 1978.

Conn, Walter. *Christian Conversion: A Developmental Interpretation of Autonomy and Surrender.* New York: Paulist Press, 1986.

Contemporary Authors 104. Edited by Frances C. Locher. Detroit: Gale

Research Company, 1982: 154.

Costello, John E., S.J., Introduction to *Reason and Emotion* by John Macmurray. Atlantic Highlands, NJ: Humanities Press International, Inc., 1991.

Crapps, Robert W. *An Introduction to Psychology of Religion*. Macon, GA: Mercer University Press, 1986.

Creamer, David G. "Faith Development in Young Adult Catholics," *Insight*, no. 4. Ottawa: Canadian Conference of Catholic Bishops (1991): 56–73.

Crowe, Frederick E. *Lonergan*. Outstanding Christian Thinkers Series. Series Editor Brain Davies, OP. Collegeville, MN: The Liturgical Press, 1992.

———. *The Lonergan Enterprise*. Cambridge, MA: Cowley Publications, 1980.

———. *Old Things and New: A Strategy for Education*. Atlanta: Scholar's Press, 1985.

———. *Appropriating the Lonergan Idea*. Edited by Michael Vertin. Washington, DC: The Catholic University of America Press, 1989.

Crysdale, Cynthia S. W. *Lonergan and Feminism*. Toronto: University of Toronto Press, 1994.

Davies, Brian. *God and the New Physics*. New York: Simon and Schuster, 1983.

Dictionary of Jesuit Biography: Ministry to English Canada 1842–1987. Toronto: Canadian Institute of Jesuit Sources, 1991.

Doran, Robert M. *Theology and the Dialectics of History*. Toronto: University of Toronto Press, 1990.

———. "Collected Works of Bernard Lonergan, S.J.," *America* 165, no. 2 (July 27, 1991): 46–48.

Droege, Thomas A. *Faith Passages and Patterns*. Philadelphia: Fortress Press, 1983.

Duncan, A. R. C. "No Man is an Island . . .," *Listening: Journal of Religion and Culture* 10, no. 2 (Spring, 1975): 40–53.

Dunne, Tad. *Lonergan and Spirituality: Towards a Spiritual Integration*. Chicago: Loyola University Press, 1985.

Dykstra, Craig, and Sharon Parks, eds. *Faith Development and Fowler*. Birmingham, AL: Religious Education Press, 1986.

Eigo, Francis, ed. *From Alienation to At-Oneness*. Villanova University Press, 1977.

Erikson, Erik H. *Identity and the Life Cycle*. New York: W. W. Norton & Company, 1980.

———. *The Life Cycle Completed: A Review*. New York: W.W. Norton & Company, 1982.

———. *Young Man Luther: A Study in Psychoanalysis and History*. New York: W. W. Norton & Company, 1958.

Flannery, Austin, ed. *Vatican Council II: The Conciliar and Post Conciliar Documents*. Vol. I. Northport, NY: Costello Publishing Company, 1988.

Fleming, D. L. *The Spiritual Exercises of St. Ignatius: A Literal Translation and a Contemporary Reading*. St. Louis: The Institute of Jesuit Sources, 1978.

Ford-Grabowsky, Mary. "The Concept of Christian Faith in the Light of Hildegard of Bingen and C. G. Jung: A Critical Alternative to Fowler." Ph.D. dissertation, Princeton University, 1985.

―――. "Flaws in Faith-Development Theory," *Religious Education* 82, no. 1 (1987): 80–93.

―――. "The Fullness of the Christian Faith Experience: Dimensions Missing in Faith Development Theory," *Journal of Pastoral Care* 41, no. 1 (1987), 39–41

―――. "The Journey of a Pilgrim: An Alternative to Fowler," *The Living Light* 24, no. 3 (1988): 242–254.

―――. "What Developmental Phenomenon is Fowler Studying?", *Journal of Psychology & Christianity* 5, no. 3 (1986): 5–13.

Forest, Jim. "A Very Public Hermit," *The Tablet* (December 25, 1993/ January 1, 1994), 1685.

Fowler, James W. *Becoming Adult, Becoming Christian: Adult Development and Christian Faith*. San Francisco: Harper & Row, 1984.

―――. *Faith Development and Pastoral Care*. Philadelphia: Fortress Press, 1987.

―――. "Fowler on Faith," in *Christianity Today* (June 13, 1986): 7-I–8-1

―――. "Keeping Faith With God and Our Children: A Practical Theological Perspective," *Religious Education* 89, no. 4 (Fall, 1994): 543–60.

―――. "Stages of Faith: Reflections on a Decade of Dialogue," *Christian Education Journal* 13 , no. 1 (1992): 13–23.

―――. *Stages of Faith: The Psychology of Human Development and the Quest for Meaning*. San Francisco: Harper & Row, 1981.

―――. *To See the Kingdom: The Theological Vision of H. Richard Niebuhr*. Nashville: Abingdon Press, 1974.

―――. *Weaving the New Creation: Stages of Faith and the Public Church*. San Francisco: Harper Collins, 1991.

Fowler, James W. and Sam Keen. *Life Maps: Conversations on the Journey of Faith*. Waco, TX: Word, Inc., 1978.

Fowler, James W., Robin W. Lovin, et al. *Trajectories in Faith: Five Life Stories*. Nashville: Abingdon, 1980.

Fowler, James W., Antoine Vergote, et al. *Toward Moral and Religious Maturity*. Morristown, NJ: Silver Burdett, 1979.

Fowler, James W., Karl Ernst Nipkow, and Friedrich Schweitzer, eds. *Stages of Faith and Religious Development: Implications for Church, Education, and Society*. New York: The Crossroad Publishing Company, 1991.

Frankl, Viktor. *The Unconscious God*. New York: Washington Square Press, 1985.

Freire, Paulo. *Pedagogy of the Oppressed*. New York: Seabury Press, 1970.

Freud, Sigmund. *The Future of an Illusion*. Edited and translated by James

Strachey. New York: W. W. Norton & Company, Inc., 1961.

Fromm, Erich. *Psychoanalysis and Religion.* New Haven, CT: Yale University Press, 1950.

Gandhi, M. K. *My Autobiography.* Boston: Beacon Press, 1957.

Gilligan, Carol. *In A Different Voice.* Cambridge, MA: Harvard University Press, 1982.

Goldman, Ari L. *The Search for God at Harvard.* New York: Times Books, 1991.

Goldman, Ronald. *Readiness for Religion: A Basis for Developmental Religious Education.* London: Routledge & Kegan Paul, 1965.

Gregson, Vernon, ed. *The Desires of the Human Heart: An Introduction to the Theology of Bernard Lonergan.* Mahwah, NJ: Paulist Press, 1988.

Griffin, David Ray, ed. *Spirituality and Society: Postmodern Visions.* New York: State University of New York Press, 1988.

Groome, Thomas H. *Christian Religious Education.* San Francisco: Harper & Row, 1980.

————. *Sharing Faith: A Comprehensive Approach to Religious Education and Pastoral Ministry.* New York: Harper Collins Publishers, 1991.

Haughton, Rosemary. *The Catholic Thing.* Springfield, IL: Templegate Publishers, 1979.

Helminiak, Daniel A. *Spiritual Developemnt: An Interdisciplinary Study.* Chicago: Loyola University Press, 1987.

Hennessey, Thomas, ed. *Values and Moral Education.* New York: Paulist Press, 1976.

Herberg, Will. *Protestant-Catholic-Jew.* Garden City, NY: Doubleday, 1960.

Hiebert, Dennis Wayne. "Schools of Faith: The Effect of Liberal Arts, Professional, and Religious Education on Faith Development." Ph.D. Dissertation, University of Manitoba, Winnipeg, MB, 1992.

How Faith Grows: Faith Development and Christian Education. London: National Society/Church House Publishing, 1991.

Kegan, Robert. *The Evolving Self: Problem and Process in Human Development.* Cambridge, MA: Harvard University Press, 1982.

King, Coretta Scott, ed. *The Words of Martin Luther King, Jr.* New York: Newmarket Press, 1983.

Kung, Hans. *Freud and the Problem of God.* New Haven: Yale University Press, 1990.

Largo, Gerald A. "Two Prophetic Voices: Macmurray and Buber," *America* 128, no. 12 (March 31, 1973): 283–86.

Lawrence, Jerome and Robert E. Lee. *Inherit the Wind.* In Cy Groves *Plays on a Human Theme.* Toronto: McGraw-Hill Ryerson Limited, 1967.

Lawrence, Linda. "Stages of Faith," *Psychology Today* 17, no. 11 (November, 1983): 56–62.

Leddy, Mary Jo and Mary Ann Hinsdale, eds. *Faith That Transforms.* New York: Paulist Press, 1987.

Leddy, Mary Jo, Bishop Remi de Roo and Douglas Roche. *In the Eye of the Catholic Storm*. Toronto: Harper Collins Publishers, Ltd., 1992.

Lewis, C. S. *Surprised by Joy*. London: Collins Fount, 1977.

Liddy, Richard M. *Transforming Light: Intellectual Conversion in the Early Lonergan*. Collegeville, MN: The Liturgical Press, 1993.

―――. *Collection*. Vol. 4 of the *Collected Works of Bernard Lonergan*. Edited by Frederick E. Crowe and Robert M. Doran. Toronto: University of Toronto Press, 1988. *Collection* was first published in 1967.

―――. *Insight: A Study of Human Understanding*. Vol. 3 of the *Collected Works of Bernard Lonergan*. Edited by Frederick E. Crowe and Robert M. Doran. Toronto: University of Toronto Press, 1992. *Insight* was first published in 1957.

―――. *Method in Theology*. Toronto: University of Toronto Press for Lonergan Research Institute, 1990. *Method in Theology* was first published in 1972.

―――. "Questionnaire on Philosophy," *Method: Journal of Lonergan Studies* 2, no. 2 (October 1984): 1–35.

―――. *A Second Collection*. Edited by William F.J. Ryan and Bernard J. Tyrrell. Philadelphia: The Westminster Press, 1974.

―――. *A Third Collection: Papers by Bernard J.F. Lonergan, S.J.* Edited by Frederick E. Crowe, S.J. New York: Paulist Press, 1985.

―――. *Topics in Education*. Vol. 10 of the *Collected Works of Bernard Lonergan*. Edited by Frederick E. Crowe and Robert M. Doran, revising and augmenting the unpublished text prepared by James Quinn and John Quinn. Toronto: University of Toronto Press, 1993. These lectures were delivered at Xavier University, Cincinnati, in August, 1959.

―――. *Understanding and Being*. Vol. 5 of the *Collected Works of Bernard Lonergan*. Edited by Elizabeth A. Morelli and Mark D. Morelli; revised and augmented by Frederick E. Crowe with the collaboration of Elizabeth A. Morelli, Mark D. Morelli, Robert M. Doran, and Thomas V. Daly. Toronto: University of Toronto Press, 1990. *Understanding and Being*, the Halifax Lectures on *Insight*, was first published in 1980.

―――. *Verbum: Word and Idea in Aquinas*. Edited by David B. Burrell. Notre Dame: University of Notre Dame Press., 1967.

―――. *The Way to Nicea: The Dialectical Development of Trinitarian Theology*, a translation by Conn O'Donovan from the first part of *De Deo trino*. London: Darton, Longman & Todd, 1976.

Lonergan Research Institute *Bulletin*, nos. 4–6, November 1989–91. Toronto: Lonergan Research Institute.

Lovelock, J. E. *Gaia: A New Look at Life on Earth*. Oxford: Oxford University Press, 1979.

Macmurray, John. "Address to Wennington Students," June 12, 1949, John Macmurray Collection, Regis College, University of Toronto, Canada.

―――. "Beyond Knowledge," in *Adventure: The Faith of Science and the Science of Faith*. Edited by B. H. Streeter. New York: Macmillan, 1928,

21–45.

———. *The Boundaries of Science*. London: Faber & Faber Limited, 1939.

———. *Challenge to the Churches*. London: Faber & Faber Limited, 1941.

———. "Christianity — Pagan or Scientific?," *The Hibbert Journal* 24, no. (1926): 421–33.

———. *The Clue to History*. London: Student Christian Movement (SCM) Press, 1938.

———. *Conditions of Freedom*. Atlantic Highlands, NJ: Humanities Press International, 1993. Based on the 1949 Chancellor Dunning Trust Lectures delivered at Queen's University in Kingston, ON and first published in Toronto: The Ryerson Press, 1949.

———. *Constructive Democracy*. London: Faber & Faber Limited, 1943.

———. *Creative Society*. London: Faber & Faber Limited, 1935.

———. *Freedom in the Modern World*. Atlantic Highlands, NJ: Humanities Press International, 1992. *Freedom in the Modern World* was first published in 1932.

———. "Here I Stand," John Macmurray Collection, Regis College, University of Toronto, Canada. It is not dated.

———. *Interpreting the Universe*. London: Faber & Faber, 1933.

———. "Is Art a Form of Apprehension or a Form of Expression?," *Proceedings of the Aristotelian Society* (Supplement 5, 1925): 173–89.

———. "Logic and Psychology," an unpublished paper in the John Macmurray Collection, Regis College, University of Toronto, Canada.

———. "The Nature of Reason," *Proceedings of the Aristotelian Society* 35 (1934–35): 137–48.

———. "Objectivity in Religion," in *Adventure: The Faith of Science and the Science of Faith*. Edited by B. H. Streeter. New York: Macmillan, 1928, 177–215.

———. *Persons in Relation*. Atlantic Highlands, NJ: Humanities Press International, 1991. *Persons in Relation* was first published in 1961 by Faber & Faber, London.

———. *Philosophy of Communism*. London: Faber & Faber Limited, 1933.

———. *The Philosophy of Jesus*. London: The Society of Friends, 1973.

———. Postscript to *Green Pastures* by Mark Connelly. London: Delisle, 1963.

———. *Reason and Emotion*. Atlantic Highlands, NJ: Humanities Press International, 1991. *Reason and Emotion* was first published in 1935.

———. *Religion, Art, and Science*. Liverpool: Liverpool University Press, 1961.

———. "Science and Objectivity," *Listening: Journal of Religion and Culture* 10, no. 2 (Spring, 1975): 7–23.

———. *Search for Reality in Religion*. Swarthmore Lecture Pamphlet. London: Friends Home Service Committee, 1969. The Swarthmore Lecture was first published in 1965, the year of its presentation, by

George Allen and Unwin Limited.

————. *The Self as Agent*. Atlantic Highlands, NJ: Humanities Press International, 1991. *The Self as Agent* was first published in 1957 by Faber & Faber, London.

————. *Structure of Religious Experience* (Terry Lecture at Yale). London: Faber & Faber, 1936.

————. *To Save From Fear*, a BBC Lenten talk. London: Friends Home Service Committee, 1964.

————. "They Made A School," a handwritten manuscript, dated December 4, 1968. It is found in the Macmurray Collection, Regis College, University of Toronto.

————. "Ye Are My Friends," a 1943 address to the Student Christian Movement, issued as a pamphlet by the Friends Home Service Committee in 1943 and reprinted many times.

Marney, Carlyle Marney. *The Recovery of the Person*. Nashville: Abingdon, 1979.

Maslow, Abraham H. *Religions, Values, and Peak-Experiences*. New York: Penguin Books, 1970.

McBrien, Richard P. *Catholicism* (Study Edition). San Francisco: Harper & Row, Publishers, 1981.

McCarthy, Michael H. *The Crisis of Philosophy*. Albany, NY: State University of New York Press, 1990.

McLuhan, Marshall. *The Gutenberg Galaxy*. Toronto: University of Toronto Press, 1962.

McShane, P., ed. *Foundations of Theology* Dublin: Gill and Macmillan Ltd, 1971.

Merton, Thomas. "Is the World a Problem?," *Commonweal* 84, no. 11 (1966): 305–309.

————. *The Seven Story Mountain*. New York: Harcourt, Brace and Company, 1948.

————. *The Sign of Jonas*. New York: Harcourt, Brace and Company, 1953.

Meynell, Hugo A. *An Introduction to the Philosophy of Bernard Lonergan*. Toronto: University of Toronto Press, 1991.

Moltman, J. et al. *Hope for the Church*. Nashville: Abingdon, 1979.

Mooney, Philip. "Freedom Through Friendship, John Macmurray: In Memoriam (1891–1976)," *Friends Journal* (January 1, 1977): 4.

Moseley, Romney M., David Jarvis, and James W. Fowler. *Manual for Faith Development Research*. Atlanta, GA: Centre for Faith Development, Emory University, 1986.

Munsey, Brenda, ed. *Moral Development, Moral Education, and Kohlberg: Basic Issues in Philosophy, Psychology, Religion, and Education*. Birmingham, AL: Religious Education Press, 1980.

Nephew, Albert H. "The Personal Universe," *Listening: Journal of Religion and Culture* 10, no. 2 (Spring, 1975): 99–108.

Newsletter of the Center for Research in Faith and Moral Development, no.

7 (January 1989).

Occhiogrosso, Peter. *Once A Catholic.* New York: Ballantine Books, 1987.

O'Conner, D. "John Macmurray: Primacy of the Personal." *International Philosophical Quarterly* 4, 1964: 464–84.

Orr, David W. *Ecological Literacy: Education and the Transition to a Postmodern World.* Albany, NY: State University of New York Press, 1992.

Palmer, Parker. *The Promise of Paradox: A Celebration of Contradictions in the Christian Life.* Notre Dame, IN: Ave Maria Press, 1980.

————. *To Know as we are Known: A Spirituality of Education.* New York: Harper Collins, 1983.

Parks, Sharon. *The Critical Years: The Young Adult Search for a Faith to Live By.* San Francisco: Harper & Row, 1986.

Pascal, Blaise. *Pensées.* Translated by A. J. Krailsheimer. London: Penguin Books, 1966. *Pensées* was first published soon after Pascal's death in 1662.

Peck, M. Scott, M.D. *The Different Drum: Community-Making and Peace.* New York: Simon & Schuster, 1987.

————. *The Road Less Travelled: A New Psychology of Love, Traditional Values and Spiritual Growth.* New York: Simon & Schuster, 1978.

————. *In Search of Stones: A Pilgrimage of Faith, Reason, and Discovery.* New York: Hyperion, 1995

Postman, Neil. *Teaching as a Conserving Activity.* New York: Delacorte Press, 1979.

Postman, Neil and Charles Weingartner. *Teaching as a Subversive Activity.* New York: Dell Publishing Co., Inc., 1969.

Pregeant, Russell. *Mystery Without Magic.* Oak Park, IL: Meyer Stone Books, 1988.

Rahner, Karl. *Theological Investigations* 3, The Theology of the Spiritual Life. London: Darton, Longman & Todd, 1967.

Rausch, Thomas P. "Thomas Merton: Twenty-five Years After," *America* 170, no. 1 (January 1–8, 1994): 6–12.

Redfield, James. *The Celestine Prophecy: An Adventure.* New York: Warner Books, 1993.

Rolheiser, Ronald. "Chronicle," *Catholic Herald.* London: Herald House, (June 3, 1994): 10.

Ronda, Bruce A. *Intellect and Spirit: The Life and Work of Robert Coles.* New York: The Continuum Publishing Company, 1989.

Roof, Wade Clark. *A Generation of Seekers: The Spiritual Journey of the Baby Boom Generation.* San Francisco: Harper Collins, 1993.

Russell, Peter. *Global Brain.* London: Routledge & Kegan Paul, 1982.

Sala, Giovanni. "The *A Priori* in Human Knowledge: Kant's *Critique of Pure Reason* and Lonergan's *Insight,*" *The Thomist* 40, no. 2 (April 1976): 179–221.

Sawicki, M. and B. Marthaler, eds. *Catechesis: Realities and Visions.* Washington, DC: U.S. Catholic Conference, 1977.

Schumacher, E. F. *A Guide for the Perplexed.* London: Sphere Books Ltd., 1977.

Siepmann, C. A. Foreword to *Freedom in the Modern World* by John Macmurray. Atlantic Highlands, NJ: Humanities Press International, 1992.

Spretnak, Charlene. *States of Grace: The Recovery of Meaning in the Postmodern Age.* San Francisco: HarperCollins, 1991.

Stokes, Kenneth. *Faith Development in the Adult Life Cycle.* New York: W. H. Sadlier, 1982.

Sullivan, Edmund V. *Critical Psychology and Pedagogy: Interpretation of the Personal World.* Toronto: OISE Press, 1990.

Swain, Bernard F. "Lonergan's Framework for the Future," *Commonweal* 112, no. 2 (January, 1985): 46–50.

Swimme, Brian and Thomas Berry. *The Universe Story.* New York: Harper Collins Publishers, 1992.

Tillich, Paul. *What is Religion?* New York: Harper Torchbooks, 1973.

Tracy, David. *The Achievement of Bernard Lonergan.* New York: Herder and Herder, 1970.

Veltri, John, S.J. *Orientations: A Collection of Helps for Prayer* (vol. 1, revised). Guelph, ON: Loyola House, 1993.

Vertin, Michael. "Lonergan on Consciousness: Is There a Fifth Level?," *Method: Journal of Lonergan Studies* 12, no. 2 (Spring, 1994): 1–36.

Wren, Thomas E. "John Macmurray's Search for Reality: Introduction," *Listening: Journal of Religion and Culture* 10, no. 2 (Spring, 1975): 1–6.

Wulff, David M. *Psychology of Religion: Classic and Contemporary Views.* New York: John Wiley & Sons, 1991.

Scriptural quotations are from The New Revised Standard Version, 1989.

Index